What Silver Disobedients™ Say About Dian Griesel aka @Silver Disobedience®

"My best friend turned me on to the Silver Disobedience blog. Now I enjoy reading it every day and consider it part of my daily devotional time. I'm constantly stopping to think: I'm 59 but feel the same as I did at 20- or 30-something, at least in my head! My body is different but my spirit is the same. Dian reinforces that belief with every post. I'm the happiest I've ever been because my lifelong dreams have come true after much hard work and sacrifice. It's never too late to go for it. I love the way you encourage people to be present, kind and brave. Thank you." @kim.rountree

"Aging is inevitable but Silver Disobedience never fails to inspire excitement, possibility and quality of life at its best along with a dose of thoughtful reflection in every post! Vibrant and visible, the sparkle that shines through in Dian's stunning photos define our demographic in the best possible way! @ SilverDisobedience is a 'must read' and a very bright voice for many!" @glitterinthepasture

"Silver Disobedience is just amazing! Always hits home with me and is a daily inspiration that I look forward to reading. I reread them, too, and get inspired all over again!" @patsypeterman01

"Authentic and refreshing points of view that are uplifting and inspiring. Great way to start my day: A cup of coffee and Silver Disobedience!" @ngrdner

"When so many post monologues on social media are written by people trying to make themselves look good, Dian opens a gentle conversation in an effort to encourage us all to be well and live well. She unselfishly puts raw photos and sometimes raw thoughts out here for us to consider and even dialogue about. She risks saying what so many of us are thinking. @SilverDisobedience gives me the daily nudge to go deep, pay attention and participate in this wonderful life." @a_diprima

"Coming to us in a time when shallow memes and pat answers are the norm, Dian Griesel draws us in by getting to the heart of who we are as humans, reinforcing the reasons we are special and reminding us of our power. Her posts delve into the complexities of relationships, emotions, social situations and aging, while inviting us to explore what makes us tick. Her love of life and sassiness shine through as the fierce spirit behind Silver Disobedience!" @margaretkerbs

"Silver Disobedience is redefining the rule book for stepping away from that 'number,' or our age, as a definition of who we are while providing insight into our endless possibilities of what we can still can be." @melissa.loehle

"I love reading Silver Disobedience posts because they open our eyes to what could be possible for us all if only we would believe in ourselves. Dian removes our doubts, fears and insecurities." Mike Henderson

"Inspiring, uplifting, interesting, reassuring and thought-provoking in a good way, Silver Disobedience is like opening a special present every day." Theresa Marie Loder

"Since I've been disobedient my entire 56 years, having swiped to find @SilverDisobedience, of course I had to stop and read. The words and thoughts resonate while never failing to make me smile." @panamadiva62

"A part of my morning ritual that somehow feels as if I have a friend who knows my heart, tells the truth, encourages and assures that we are a community." Cheryl Taylor

"I'm 56 and life seems to keep getting better and better. My takeaway? That is the spirit of Silver Disobedience posts and I love it!" Scott Detweiler

"Nurturing personal growth and innovative thinking that is naturally within all of us, Silver Disobedience activates the blossoming forth of this awareness and in so doing brings hope to these interesting times in which we live. I am grateful." @smith.evy

"Reading Silver Disobedience has made me reframe what I used to deem problematic and transformed it into a challenge to accept or possibly even a positive. Each essay provides sage advice to help navigate the waters of aspiring to our highest selves while finding our own answers." @_bigasia

"Dian is redefining the culture around aging while helping to establish new ideas and attitudes about age. Through Silver Disobedience, Dian is changing the paradigm of how we view our years so that people can continue being productive, positive, happy and healthy!" @sistersofthemoon22

"What stands out for me about Dian is her unrelenting spirit and refusal to allow aging to define herself or anyone else. This disobedient philosophy breeds hope, encouragement and guidance through spunk, warmth and truths. I like it and I'm looking forward to walking that walk and inspired to pay it forward." @charlenealofs

"Thought-provoking narratives cause us to stop and question the perceptions and limitations our society, and more importantly we ourselves, so often place upon what is expected of living out our midlife years and beyond. Silver Disobedience provides us with a bright, inspiring beacon to help us live our silver years joyfully, boldly, loudly and courageously to their fullest potential!" Carter Siverson

"Silver Disobedience shows us how to accept our years graciously…with hope, with faith, with joy. That's why I read what Dian has to say every day." @juliluinst

"Sometimes this odd journey through space and time encased in an ever-changing flesh vessel gets scary. How lovely it is to connect with other beautiful souls for support, inspiration and confirmation we are not in this alone. Thank you @SilverDisobedience for being a guiding light on this wild ride!" @janetleeyyc

"Dian writes about our life journey in a tender, educational and humorous way. She encourages us to express or question her thoughts. It gives me a sense of relief as I feel a sincere camaraderie with her and the other Silver Disobedience followers who share their thoughts." @annahbell9120

"Silver Disobedience is a village made up of thousands of people learning something new about themselves each day, not only from Dian but also from one another." @ram_duke.56

"Silver Disobedience reminds us to live life to the fullest because we get out of it what we put in." @Eddie_bassist

"Your writing, your perception of age and simply just your positivity reinforces one thing we learn to realize as we grow: getting older is an honour and a privilege, NOT something to dread." @lorigriffs

"Silver Disobedience is life lessons for a life well lived." @beyondjan18

"Raw, honest, sometimes flashy and wild...but grounded...messages that encourage us to be comfortable in our own skin!" @dgrunner3

"As a 50-something man, I find it easy to feel down as 21 years of military service left me with injuries that prevent me from doing the hardcore fitness that I love. @SilverDisobedience encourages and helps me remember I am not alone in my feelings and that there are blessings in being older." @fredlgmefic

"Sometimes, the reflections by Dian are short and sweet; sometimes, they are deep and philosophical— but always, they are wise and insightful." @stormlaurie

"I love Dian's perspectives about 'growing' young, and her reminders that our best years are now! Thanks to reading @SilverDisobedience daily, my life is taking a positive turn as it is injected with new ideas for living our best day, every day!" @oliveinthedesert

"Silver Disobedience topics resonate with me each and every time while inspiring me to think about life, growing older and finding balance." @carolyn_jones11

"Baby boomers have often rejected their pasts, have forgotten to live in the moment and are surprised they have arrived in their future.... Silver Disobedience brings life and reality to such a large community that is continuing to find their way in a world they've tried to change." Shirley Klima

"By far your Silver Disobedience post about anger being the purest display of another's hurt was eye-opening. I shared that with everyone." @sococake3

"No matter what age one is, Silver Disobedience helps us consider new perspectives with positive motivation to not be scared of change." @stadick17

"Silver Disobedience asks us to 'Remember when we all thought gray hair was getting old!'" @debbierichardson913

"Dian reminds us to breath and examine who we are and how want to do positively live our silver years." Harry Anderson

Comments continue on page 271...

The  Playbook

365 Inspirations for
Living and Loving Agelessly

The  Playbook

365 Inspirations for
Living and Loving Agelessly

DIAN GRIESEL

The Silver Disobedience® Playbook
365 Inspirations for Living and Loving Agelessly

by Dian Griesel a/k/a @SilverDisobedience

For information, contact the publisher:

DGI
335 W. 38ᵗʰ Street, Fl. 3
New York, NY 10018
212-825-3210

Published in the United States of America
Printed and Bound in the United States of America
<u>Library of Congress Cataloguing-in-Publication Data</u>
Griesel, Dian 1961 -
ISBN: 978-1-7329669-1-8

1. Self-Help 2. Relationships 3. Self-Help & Psychology 4. Philosophy
5. Sociology & Social psychology 6. Family, Marriage, Home 6. Success 7. Motivational
8. Business & Professional Growth 9. Motivation & Self-Improvement

Thanks to:
Cover Design: Tony Iatridis of Innovation Design Graphics
Manuscript Editing: Sebastian Thaler of DGI
Insightful Feedback & Strategic Edits: Judy Katz of Katz Creative

Front Cover Photo: Peter Hurley • Back Cover Photo: Susan Bowlus

DEDICATION

To my fearless, ageless Silver Disobedients.
You read my blogs regularly.
You write me long, heartfelt, and equally inspirational responses.
Our connection inspires me daily!
You have become the reason I write my essays and my books.
Love you all!

Thank you to Rory, Chamonix and Steel.
I love you. Thanks for inspiring me to practice "walking the talk" daily.

To my Mother and Father and Bernie
You have taught so many so much by living exemplary lives. We all love you.

To Judy Katz
Your unflagging support energizes me to keep the creative juices flowing.

PLEASE READ THIS FIRST...

No matter how old we are today, we have never been this exact age before. So, what does it mean when we are told: "Act your age?" How are we supposed to act? Did we cross invisible aging thresholds throughout our lives? If so, were we supposed to change our style and dress differently? What does *that* look like? Did the age rules change when we had children? What if we never had kids? Would this then mean we would never have to act our age? And, if a day is declared, when we are all suddenly supposed to "act our age," what behaviors need to be tweaked? Are the changes mandatory? Are there penalties for non-compliance? Is somebody watching? Who is the judge?

It seems that throughout our lives, we are either told to "act our age" or we spend time worrying about "becoming our age." What's up with our cultural issues regarding aging? Why don't we just relax, welcome and embrace the benefits of the years we have lived?

As a businesswoman, wife, mom and author who recently became a "silver" model with Wilhelmina Models, I have always challenged life and have never been easily contented. I've lived with a ferocious curiosity, hunger for knowledge and most of all a deep desire to understand human connection—all of which combined together have resulted in a life full of experiences. In light of this, as I wrote my first @SilverDisobedience blog, I began questioning a range of societal beliefs about aging, as well as attitudes towards life after age fifty.

To confirm our cultural distaste for getting older, look no further than a thesaurus— which cites synonyms for "old" that include "ancient," "decrepit," "tired," "fossil," "broken

1

down," "depilated," "enfeebled," "exhausted," "antiquated," "archaic" and "geriatric."

These words surely don't describe my feelings about myself in the latter-half of my 50s, nor do they reflect any of what my peers and far "older" friends express to me. To the contrary, it is the antonyms of "old" that I hear most commonly referenced.

For most, our 50s and beyond are accompanied by an unanticipated element of excitement—a newness and sense of freedom distinguished from and wholly different than any earlier time of our lives. Our cumulative years seem to become a catalyst to release energy that allows us to blossom in entirely new and unexpected ways. We seem to grow into the versions of ourselves we've always wanted to be. Slowly but surely, we're getting comfortable with shedding standards of our younger years that no longer hold any meaning for us. We're relinquishing the need to question ourselves, or our wants and desires, and entering a stage where we aren't as worried about societal norms as to "how we're supposed to be or act." Suddenly, age is revealing itself as a more free-spirited time—in much the same way that youth is idealized to be, yet rarely is because youth is so often for many a quagmire of insecurities.

I'm not saying that we are all having a love-fest with our wrinkles nor that there aren't certain personal, health, financial and other challenges that accompany aging. But having now read hundreds of thousands of detailed, heartfelt responses to my blog posts, I can firmly declare that most of us are very glad to have lived long enough to get wrinkles, and we recognize it would have been worse to not have had the opportunity to deal with those wrinkles-in-the-plans that life delivers. The majority of us feel that we are honored and happy to be alive.

All of this, plus countless additional conversations and observations, constructed the foundational idea upon which Silver Disobedience is built: Perhaps aging is, in essence, the evolving process of getting to know ourselves more deeply and with greater acceptance and kindness over time.

SO WHY THIS BOOK?

The goal for each of my essays—both for this book and for my daily blog—has remained constant: By sharing what my readers view as "practical, relatable yet challenging thoughts," perhaps others can engage with my musings and find them to be comforting as we explore our connectedness and release many of the feelings of "aloneness" that some grapple with as they age. This dream has been realized beyond my wildest imaginings, thanks to the willingness of the hundreds of thousands who participate in a daily conversation on my website and social media accounts. The comments following each Silver Disobedience blog are as insightful and honest as I hope each of my essays is. This mutual dialog continues to be immensely heartwarming and underscores the joys of unanticipated "aging" consequences. Clearly, there is a collective desire to understand ourselves, our responsibilities and our relationships—including our desire to confront our differences in constructive ways instead of simply holding on to the need to be "right." The ongoing conversation confirms that the essence of "Who we are" doesn't change very much as we age—yet, we appear to believe wholeheartedly that each year has helped us to become better in myriad ways.

I wrote this book in response to numerous requests to put my Silver Disobedience essays into a portable form that would be easy to reference, review, mark up, highlight and keep handy at the beach, at one's bedside or anywhere else where a bit of camaraderie and inspiration is desired.

NOW IT'S IMPORTANT TO NOTE...

Many books in the self-help genre promise that readers will be magically transformed: Start at the beginning, read to the end and a marvelous transformation will occur as the secrets are revealed. The pitch is always positioned as if someone else—not us—has all the answers. And of course, we need those answers revealed to us so that we too can become as evolved and enlightened as the author.

That's not this book.

Do you want to know why?

Because YOU are already a one-of-a-kind, never-to-be-replicated, freewheeling, original-thinking, rebel-with-a-cause, adventuresome, fabulous-fighting, observant, crazy creative character, lovable-being, gift to the Universe, independent, valiant superhero-in-disguise, child of God, appropriate, picky, certainly different, intelligent, extraordinary, unruly, dependable, charming, fair, fearless, encouraging, reliable, memorable, exuberant, humble, conscientious, cultured, significantly special, loveable and enlightened being.

Yup. That's you. And me. And the coffee barista, the mechanic who fixes your car, every teacher you've ever had, the plumber who keeps your toilets flushing, the firefighters, financiers, marketers, doctors, nurses, moms, dads—basically anyone and everyone you've ever encountered.

We're all our own version of a one-and-only creation.

Where it gets complicated is this: We are each coping with everyday life. AND... We're also navigating relationships with other ones-of-a-kind!

It is the "each other" part that is the best part—but also the reason we may have somehow forgotten and lost touch with the enlightened status that is automatically assigned to us at birth by divine order.

We lost connection with embracing and showcasing the essence of who we *really* are, at the heart of us, for a reason. Throughout our lives, the well-meaning people with whom we've interacted have tried to give us meaningful direction (read that as: "socialize" us). But the truth is, we are actually fine characters--exactly as we were when we were cast into this play called "Life."

So, this book is your personal "read-it-any-way-you-want" playbook for getting back to being the unique individual that you are—who is living in a world where we must cope with other equally unique and complicated-to-figure-out people.

By bringing the focus back to ourselves—by taking full responsibility for owning up to our exclusive character, characteristics and qualities that distinguish us from each other—three big benefits immediately accrue:

1. We become aware that we have most likely gotten somewhat lost on our journeys. This new awareness helps us to become more patient and understanding of ourselves and others, knowing that getting lost can be lonely and frightening.
2. We recognize that most issues are our own issues to resolve, and that what belongs to others is theirs to resolve.
3. We rediscover a wonderful newfound sense of freedom.

Embracing our "exclusive editions" enables each of us to see one another as works of art that can be declared perfect, exactly as-is. We can revisit our misunderstandings about imperfection because since we are all unique with no two of us the same, imperfections cannot really exist because it would be impossible for anything that is one-of-a-kind to be imperfect. There can be no comparison if something is singular. Yet there can be greater appreciation.

Accepting how we began (as one-of-a-kind) and who we are today (still a one-of-a-kind but someone who perhaps got a bit confused or misdirected along the way), we can become reacquainted with ourselves in a purer sense. With time and practice, we can get back to basics in our daily lives and interactions with all of those with whom we connect. Life and our communications with others become more loving, peaceful and joyful. Acceptance improves for not only our own struggles but for the challenges others are confronting as well. After all, everyone is trying to get through this thing called Life.

This book recognizes that you are already in the Statusphere of Humanity because, Baby, you were born this way. These pages simply offer words of encouragement and an important reminder: Be bold enough to share your exclusive-edition self with the world at any and every stage of life—it will make daily living a lot more fun.

Again, please enjoy this book in any order you like. These meditative essays are designed to help us remember what we already know in our hearts. Please open to whichever headings capture your attention. Linger as long as desired as you reflect on the words and how they personally connect to you. Highlight what's relevant to you. Doodle. Fold pages. Take your time.

Thank you to all who have chosen to share some of your time with me on my blogs. Welcome to all of you who are new to our Silver Disobedience movement. I hope you enjoy reading my book. Together, let us grow—and embrace age and aging—by becoming the people we were always meant to be.

Love,
Dian (a/k/a @SilverDisobedience)

ENLIGHTEN ME

Enlightenment is the act of giving intellectual or spiritual light to others; offering instruction; or imparting knowledge.

By this definition, let me assure you that you are already an enlightened being.

Now that your enlightenment has been established, let's correct a big misperception relating to enlightenment: Even if one is enlightened, this does not mean someone has complete self-power to prevent their mind from swinging wildly between good and bad; between right and wrong; and between "do it" and "not such a good idea to do it."

No matter how much we pray and meditate, thoughts will whip us around. As committed as we are to another, we may still suffer whiplash when someone we find attractive catches our attention. We can be devoted to eating healthy and exercising, yet tempted by our favorite junk foods. We may work hard to be peaceful but still feel moments of fury.

Harmony is really what we want as it improves our enlightenment. Harmony is the simultaneous combination of tones that, when blended into chords, become pleasing to the ear. The goal for a more peaceful life is to become more harmonious by allowing all of the day's high and low notes to blend together. Throughout our lives, we have dealt with pleasant and unpleasant situations and people. When we allow discord to become new "chords" blended with pleasantries, we create our own special harmonious life song.

SMASHING AGE STEREOTYPES

There are countless stereotypes as to what defines an "old" person. These are accompanied by myths as to what "older" looks like and "how old people act." However, as with all stereotypes—most of them are simply not true.

Aging does not mean that Alzheimer's and forgetfulness are inevitable. It doesn't mean we're all retired and sitting in rocking chairs (although many of us do love to rock!). Age doesn't mean we're less productive; technologically inferior; impossible to teach; void of sexuality; set in our ways and unable to change; uninterested in our physical being; lacking interest in fashion; driving 40 in the fast lane; not contributing to society; unable to make important decisions without a tribunal of family opinions; blah blah blah!

The reality is that each of us individually defines what every year of our life look likes. Just as no two people are identical, our perspectives on life at any age covers an equally vast spectrum.

THE LAW OF ATTRACTION

The Law of Attraction states: Thoughts are a form of energy and what we think about is what we attract. We all know happy people who seem to always be talking about the great things happening to them. They have down moments, but for the majority, things seem to be going right for these folks. We also know some people who always seem to be fighting their way through life, who believe everyone is lining up trying to make their lives miserable in some way or another. Then, there are those who are constantly worrying about one thing or another…and sure enough, it does seem like problems that are cause for concern constantly befall them.

Here's why: Our subconscious mind has one job. Its role is to make "reality" out of what we "believe" to be right. It's the "validator." We believe things are going great? Our subconscious' job is to support, prove and validate that belief, making it reality. However, the flip side is true as well: If we believe we can't do, have, win, meet or achieve… whatever—our subconscious will help to create the situations, find the reasons and seek the people to support our beliefs. We will prove ourselves to be miserably correct.

The point is, since the job of our subconscious is to prove our beliefs to be correct, it might be time to take a belief inventory. Otherwise, we're choosing to run on autopilot with dire consequences, as we may be heading straight toward disappointment in a number of ways.

If you get one thing out of reading this book, let it be this: 99 percent of what we want and need originates in our thoughts. (I'm leaving a one percent variable because inexplicable crap does happen.) We get what we believe we deserve, not what we want, because our powerful subconscious supports every effort to put our thoughts into action, causing things to happen. Our subconscious mind is always subservient, taking directions from our beliefs.

If we desire something but don't believe it's possible, we are stalling our own powerful engines. It's time to get our motors running! Fueling our minds with positive thoughts and with actions that support our beliefs. Try it. This is universal law. Watch what happens…and keep reading!

RESOLUTIONS

Often we begin a new year with resolutions about all we're going to change. Sometimes we just pick a day and declare: Today I'm changing Whatever!

We begin with good intentions. We reflect on our habits, life, actions and pick something(s) we're determined to change or improve upon. Some of us even stick to our goals and reach them—which is fantastic!

While I think resolutions are a good personal challenge, I also think they can be ways we beat up ourselves. I'd like to propose some simple resolutions that you can start anytime—and that are reachable for all, and that can increase possibilities and feelings of confidence. Of course, you can raise your own personal bar, but if you occasionally miss the mark please don't use it as a way to beat yourself up. Rather, go back to this list. The journey of 1,000 miles begins with one step.

- Wake and start your day with two big glasses of water. You dehydrated overnight and this one little change will improve your health.
- Eat a piece of fruit with your breakfast. The fiber, nutrition and sweetness will add greater satiation to your meal.
- Squeeze in 10 minutes of extra walking daily. Parking farther away from the entry counts toward these minutes.
- For lunch and dinner, add two vegetables to your meal. Eat them plain. You'll get used to the flavors and maybe start enjoying them! Yes, salads, fresh, steamed or frozen all count.
- Smile at the first person you see each day. If it's someone in your household, it will make your home more pleasant. If it's a neighbor or stranger, you'll both feel better as well.

Choose an inspirational quote and think about it throughout the day. Try to make it a "practical" experience. I post new ones regularly at 1440moments.com and @1440moments if you need an easy place to find one!

WONDERFUL LIFE

If only we could each realize our value to the lives of all we meet, we'd realize it really is a wonderful life. If only we could realize ways we can be important to people far removed from us who we will likely never meet, we'd realize it really is a wonderful life. If only we could realize that every encounter between ourselves and another has potential for life-changing magic as we share a part of us with another for each other's eternity, we'd realize it really is a wonderful life. If only we could always remember "This too shall pass," we'd see a lesson instead of a problem, and realize it's really a wonderful life. If only we realized how our life has impacted those around us, in ways we'll never know or understand, we'd realize it really is a wonderful life.

NO NORMAL

For much of my life, if asked, "How's it going?" My rote response was an automatic: "Fine." It was my go-to answer for two reasons:

1. Because I thought complaining was weak and ugly, and
2. I was afraid to admit that anything in my life might be anything other than fine.

The problem with insisting on what we think is "normality" or that all is "fine" when it might be otherwise, is that this somehow means deep down we are very dissatisfied with accepting life as it is—which is problem-full, because problems happen.

Having problems doesn't mean we are weak, unlucky, less than or otherwise.

If you believe others to be problem-free, it's probably because you are comparing your inner feelings to the facade of normality we all so often try to present. In reality, believing that you should never have a problem—or that problems are a sign of weakness— is painfully isolating. You can't really have any conversations in depth if you're afraid to acknowledge that sometimes life bites. Sometimes it bites hard. It is what it is...and it isn't always fine. In fact, it can be immensely painful.

At those times when life is normal—or full of trials and challenges—we hold the potential to reach new understandings of our personal capabilities. We can embrace our personal challenges and ask for the embrace and support of others. This isn't weak. It's how humans show their strength and fortitude for living.

Aging Like a Fine Wine: A Terminology Primer

Wine is cheered for aging well, so why don't we appreciate the same features in people? Whether you imbibe or not, let's look at some wine terms and imagine instead we were describing our finely aged personalities.

"Complex" simply means that when you encounter it, the flavor changes from the moment you taste it through to the moment you swallow. "Creamy" is the phrase associated with famous, very expensive wines and champagnes because they are *smooooth*. "Crisp" is uncomplicated and effortless, and would add the fun to a picnic on a hot summer day. "Elegant" resembles a former ballerina whose movements still reflect years of practicing finesse. A "Flamboyant" wine is trying to get your attention with an abundance of fruit. "Hint of…" implies a blend of characteristics that might be all over the place and even contradicting. "Intellectually Satisfying" is used to described wines that are rare, expensive and maybe a bit decadent. "Jammy" implies the wine is still a bit sticky-sweet and is reminiscent of a good homemade jam or pie. "Juicy" is retaining childlike and youthful characteristics, as in grape juice versus wine. "Opulent" is old-school rich, smooth and bold—all at the same time. "Refined" means less is more. "Silky" is a relaxed personality that could be compared to sliding into a comfy bed. "Unoaked" would describe those of us who are a still a bit tart and snappy—which could imply we've maintained or developed a very sharp sense of humor. And those of us who are "Velvety" just pour ourselves into whatever we're doing with unmistakable swagger like Jagger. (Thanks to WineFolly for helping me with some of these descriptors!)

Whether you drink or not, which positively delicious phrases would you use to describe your Silver Disobedience® self?

WEEDS

I've always been fascinated with weeds.

Weeds are marvelously inspiring examples of strength, particularly those that push their way through seemingly strong barriers like cement or tar. I so admire weeds that I always have to stop and take their pictures. Can you imagine their energy? The perseverance and determination to reach the surface and sunlight?

Weeds don't wait to get planted. No special fertilizer is needed. They grow despite the circumstances. They push through and stand tall. Some even flower beautifully, like dandelions. Then, even after their flowering days have passed, they still provide us with hope as we blow their seeds into the wind to make wishes.

It's our nature to be strong. To push through adversity even when it seems like all forces are against us. Storms make trees grow deeper roots. Adversity makes dandelions grow roots that can reach one to two feet deep into the Earth, compared to the four to six inches we see above ground.

Like the dandelions, we are much stronger than we think or might show to the world. Something beautiful will grow from whatever you are going through: It will be you—and the stuff dreams are made of.

WHO'S YOUR AUTHORITY FIGURE?

A big benefit of aging is that it tends to make us our own authority figures. Ideally, by this stage of our lives, gone are the days when we were completely vested in what everybody thought about our every action. We're old and wise enough to decide for ourselves what is right for us. This is not to say we don't respect the opinions of others. It's more that we have become much better at listening to these opinions—pulling out what we think might be valid and then more comfortably deciding what is best for ourselves. Our age seems to have helped us become more comfortable with looking closely at our lives and deciding that the only real authority figure for our actions and the life we lead is ourselves.

Of course, we all still look to other people for their opinions at times, but we know in our hearts that once we decide to start opinion seeking, we've probably already made our decisions and are instead looking for validation for our plans. Silver Disobedience is a phase of accepting utmost responsibility for our actions. We no longer want others to make our decisions. We're making them ourselves. Are you your own authority figure?

SHAKE IT OFF...

Staying angry is not healthy. It won't help you or anyone around you live longer. Anger raises cortisol, adrenaline, epinephrine and insulin—which hardens arteries and hurts our cardiovascular and heart health. Anger wrinkles our faces. When I'm not feeling angry—or the minute I realize I am—I try to imagine the distorted contortions my face makes when I am in a fit of fury. It's not pretty; actually, it's pretty ugly.

Smiling and laughter trigger polar opposites. Those stress hormones are reduced. Antibody-producing cells that raise the effectiveness of T-cells lead to a stronger immune system and greater health.

Wrinkles-wise? If we're lucky, we get to live long enough so we get wrinkles. And you know what? Those wrinkles around the eyes and upper cheeks are the best exterior indications of internal beauty.

TURN THE PAGE...

Whether it's Bob Seger's original song or Metallica's cover, whenever "Turn the Page" comes on the radio, my mood gets infinitely better. While painful to the ears of others, I start singing along. ;-)

In life, there always comes a time—sometimes many times—when you have to choose between turning the page or closing the book. To "turn the page" is to transition, to move on, to go from one role to another. It might involve making the choice to move from a negative or neutral situation to a more positive one.

We don't need momentous events to trigger a turn of the page, although it may be an event, situation or person that causes us to finish that chapter.

At any time in our lives, we can turn the page by making a choice to change something that would positively move us forward and create benefits in some way.

We could choose to "turn the page" by smiling more. Laughing freely. Embracing new friendships. Changing our work. Moving. Exercising. Eliminating an unhealthy habit. The possibilities are endless.

Maybe you've had to turn the page or close a book—maybe you've chosen to do so. Either way, you've learned lessons—because every book has at least one.

CRASHING THROUGH FEAR

I once read: "Everything you want is on the other side of fear." I disagree with the "everything." It needs an "almost" in front of it. Almost everything we want is on the other side of fear.

Fear of failure. Fear of success. Fear of embarrassment. Fear of falling. Fear of crashing. Fear of mortality. Fear of immortality. Fear of being on stage. Fear of never being recognized. Fear of what our parents would say or think. Fear of what our children will say or think. Fear of caring. Fear of not caring enough. The list is endless.

Are we really that afraid? Yes, we are. No, we are not.

Fear is a dichotomy of the self. Opposing ideas within us much like war and peace. We feel afraid—yet we know how great it feels to be on the other side of that fear. Mostly.

I was in a plane crash on October 10, 1981. After not flying for a year, understandably due to fear of flying, on October 10, 1982 I went flying again. Guess what? Another crash landing! My point? You can face your fears and go through them but life doesn't come with guarantees. I still crashed. In fact, I crashed again…and again. Hopefully not again, again, though!

Crashing isn't so bad, assuming we still get to live. We learn a lot from it. Namely, that we can survive adversity. Also, we learn through life experiences that no matter what is aggravating us, no matter what we're afraid of, no matter what fear we're experiencing, there are no guarantees—but odds favor we'll probably live through whatever the experience is.

Life actually inclines itself toward living. All life forms strive for health—and existence. Think about the crap most of us put in our bodies. If we put the equivalent of soda in an auto for gas—that would be the end of that engine. But bodies? They tolerate a lot of abuse. Stop the abuse and health will do its best to improve our overall being. Same goes for our minds.

Once we challenge our fears, they begin to lose their power. We realize we haven't died. We're still alive. Stronger.

ENVY NO ONE

In my early 20s, in a conversation with a wise friend who is 20 years my senior, I started whining about the life I didn't have. When I finished, she patiently pointed out that envy and jealousy weren't my most attractive traits. Then she said: If everyone in the world had to put their troubles in a suitcase, then had the opportunity to throw that suitcase out on the street, to grab a different one—once the suitcases all started popping open, we'd run back as fast as possible to grab back our original problems.

I'm still not immune to envy and I'm not sure I'd believe anyone who said they were. There will always be something we see, want, imagine, covet or dream of that somebody else seems to have.

But when I find envy creeping into my heart, I try to see it as an impetus to kick-start a new plan of action. If someone's got something I think I want, I should be celebrating! It means that whatever that is—if I'm alive, we both have the same 24 hours in a day— so maybe it's attainable for me as well. Instead of wasting time being envious, I try to determine a new pathway—although admittedly, sometimes as I think about the effort necessary, the attraction fades because I realize it might be "nice" but it's really not so important to me.

Steve Jobs had less time on Earth than we've had to date. During his Earthly visit, he made Apple products must-haves for many, making gazillions in the process. Do I envy that wealth? Not at all. Hey, money is better than no money—but I'm still alive and full of possibilities; he's not.

Unhappiness comes from undervaluing what we have, while overvaluing what we think others have. As Thomas Brown said, "Let age, not envy, draw wrinkles on thy cheeks."

THE SUBWAY

Lots of people will always want to ride with us in the limousines. But what do we all want? We really want and need those who will take the subway or bus with us when the limo breaks down.

Work hard; play hard; and surround yourself with the people who will walk proudly by your side in true friendship, however your life is unfolding.

POWER PLAY

Almost 2,500 years ago, Plato wrote: "You can discover more about a person in an hour of play than in a year of conversation." With insights like that, it's no wonder the guy is still a philosophical rock star today.

Without play, we become dull, tired and worn out. Sometimes we resist the idea of getting out and playing with others because we think it might be too much work. Isn't that ironic?

When we play, we're learning about ourselves and others in a relaxed way. Playtime is never wasted. As George Bernard Shaw said: "We don't stop playing because we grow old; we grow old because we stop playing."

Play at every age reinforces our easy, "try it, do it" natures. Play helps us to learn how to adapt, construct, problem-solve, process our emotions, create, explore, challenge, laugh, have fun, speak and manage stress.

Play matters. How will you play today?

A WORK OF ART

Like snowflakes, we are all unique and beautiful in our own ways. A work of art can be perfect while filled with imperfections. Yet what is imperfection when speaking about works of art like humans? If we are all one-of-a-kind, with no two of us the same, how can imperfection exist? How can a one-and-only be imperfect? It can't. There can be no comparison to something singular.

We are each a "one of a kind," therefore perfect as is. Each beautiful in our own right and way. And taking this further, it is wholly possible to admire beauty in another without it diminishing or casting doubt on our own beauty in any way.

Comparing oneself to others brings sadness and discontent. However, comparing yourself to your "yesterday self" is how personal improvement thrives and life satisfaction is most easily improved as well.

Life satisfaction has nothing to do with others. It is a personal reflection: Am I a better person today than yesterday? It matters not what others are doing. What matters is what you are doing to fulfill your own journey. Happiness flourishes when we stop comparing ourselves to other people.

FEELINGS AREN'T FACTS

Happiness is a balancing act involving our emotional state of being. No one is happy (or sad) 100 percent of the time. If you believe anyone is happy all the time, memorize this: "Do not judge your inside feelings by what other people are projecting on the outside."

Happiness is not an omnipresent feeling. Everyone experiences ups and downs. (Yes, including yours truly.) Humans have tides of emotions and feelings that ebb and flow. We all have moments when we feel sad, alone, frustrated, angry, afraid, envious and jealous. We also all have moments of immense joy, contentment, pleasure, satisfaction and happiness. None of these emotions should be confused for facts. Rather, our emotions are better understood as fleeting glimpses of intense mental activity that is rapidly trying to assess our pleasure or displeasure in a split second—not actual facts about the situation or person to whom we are comparing ourselves.

Our emotions provide us an opportunity to observe ourselves and peek into a window of our temperament, personality, disposition and motivations. It is beneficial to our health to spend time working to consciously observe our complex set of emotions, because their broad scope is closely linked to the arousal of our nervous system—which benefits from balance versus extremes.

Reflecting on an emotion—particularly when we're just not feeling it—can help us make the changes that might lead us to more moments of happiness, when those moments of extreme emotions are triggered. Happiness is a state of being that we each can learn "to be" if we decide to practice being more observant when emotions rise. Whatever the emotion—which we won't label as good or bad.

THE WORST HAS ALREADY HAPPENED

No matter what is going on in our lives, it's quite possible that the worst has already happened.

Here's where you say: "You don't know me! How can you say that?! What's the worst thing that has already happened in my life?"

The worst thing that can happen to any of us is this: Believing that exactly as we are, we are inadequate for any challenge or situation life abruptly tosses in our direction.

We've all felt this way at some point or another. It's a universal emotion. So, starting today, try being a little gentler with yourself…

Remember this: You're ready. You've had a lifetime of preparation that has all led up to this day. Stay in the moment and just take it one moment at a time. Make your choices accordingly. Do what you have to do in the moment. Stay out of the past or future. Stay present in the moment and allow yourself to blossom. You've got deep roots that have made you more flexible and stronger than you might imagine. You're firmly planted and you're flowering aboveground. You are ready for whatever happens today.

EVERYDAY LIFE IS LIFE

Everyday life is life. 'Nuff said, really. As John Lennon, on *Double Fantasy*, the last album before his death, sang: "Life is what happens to you while you're busy making other plans."

This is it. Right now. Not tomorrow. Not next week. Not next year. This is life. With all the work, chores, aggravation and annoyances. It's also all the fun, laughter, accomplishments and smiles.

Every day we wake, we are experiencing everyday life. Children know it. They don't want the day to end. They burn their energy to the last second possible before collapsing into sleep. Teenagers and 20-somethings love the moment and want the party to last forever—but are also more likely to do stupid stuff because they don't yet grasp the brevity of life and its value. By our 30s, life is becoming real. Rent, bills and work responsibilities are in full swing. Our 40s accelerate our awareness and we're often so worried about doing, achieving, reaching and getting through that we are not even noticing life's precious moments. By our 50s, a realization strikes: This is it. And although we never know how many days of life we will have, we (hopefully) start to recognize the value of the moment.

Everyday life is life. 1440 moments—which is how many minutes there are in a day to spend. Forget bitcoin; we're spending something more valuable: time.

GREATNESS IN THREE STEPS

If we want to take charge of our lives, we all need to keep honing our personalities, move our ideals and hopes ahead, fight for our dreams and live our lives around our personal purpose. Our ideal life is not something we "find"—it is something we "create." The business of being a person is to take our existence and organize it around our plans and purpose so that we create the life we want to live.

Here are three steps to building your greatness.

1. Imagine what you want. Use your most vivid imagination possible. Hold the image in your mind's eye so that you are drawn to it. Be bold and imagine yourself being knocked down and defeated—and victoriously rising like only you can do. See how you are contributing to whatever success you imagine.
2. Use your common sense. Don't try to shove round pegs in square holes. If you want to be an artist, start acting like an artist! You've got to start doing what you want to do.
3. Put on your super suit. Greatness takes faith, courage and the ability to ignore ignorance, neglect, negativity and disrespect from others regarding your ideas. Believe that whatever it is you want to do will benefit not just yourself but others as well. If you think this sounds grandiose, remember: Because you are working to fulfill your dreams, you will change others simply because you'll be more pleasant to be around.

Even a moderate dose of all of the above will set you on a new journey. When we chase pleasure alone, we won't necessarily win. When we live to make ourselves greater, every day we push forward is another win.

ADVERSITY

Someone once said that the trouble with using experience as a guide is that the final exam often comes first and then the lesson. Oscar Wilde wrote: "Experience is the name everyone gives to his mistakes." Aldous Huxley wrote: "Experience is not what happens to a man. It is what a man does with what happens to him."

Adversity introduces us to our strengths—including those that we may not even know we had. Although everyone would like a warranty that gets us through life without any accidents, damage or adversity—this is just not how the game of life gets played.

At this stage in our lives, we've all had plenty of tests that have challenged our strength and fortitude. Certainly, there were times we questioned whether we could handle the load. Some situations and people may have even made us question whether we could trust ourselves.

Our years add experiences: good, bad and ugly. It's all a numbers game as we grow and learn, becoming different people than we were yesterday. Everyday we're absorbing new information, forming different ideas and expanding our possibilities. Today, congratulate yourself. You're reading this today so you still have a working mind. Things are looking up!

HAPPILY EVER AFTER

Past our glorious half-century mark, we've realized that life is not one great fairy tale. However, we can still "live happily ever after."

Experience and time have taught us that happiness comes from our choices on a moment-to-moment basis that builds to our overall sense of acceptance of others, our daily situations and our circumstances. None of this means we've retired from living and we're sitting around doing nothing to better ourselves. Rather, it means accepting that if we want something to be better in our lives, it's up to us to figure out how to make that happen. It is from this ownership of our choices and actions that our sense of serenity builds.

When we're doing anything that feels like it is moving us forward in a positive way—it's as if a renewed life force of energy courses through our veins, reinvigorating our spirits.

"The rest of our years will be the best of our years." Life is for the living. No matter what is going on in our lives, today is a perfect day to do whatever is within our power to create our own best version of "happily ever after."

FUNKY TOWN

Everyone visits Funky Town at some point. I'm not talking about "Uptown Funk" where Mr. Mars grooves: I'm talking about tough times when we really need to get ourselves out of the mental muck.

Here's a list of 10 things to get your mojo back when it seems to be hanging in the wrong neighborhood:

1. Get out of your house and closely observe the scenery outside your home. Say "hi" to strangers you pass.
2. Take a brisk walk. Go as fast as you can, as far as you can, as long as you can. See #1 about saying "hi!"
3. Volunteer to do something for someone else.
4. Call a friend to meet in person. Together, leisurely enjoy a coffee or tea and some cookies.
5. Wake up early enough to watch a sunrise.
6. Read a good fiction short story in whatever genre you like.
7. Listen for 10 minutes to classical music like Mozart, Vivaldi, Beethoven, Chopin. Try to identify as many instruments as you can.
8. Turn on the music and dance for 10 minutes all by yourself. Get your groove on. Listen to "Uptown Funk" or "That's What I Like" by Bruno Mars; flick your hair and dance!
9. Take a drive in a car and sing stadium-loud to whatever song you like. Channel your inner rock star…or Sinatra!
10. Learn a new vocabulary word and try to use it throughout the day.

CALCULATED RISKS

It's healthy to take calculated risks and push ourselves into uncharted territory. By doing so, we can work toward the goal of giving up our fears of failure and our fears of success: They are equally powerful.

The more we can accept that there are no guarantees of failure or success, the more acceptable the prospect of making a mistake becomes.

Anytime we decide to take a risk, it is normal to consider the downside. It's equally normal to fear the "what ifs" and changes that might occur if we were to actually succeed. Both can be paralyzing.

It's uncomfortable to feel trapped by fear. However, it's worth considering that it is actually more comforting to act than not. Yes, in action we may make mistakes. But we make a bigger mistake if we think we can get some kind of guarantee of success.

The goal is to live life to your personal definition of "the fullest" at every age. Go for the gusto. There's no shame in taking a risk. Don't worry about what others say or how they might try to discourage you. Don't wait. Find the time. Never allow waiting to become a habit. Life is happening now. What are *you* doing?

OWNING OUR ECCENTRICITY

A dictionary search defines "eccentricity" as unconventional and slightly strange behavior. "Strange" is defined as unsettling and hard to understand. Personally, I define "eccentricity" as any and every form of self-expression—from bow ties and suits to tattoos and mohawks—because it all depends on individual persuasion.

Depending on our perspective, any aspect of the full range of expression could be deemed "strange." But it is these nonconforming, fantastic, mystifying, marvelous, offbeat, atypical, perplexing displays of human expression that make day-to-day living so interesting and refreshing.

Who wants a cookie-cutter life? Don't we all crave a bit of extraordinary entertainment? Imagine a world in which everyone shared their hidden bit of eccentricity that's been bottled up. More smiles, more laughter, less judgment, more acceptance—because more unusual would be embraced. As we age, many of us begin to appreciate eccentricity in ourselves and others. When we accept eccentricity in others, we are actually giving ourselves greater freedom as well. How can you express *your* eccentricity?

TIME TO SHINE

Life is a constant self-improvement test whereby we steadily grow into the best version of ourselves. With this as a personal meaning of life, there's plenty to keep us categorically busy emotionally, physically, intellectually and spiritually. If we each identified daily tests of endurance—not just those that we design, but including those that surprise us along the way—we'd see that every day holds the possibility for us to become our own better version. This is a "self-ish" pathway that really benefits everyone. Committing to whichever areas we want to improve moves our focus away from judging others and puts it squarely back on ourselves. Dammit—we've got nobody else to blame! ;-)

Possibilities to reach our best have not passed us because of age. Ben Franklin invented bifocals at 79; Nelson Mandela was elected president of South Africa at 72; Michelangelo designed the Basilica at 72; Tim and Nina Zagat started their restaurant guides in their 50s; Frank Lloyd Wright completed his Guggenheim Museum work at 91.

Whatever is happening in our lives, wherever we are living, whomever we are living with—we can still release and embrace our own best purpose that is unique to us.

Grandiosity is subjective: Being the most fun grandparent (or parent); the best listener; the most likely to laugh and tell a good joke; the plumber or electrician who can solve any challenge; the best-est, most fun-est, most-wonderful whatever! Making healthier food choices; exercising in some way every day to stay strong and flexible; reading or doing crossword puzzles or anything else to keep our minds strong.

Doing those things we've wanted…but have been waiting to do…whatever they are… all count toward becoming our personal best. The world needs each of us to strive toward whatever we each define as our personal best. Own the fact that today, tomorrow and the next day are all your time to shine.

AHEAD

When we feel overwhelmed or threatened by change, we are hoping we can freeze time—because we somehow believe life can't get better. Faulty thinking is in abundance here because everything we believe to be real in our world changes as we change our thinking about change. With each change, something within us dies a little, yet we also have the capacity to grow a lot. Life is change. Growth follows change. Change + Growth = Life. That's my only favorite mathematical equation. Keep looking forward. Great changes are ahead of us all!

RETHINK WHAT YOU THINK MATTERS

Some things do matter. Illness and death are big matters. Having an income matters and it's very stressful when money seems to be flowing in the wrong direction. But other than these, not much else really matters.

What you said or neglected to say; how you acted or didn't; what you wore; that expression on someone else's face; that prize; that job; that comment; makeup; no makeup; bad hair days; no hair days; that parking spot somebody just took; the rude person who "didn't let you in"; stepping in dog poop; pigeon poop on your hair; coughing without covering a mouth; cold-callers; poor customer service; slow internet connections; annoying people shouting into their phones; celebrity drama; people reading over your shoulder on the bus; sycophants; complainers; stepping on chewing gum; feeling bloated; five extra pounds; delays in traffic; late trains; airline cancellations; people who don't answer your calls; junk mail; broken dishwashers; unflushed toilets; politicians; paper cuts; bad parkers; acronym text messages that need deciphering; long waits at traffic lights; slow-closing elevators; uncut lawns; grocery store lines when you only need one thing; Christmas lights in March; weathermen who are right only 50 percent of the time; the speed police; dieting celebrity sagas; burnt toast; and pimples and wrinkles at the same time…

It all doesn't matter as long as you're healthy and alive—that matters. Changes can happen with life.

BUCKING UP

It takes lots of courage to do what we want, whether it's something as simple as getting a new haircut or changing to a new job or moving. Sometimes we don't make the moves we want because we're too guilt-ridden. It's easy to become too concerned about what others might think or if they'd approve of our change in direction. The problem becomes that we forget to live life on our own terms. We tell ourselves we'll "get to it."

When we're getting "ready" to live, we're not really living (paraphrasing R.W. Emerson.) On some level, we all know this. Nike built an empire with one of the most successful tagline campaigns based on this concept: Just do it. There's a reason we all responded to it: Instinctually we know how important it is to "Just do it."

We all have responsibilities. But a life well lived in the end is more than just paying the rent, going to work, checking off the bills, shuffling kids to and from, saving for rainy days.

Today is a good day to buck up our courage and bridge the chasm between how we spend our time and what is fun and important to us.

It takes courage to live our dreams. But doing the extra-over-the-ordinary feels better than anything describable.

Today, decide to do something you've been afraid of doing—and take the first step toward doing it. The size of the choice is irrelevant. It could be as simple as choosing red nail polish when you always select nude; or growing or shaving your mustache. The point is that you are summoning your courage to do something out of your everyday norm—just for you.

Just do it!

RAINY DAYS

When we're having a good day, we often want everyone to be in the same mood we're in. Often, in day-to-day interactions, it bums us out when we're feeling cheery and others around us are moping about whatever. Sometimes it even makes us feel angry. We want everyone to be in the same mood we're in at the exact same time with the same amount of enthusiasm.

Admittedly, if we are honest, we might be chagrined to notice that such thinking is a bit selfish.

Perhaps we can practice understanding that just because we're having a good moment, this does not mean that those around us are feeling the same way. They may be struggling or frustrated with something we're completely unaware of. In fact, our energetic exuberance may be adding to their bad mood.

Accepting these moments is essential to maintaining any long-term relationship. If we don't adversely act on or put up a wall to the sudden resistance we feel when another is not on our same mood elevation, we can still be happy.

When others are ready, they'll join our moment—which may have shifted in its mood as well because this is life.

STICK TO THE FACTS

While imagination is a wonderful thing, it can also be the root cause of much of the stress in our lives. As we get older and continually deal with more challenging life experiences, it can be our imagination that derails us.

If we find ourselves worrying and experiencing stress about what might happen, our imaginations have gotten the better of us. We need to stop and stick to the facts.

For example, let's imagine someone is perpetually late or owes us money and hasn't paid us on time. Our imaginations say: "He thinks I'm stupid. She's selfish. They don't respect me. I must be a weak pushover if they're treating me like this." Facts say: "They're late." Or, "The payment is late; I wonder why?" Then it's time for questions and answers.

Sticking to the facts is not being emotional. It is viewing a situation, your health, a relationship, our work, the economy, whatever—in a factual way without confusing it with emotional, imaginary ideas.

When we start adding emotions to a situation, our imaginations are drawing references from the past.

Today is a different day. Stick to the facts of the moment, ask questions and do whatever you can do to make life unfold as best as you can.

New Collaborations

Do you remember when you were a child and you'd meet other kids, play with them and instantly feel like you had a new best friend? It wasn't the length of time that established the friendships—it was a connection of energy that upon reflection seems so magical.

Sadly, as our teen years descended upon us, friendships became more complicated. Gossip entered the picture. Later, as we dated, relationships became even more puzzling as we tried to find that partner who would love us for who we were. In many ways, this is a giant compromise, since we're all unique and have a different set of experiences that have combined to merge the nature and nurture aspects of our complex personalities.

Sometimes for sure it all seemed just so difficult to relate and connect.

Although many people would describe me as outgoing, I remember breaking into hives 20 years ago on the night of my 20-year high school reunion. I had to wear a turtleneck on a hot June night! To my amazement, it turned out to be a completely comfortable, very relaxing and fun evening. It seemed everyone had mellowed. The conversation was easy and kind. As I've reflected on this, I've observed that age has somehow enabled me to make new friendships that resemble those spontaneous friendships of youth. I connect more easily. The conversations seem to reach a deeper level more quickly—almost as if I've known the other person for years. Gone are the days of worrying about every word. This has been replaced with a sense of valuing collaborations and a greater appreciation of the wisdom and experience that others can bring to my life. It is marvelous to be at a stage when if we are attuned, we can embrace the connectedness, the oneness, we have with others. Time loses its impact. Instead, love seems to rule the day. How are you experiencing yourself within new collaborations, friendships and moments of every kind?

Timeless

Is there something you love to do that makes time fly by? Something that when you're doing it, you are almost startled when you hear your name or you look at a clock and realize how much time has passed?

Whatever that is, do more of it.

DUALITIES

When we start to think in opposites, it's helpful to try to recognize we are in opinion mode and it's quite likely that we're heading for trouble or an argument. Zen philosophy says: "When the opposites arise, the Buddha-Mind (your inner connection with God) is lost."

Dualities are learned thinking. They look like this: "I'm right so you must be wrong" or "That's pretty, so something otherwise is ugly."

There are dualities everywhere and in much of our daily thought processes.

What happened is, as children, our duality-mind formed to help us cope—because society teaches duality as a way to control the masses.

The result?

When someone disagrees with how we feel, think or see something, we've been conditioned to believe that one of us must be wrong. We think that all we need to do is explain our position—and the other will understand their wrongness and our rightness. The argument develops because we think the other cannot possibly be listening to us if they don't "get our point…our rightness" … or worse, that we haven't been clear so we start monologuing ad nauseam—or until everyone's anger starts to elevate.

If we see our dual-mindedness as a conditioned mind, one that has been taught that opposites are absolutes (incorrect!), we can try to release this thinking and stop assuming that one must be right or wrong. Instead, maybe we can see different perspectives—allowing them to coexist with all being "okay"—whether we agree or not.

Releasing the restrictions of the dual-mindset is the only way that we can really be open to all the possibilities of life and relationships—which are made up of people who have come from different experiences than us, and are quite likely to think differently from us as well.

When we only want to be right, we are choosing our rightness over the importance of the other person in our life. In our hearts, we know this is wrong.

Understanding Another

By this stage of our lives, many of us have married, divorced and married again or opted for singledom. Every year that passes, relationships change whether with spouses, "significant others," children, friends, coworkers—and ourselves. The Bible and every religious text, regardless of religious persuasion, tells us to "Love one another." We all know this is not always easy.

The love part starts with trying to understand one another. Only by working hard to understand another can we actually start to love them or keep on loving them. When we cannot love someone or something, it's because on some level we simply don't understand them, their thinking, their actions and motivations. So, they/it become(s) unlovable. Yet the more we try to know or understand someone or something, the more we access the potential for feeling love (or at least acceptance of another or a situation).

All of us do things that are completely incomprehensible to others. Does this make us all unlovable? Let's hope not. Rather, it just goes to show the human condition is complex, diverse and ever-changing.

To feel love means we have to constantly try to understand one another. If we understand another, we can forgive them, as we are all hoping they forgive us as well.

As years go by, if we've really put any effort into growing, we've tried to understand others—many who see life and the world far differently than we might. If we only love those similar to us, we've made our worlds smaller.

If this seems to be confusing at all, think about what makes us each feel loved: It gets down to feeling that we've been heard and understood. If we've kept ourselves youthful by maintaining flexibility toward our stances and opinions of others, we're likely aging quite well with love continuing to expand the capacity of our hearts—and a big heart capacity is a very healthy thing.

POSSIBILITY

Possibility is the condition or fact of being possible. It is one's utmost power, capacity or ability. Possibility provides us with a chance to change our circumstances for the better at any point in our lives. Possibility can happen in most unexpected ways. While there may be certain possibilities that pass with time, infinite, new and different possibilities for wonderful unexpected potential experiences present themselves almost daily—if we're open to the possibility.

Age does not diminish the likelihood of possibilities presenting themselves; however, our minds may, if they are closed to possibility or believe it no longer exists.

I can assure you, possibility still exists for every one of us, just differently. This is fine. We're all different; our desires to experience certain possibilities are different from each others' and our dreams for ourselves have likely changed over time. As such, be watchful and open to seeing possibilities, as they often come disguised in unexpected ways.

Since we can never predict when or how life will present our exciting possibilities, prospects, opportunities, adventures and friendships, we must practice accepting that possibility exists today and every day.

The existence of possibility for each of us today is a fact. There's nothing "whoo-whoo" about it. Through meetings of chance with others throughout my life, door after door has opened. As unprepared as I might have felt, as uneducated to the opportunity as I may have been—I've entered every door that was graciously opened. I'm grateful for every person I've ever met. Some offered me entry directly, others in more circuitous ways.

If we want to exponentially increase our own possibilities, we must start believing in the possibilities of others as well. By helping other people whenever we can, in any ways we're capable, we increase our own possibility in spades.

Believe me—if you don't yet believe this yourself. Stay on the lookout for opportunities to do unto others and watch what comes back. Be open to the possibilities.

CALENDAR SHMALENDAR

Calendars are handy when it comes to reminding us what day it is, when we have to do something or when we might want to celebrate an occasion. Other than that, being overly vested in the days, weeks, months and years that are declaring our chronological age may prevent us from being open to untold opportunities and possibilities.

We are really never too old to try whatever it is we want to do, assuming it is physically attainable. My best friend is 78-year-old "Aunt Judy" to my children. They've always thought that she's a bigger kid than they are! And you know what? They're right! Judy is a lot of fun, always up to get out and meet people and her exuberance toward life — along with her very active career as a ghostwriter—make her seemingly ageless to anyone who meets her. Abraham Lincoln understood this idea. He said, "It's not the years in your life that count. It's the life in your years."

Since we all woke up today, we still have time to get living. The calendar, other than reminding us where we might need to be at some point today, is irrelevant to our degree of life satisfaction. Our satisfaction is best measured in other ways.

As *Rent* playwright Jonathan Larson (who died the day before the first preview performance of his ultimately blockbuster play) asked, "Five hundred twenty-five thousand six hundred minutes. How do you measure, measure a year?"

SCORING 100 PERCENT

Everyone has days when we feel like we just want to quit. On particularly rough days when we feel that we've reached the end of our capacity to give, love, care, think, act, change, try, hear, or do whatever else is demanding more and more and more from us, it is helpful to remind ourselves that our track record for getting through bad days so far is 100 percent!

Congratulations!

Now go easy on yourself, notice all the things you're doing right and remind yourself that: Life is a test. We're doing our best and that's just fine. More than half of our grade each day is earned just by waking up!

ANGER, EMOTIONS AND HEALTH

Our mental state can upset normal physical functions, weaken resistance to infections and actually change the structure and functioning of our vital organs.

For example, emotional upsets affect the flow of hydrochloric acid, which in turn aggravates stomach ulcers. When I worked as a nutritionist and hypnotherapist in private practice, upsetting conversations could make people buckle with stomach pain. Anger can send blood pressure skyrocketing. Essential hypertension or chronic high blood pressure with no other apparent physical cause is associated with bottled-up anger. Considering how many deaths after 50 are related to blood pressure, this is significant. Hypertension patients often appear to be easygoing, yet these very same people may be smoldering. Once taught how to release pent-up emotions, blood pressure resumes at normal ranges. Diabetes has also been associated with emotional shock. Arthritic and autoimmune flare-ups can parallel emotional upsets and worry can accelerate tooth decay.

Understanding frustrations and fears is just as important as what blood tests or x-rays might reveal. Many of us bury distress in the crypts of our minds at the expense of our health.

Learning to relax can reduce or eliminate a plethora of problems. E-motions (think E= energy in motion) need conscious release or they express themselves in terms of flesh and blood. Allowing emotions release—without judgment, without labeling them good or bad but just as normal human emotions—gives us a chance to work through these fleeting feelings before they cause us physical hurt as well.

Some difficulties are real and cannot be ignored or meditated away. But facing challenges head on; accepting a situation; and talking with others or asking for help are steps to solutions that also give us new ways to cope with our challenges. Taking personal time-outs will release pent-up energy, while simultaneously filling us with a new kind of energy that enables us to live richer lives. Timeouts aren't wastes of time; they're time energizers that get our minds back in line to keep our bodies healthy.

Hint: When you're so busy that you think you have absolutely zero time to take a break—that's the time to take one.

NEED TO BREATHE

Here's the absolute best solution for feeling better when the tides of emotion from any situation begin to feel overwhelming: Breathe.

Breathing is essential to life and emotion management. Breathing impacts our respiratory system and our circulatory system as well, which impacts heart function.

There are times that we experience stress at such levels we forget to breathe. Actually, we can't really forget to breathe, because breathing is an involuntary action that the body is so perfectly designed to execute without our input.

Still, the reality is, when consciously or unconsciously experiencing stress, we tend to take shallow, short breaths. Yet the importance of strong breathing correlates directly to greater health, longevity and well-being.

Taking deep solid breaths, instead of the shallow ones we usually tend to take, can immensely improve our ability to manage all our interactions and positively curtail any negative feelings that might arise.

Throughout the day—whether at work, waiting in line, while relating with friends, family and everyone else—make a conscious, voluntary effort to breathe deeply. If tensions rise, before answering any question or providing a response, take the time to breathe in deeply and release. A plus is that others will perceive us as calm, rational and thoughtful—even if we're not feeling that way at all and are simply catching our breath!

Every day, as often as necessary, take a breathing respite. Find a private spot where nobody will bother you. Take five to 10 deep breaths in and out—but this time with your eyes closed. Reflect on how you can handle any situation sent your way. Try adding a deep sighing vibration as you let out your breath, doing your best Darth Vader imitation. This additional vibration will make you feel extra-great both mentally and physically. The Force will be with you!

INSTRUCTIONS

We instruct the world on how to see us.
That's it. I think it says it all.

CONTROL ISSUES

People are so colorful, expressive, wild, crazy and possibly even more intelligent when they allow themselves to just "be": Relaxing into the moment, be-ing themselves.

In the moment, people laugh, cry, feel and share the full wonderful range of emotions that make humanity accessible and real. I once read that "Being too sane is a sign of madness." Something about that really resonates. In some ways, "too sane" reminds me of being too worried about being too in control. Of everything. The "madness" part of that could also be interpreted two ways: As in "angry" because trying to be too perfect (sane) could make you "crazy!"

With age, it helps to reflect on what we might call our "control issues." Having "control" is illusory. The older we get, the more this becomes apparent. While controlling certain actions and choices may make us feel more powerful, there are still no (and never were) associated ironclad guarantees. Our control issues may have gotten us to work on time, but were not guarantees we got to keep the job. They may have kept us eating well and exercising, but did not guarantee our good health. They may have made us good communicators, but haven't guaranteed that everyone wants to hear and do what we say. The list is endless.

Control issues are not a bad thing to have: They've likely served a purpose and helped us to become more observant and action-oriented. But they may also have created unrealistic expectations and disappointments.

Today is as good a day as any to think about what we're trying to control. Maybe it's a good day to just let ourselves just be. Be who we've become from years of living and experiences: Knowing we don't have to worry about controlling anything because 1) we really can't and 2) because we can handle whatever happens.

RESTING UP

Throughout our lives, rest has been important, but now that we're older, it's more essential to our health than ever. We must get the rest necessary to keep us going for the long haul.

Rest is any period of inactivity during which our bodies can restore expended nerve energy. Anytime we're under excessive stress, we build up cellular waste faster than our body can eliminate it and we're depleting our energies faster than our bodies can restore it. To stay healthy, in our 50s and beyond, we have to give ourselves permission and time to rest.

There are four kinds of rest and each is essential.

1. Physiological rest or sleep is when our bodies are primarily inactive and we're able to catch up on building nervous energy for future expenditures.
2. Sensory rest refers to meditation and also sleep. During sensory rest, the nervous system and brain are relaxed or not normally exerted. Closing our eyes is sensory rest. It saves a great deal of energy and removes about 80 percent of energy-draining distractions.
3. Emotional rest comes from withdrawing from real or perceived stressors that drain our emotions. If we want to be healthy, we each need to give ourselves permission to remove ourselves from situations in which our emotions are being raised to unhealthy, stressful levels.
4. Mental rest happens when we allow ourselves to leave the office behind; accept that tomorrow is another day; and give ourselves credit for the fact that we really can handle life if we take it one step at a time.

Rest in each of these forms is essential for maintaining peak health. It is also during rest that our minds can dream and create new possibilities, as well as when our bodies can reap peace and experience recuperation.

We're all busy. Many of us are living extremely full lives, caring not just for ourselves but others as well. However, life is a balance between rest and movement. If we want long lives, we'll need to figure out how to strike that balance.

REFEREE ADVICE ON BEING HAPPY

Many years ago, a professional referee who works for a big-name sports franchise shared a story with me. (I'm protecting his privacy by not disclosing any more information.) He was early on in his career and one day he complained to his boss (the head of all the referees) about his wife, who is a very lovable woman, and who was working full-time as a teacher while also raising their three young children while her husband was often traveling for work.

His boss gave him this advice:

"If you want to be successful in this highly competitive business, and manage to stay happily married with all the traveling you'll be doing—a stable home is essential. Before you tell your wife one thing you don't like about her, before you complain about anything she does—make sure you've first told her 50 things you admire about her. If you can do that first, then go ahead and complain about whatever you want. But remember, this is an 'every 24-hour requirement': Find and tell her 50 positives every 24 hours before you start complaining. I expect you to report your progress to me."

Can you imagine? Wow! What a wise man who clearly valued the worth of a partner and family; understood human nature; and knew the effort (and kindness) essential to maintaining relationships. I never forgot this story. Its lessons can be applied to so many of our interactions with others as well as with ourselves. What an effective practice to get rid of those thoughts, such as: If only she didn't…If only he could… If only I weren't…If only they would…

What if we all stopped thinking about what we aren't happy with and instead required ourselves to list 50 things we are happy about before we're allowed to complain? Just an idea…

BURN OUT

Whether it was Neil Young, Def Leppard, Kurt Cobain, Oasis or anyone else who got us singing: "It's better to burn out than to fade away"—it's a thought worth contemplating.

When we were younger, the words likely had one meaning; now that we're older, possibly another.

Today, burnout is more likely associated with excess stress. Stress isn't necessarily negative. Positive mental and physical benefits come from exercise that stresses our muscles, respiration and circulation. High blood pressure, accelerated heart rate, abnormal increase or loss of appetite, excessive sweating, dilated pupils, lumps in the throat or in the pit of our stomachs, skin outbreaks, reduced immunity and tightness in our chests indicate the negative effects of stress.

Whether the stress in our lives is positive or negative, our bodies react the same. The crucial factor is how much demand is placed on our bodies and minds to adjust.

There are basically only two ways to deal with stress: 1) Remove ourselves from the stressor (which can be complicated) or 2) Build our resistance to stress by improving our diet, exercising regularly and getting adequate rest and relaxation.

Here are basic, easy things you can do, starting right now, to cope better with stress:

Drink more water. Not sipping, drinking whole glasses of H_2O starting the minute you wake up. Walk more—whenever, wherever you can. Eat your veggies: Steamed or in salads without drowning them in globs of commercial dressings. Try your salads undressed or make an olive oil, vinegar and mustard blend. Add one to two pieces of fruit a day to your daily diet, eating it in the late afternoon and evenings when you're tired and craving junk. Go to bed before midnight whenever possible. And remember: It's not stress that kills us; it's our reaction to it.

TURNING POINTS

Turning points are those moments when our world seems to turn upside down—whether we like it or not. Crisis often accompanies our turning points, and difficult or important decisions must be made. Suddenly we are challenged to adapt, reach, grow—and maybe even rebirth ourselves into what feels like a new life.

Events and people can both spark turning points. Dilemmas arise when choices must be made. We doubt ourselves. We worry. We seek the opinions of others. Will we make the right decision? Life is demanding that we move through our fears.

It is at the end of our comfort zone that life begins again. Our commitment to seizing the moment, owning it and defining our destiny with our utmost conviction will largely define life as we know it. We're forced to draw upon and use all of the skills, talents and energy that we've accumulated throughout our lives. Then, ultimately, we must face that moment when we will realize that nothing will ever be the same: Life will become divided into before and after this. There is no wrong way; no right way. There is only your way.

CYNICISM

Cynicism might be the only thing that can make us really old.

Cynicism happens if we allow bitterness to replace contentment.

Distrust to replace trust.

Doubt to replace belief.

Pessimism to obliterate our optimism.

Sarcasm to dominate our kind words and gentle communication.

We must work to maintain our faith and belief in others just as we'd like them to work to maintain the same with us. Old can happen at any age; dodging cynicism holds the secret to staying forever young.

LESSON LEARNED

At any and every stage of life, an optimistic outlook toward our challenges, adversities, losses and setbacks is beneficial. If we can look at everything that happens as a necessary lesson—whether we like it or not—our mental and physical health will benefit. Even the most unanticipated and unpleasant situations can be seen as a chance to learn about what we want to improve upon going forward, healing physically, mentally or spiritually. Utilizing our optimistic powers, seeing life as a series of lessons, can make our disappointments new opportunities to build our resiliency.

A career loss can expand our sights into new work directions, possibly with a new focus set on something we would prefer to be doing. Relationship pain offers lessons in improving communication, setting boundaries, developing trust and releasing doubts. A health setback holds lessons in making self-care a priority—improving diet, stress management and physical activity.

When we opt to find the lessons in adversities, we are choosing healthy personal growth. We are making the decision to define our situations instead of letting such situations define us.

Do Less; Accomplish More

There's only one way to get done everything that we need to do. We must learn to do less to accomplish more. While this may sound counterintuitive (or lazy), it's actually an essential strategy for every phase of our lives. Establishing top-down priorities so we can maximize our energy and stay healthy for the long haul is the goal.

To accomplish more by doing less, we need to start writing "Must Do Today" lists. While some of us may already be "listers," the idea is to refine the process by making sure each task on our list is essential and will have maximum impact. We've got to take care of the things that count the most, first. Save the rest for another day when you're making a new list, or figure out how to delegate tasks to others. Doing this will not only relieve stress; you'll be surprised that some things you thought you'd have to do will take care of themselves—or maybe they aren't really necessary.

Doing less but accomplishing more is one of the best ways we can help our mental and physical health, which benefits others in our lives as well. Don't feel guilty! Ultimately, these daily lists will help to better manage the life that keeps coming at us. Priorities, objectives, specifics, deadlines should be divided into short- and long-range goals. Focus intensely on the moment and reap the future rewards of more time for fun. Do Less, Accomplish More.

You Get What You Need

"You Can't Always Get What You Want" by The Rolling Stones is often playing in my head. I think there's a lot of truth in that title, but I particularly like the subsequent line that holds a bit more insight about a life philosophy: "You get what you need."

Being comfortable with aging is closely associated with a kind of wisdom that embraces our years as a necessary byproduct of growth. The Silver Disobedience® mindset can be defined as one that acknowledges and accepts our past mistakes and all kinds of losses— physically, emotionally and external to us—while still believing we can improve and grow.

We can all learn to recognize the good and the bad within ourselves and outside of ourselves, yet still try to learn from it all. We know our bodies are changing—and maybe we're more forgetful than we once were. Still, we're adaptable, bringing lighthearted humor to our lives as we recognize what we can change and accept what we cannot.

We're not giving up nor settling for less: Instead, we are challenging ourselves in new ways, by redefining our goals without feeling the need to justify them to others. This is the freedom inherent in Silver Disobedience®.

Spend some time thinking about how you can get your ya-yas out!

POWERING UP TRIAL AND ERROR

Much of what we know has been learned by trial and error. While we've had successes and enjoyed glory, we've also experienced failures. Some failures may have been accompanied by ridicule, pain, humiliation and other uncomfortable feelings.

Upon achieving success, our unconscious mind does not wipe out our memories of pain and failure. The unconscious dreads pain, humiliation and fatigue, and will avoid such emotions at all costs. This explains our inertia when action would be to our advantage.

Rather than face the possibility of pain, unconsciously recollecting our past failures, we decide not to act at all or we choose an easier task—often without finishing because we stop before we risk the possibility of yet another failure.

The secret to breaking a spell of inertia is this: Act as if it were impossible to fail. This act of imagination turns failure to success. Note I said "act." So you do have to *do* something. You must imaginatively capture the state of mind you'd be in "as if" your success was inevitable.

Sigh with relief, knowing that by acting "as if," you can allow your mind to use its already existing aptitude that in the past you may have lacked the energy to exploit! Insist to yourself you must reach the goal as soon as possible. Hold the mood of how you'll feel, as if waiting for a word of command. Imagine the energy and let it release. Give yourself working orders with the indisputable knowledge that your Higher Power (whatever you believe in) wants you to live life to the fullest. While doing this, act to make yourself more focused yet flexible.

Change up your routines. If you need to exercise, get sneakers on at a set time. Put fruit on the counter—so you grab it before junk. Go to yard sales and bookstores. Buy all the books about whatever you want to accomplish. Pile them in a place so you can't resist the temptation to open them and learn. Take selfies in your power suits for your new career. Whatever! Visualize. Feel it. Imagine. Act. Succeed. You can do it! Today's a good day to write out your plan of action detailing whatever it is that you want to do.

FEELING LUCKY

Do you believe in luck or are you a fatalist (a believer in fate)? Undecided? Let's look at how they're both defined:

- Luck is having been favored by good fortune.
- Fate is something that befalls a person; a prophetic declaration of what must be; an inevitable predetermined destiny.

The feelings we have regarding whether luck or fate has most impacted our lives, possibly align with our thoughts regarding the proverbial "Is the glass half full or half empty?" conundrum.

Both luck and fate are possible simultaneously and they are intimately intertwined by attitude. When suffering with a pessimistic and gloomy attitude toward life, circumstances or another person, fate seems to fulfill itself and unfold in almost prophetically negative ways. It seems like we had no control and things were just destined to unfortunately happen. Conversely, when a positive attitude rules our mental state, luck seems to keep appearing in almost miraculous ways.

While neither of these scenarios is always the case, as rarely in life are things ever so clear-cut, one could conclude this: Our luck or fate will be determined by our attitude. What do you think?

WHAT GROWS AROUND, COMES AROUND

We are what we think. Whenever I say this to my kids, it gets them as angry as it used to get me when my mother said it to me. But now I know it to be an accurate statement.

We reflect the images we hold of ourselves. We are who we think we are. We become who we think we can become. What we think about every day, our contemplations, make us who we are. Resumes are nice and we all like clothes. But no "things" define who we are. (You could read that "no thing" equals "nothing.") It is our thoughts that make our realities.

All that exists is based on thought. And thoughts are real only in that what you think should happen is usually the result of how you thought something would. We're our own best or worst judge and jury. Whether your future will be positive or negative, happy or unhappy, largely depends on how you choose to think it will be. Thoughts are seeds. Those that you pay attention to grow. Certainly, if you had a garden that you relied on for your food and welfare, if it was getting taken over by poison ivy—you'd stop it. Today is a good day for weeding out the poison vines and giving your optimism plenty of fresh soil to grow.

A RACE CAR LIFE

The idea of a race car triggers all kinds of excitement. (Did you know that "race car" is spelled the same way forward and backward?) So, what if we talked about aging using auto racing terminology?

There would be the "200 Mph Club" for those who've broken records driving a specified distance at 200+ mph.

Getting a "bye" would allow us to advance to the next stage or heat of an event without competing (cause we're so dang experienced and good).

Our "E.T." is the elapsed time it's taken us thus far from our start to now.

We'd celebrate "flag-to-flag coverage" recognizing our entire race and not just the packaged highlights.

We'd enjoy "laps of honor" or "victory laps," which are non-competitive laps taken before or after races to celebrate a driver's win or history of successes.

We could say we're looking at "photo finishes," whereby we're all doing so great you'd need a photograph to determine finishing order as to where we're all lined up crossing the line.

We'd respect "horsepower," our total power output, and our "torque," the superior turning ability of our engines.

We're already "pre-qualified" due to our lifelong experience with all kinds of challenging and hazardous situations along the road.

Checkups are merely "pit stops" necessary to keep us racing at optimum speed.

We've earned the "pole position" or our spot on the grid closest to the starting line, reserved for those who've had the best times.

We'd be recognized for our ability to "short shift" or regain control at high speeds around unforeseen corners in life.

Heck, if we could add humor to the age conversation, even "awful awful" is hot rod slang for a drag racer!

Personally, at this stage of life, I believe I haven't come close to hitting my full acceleration—how about you?

COURAGE: MORE THAN A CAPE

Black Panther, Wonder Woman, The Avengers, Deadpool, Ant-Man, Wasp, Aquaman, X-Men, Spider-Man, Batman, Superman and the Incredibles: Hollywood knows the appeal of superheroes and there's no sign of a slowdown for death-defying, courageous acts on the big screen.

Action movies make it seem like all we need is a cape, bulging muscles, character and courage to deal with adversity—regardless of the nemesis. In reality, when facing personally traumatic events, summoning courage is a lot more complex. It takes tremendous courage to rush into a burning building, arrive at the scene of an accident, fight wars, deal with trauma and care for ill people. It also takes courage to stand up for ourselves at work, share feelings with loved ones, confront unforeseen health issues, deal with financial setbacks and imagine our later years in life on a budget.

Courage is more than putting on a cape. To strengthen daily courage, keep these ideas in mind: Courage begins with thinking versus action. Rational thoughts conquer emotional and physical fear. Action will be necessary (that's why they're called action heroes!). We can't just hope for a solution. It will take courage to face the truth and figure out what actions are necessary for us to win the battle at hand. Stop procrastinating. Superheroes make decisions and move—even if it triggers all kinds of other twists and turns! At least they're not just standing around thinking about the situation while the world collapses. Forget Doomsday! There's no time for catastrophic thinking in our super suits!

Like Star-Lord (my favorite!) or Captain America (my second fave), we must draw on our very human emotional strength. Accept our limitations, recruit help, stay calm and find ways to comfort ourselves. Keep a moral compass. We can do the right thing because we have experience with adversity. Knowing what we value will serve as a huge source of strength. Life takes courage. But my bets say your super powers will come to the rescue.

'NO' IS A COMPLETE SENTENCE

"No" is a complete sentence. "No" is one of the shortest words in the human language—likely the first word issued by most of us as babies. "No" is an almost universal word, understood regardless of other language barriers.

Both "yes" and "no" are words that make us responsible for our thoughts and actions. If we say "yes," we're responsible for fulfilling whatever we agreed to. If we say "no," we must accept that another may be upset.

It is OK to say "no" to conserve our energy and define our priorities.

Because we've developed and collected a large scope of experience and connections over the years, we're often in great demand! So learning to determine when we need to say "no" is very important. The fact is, we really can't do all that we're asked for a variety of reasons—and if we try to, we're potentially increasing our likelihood for illness triggered by physical and emotional stress.

When we need to say "no," there is no need to over-explain or justify our position. "No" is "no." But if, like many of us, we've said "yes" throughout life when we really wanted or needed to say "no," here are four strategies for getting comfortable with using the word when we need to conserve our energy:

1. Just practice saying "no." Get used to the sound of it coming out of your adult mouth.
2. If "no" still feels too hard, practice saying this with a smile: "Thank you for asking. I'm flattered but I can't do it. I appreciate your understanding."
3. When possible, offer a suggestion. Maybe there is someone else or some other way you can envision the request being fulfilled: "I'd love to help but I can't. Perhaps you can…"
   Then,
4. Remove yourself or change the subject.

It is OK to say "no." We have every right to think about our response and respond within our own timeframe if we need to think about our answer as well. Before jumping to say "OK" (another short word), stop and choose. It is OK to say "no" and move on guilt-free. Try it.

BREATHE? HERE'S WHY...

Breathe to be healthy. Breathe to be beautiful. Breathe to walk taller, think smarter and live better. Every posture expert will tell you to fill your lungs. Beauty gurus (and cardiologists!) advise that better breathing increases circulation, which is good for our complexions (and hearts!). Psychiatrists will tell you short breaths increase anxiety. Doctors listen to your chest and back to make sure oxygen is properly flowing through our hearts and lungs.

While we all take in enough air to sustain our lives, are we taking in enough to live life vigorously—whether for what it demands or what we demand of it? Too often we don't take in enough oxygen. If you don't believe me, notice the physical fact of the lightheadedness experienced if we've stressed our lung capacity beyond our norm. Your lungs won't collapse. We need to allow them to expand all the way down our rib cages.

Nervousness, anger, excitement and basically every emotion can be managed through breathing. The calming effect of steady breathing is a miracle.

As we get older and bone density tends to decline, breathing becomes even more important—as people who breathe poorly tend to slump and develop concave chests. This impacts all aspects of health.

Breathe, move, fill your lungs with oxygen. The more oxygen in your body, the brighter your skin and moods will be; the more rev in your engine; the more smarts in your thoughts; the more peace in your mind.

IMPORTANT

If some aspect of our lives isn't working, we need to figure out what it is—and if it is due to something we mistakenly believed was unimportant.

In the big scheme of life and all our relationships, more problems originate from little things than big things. It is the things we overlooked because we thought they weren't so important that are usually at the root of our troubles.

When something isn't going quite the way we'd like, it's time to get back to basics and reassess what's important.

Brain Power:
How to Stay Mentally Sharp

The same factors that prolong life are proven to keep minds sharp as well.

Studies of those who have lived to be 100 show behavioral commonalities among the 25 percent showing no signs of cognitive decline. Also, among these elders, many didn't exhibit any form of dementia until age 92 or later.

Here's a collection of their aging secrets for a long life and a healthy mind:

Stay lean. A study of twins over a 40-year period found that those who were overweight in midlife were 1.5 times more likely to experience dementia by age 65. It is never too late to drop those extra pounds.

Eat for a healthy heart. A diet built on fish, vegetables, whole grains, nuts and fruits seems to reduce the risk of cognitive impairment. One study showed a 28 percent improvement in cognitive function over a four-year period for those who positively altered their diets.

Move that body. A one-mile walk daily reduces the likelihood of dementia by 50 percent, according to research.

Change up activities. A study of 1,300 people aged 70 to 89 asked participants about their daily activities starting in middle age. Those who read, painted, played games, did arts and crafts, and stayed physically and mentally active were 30 to 50 percent less likely to be experiencing memory loss.

Sleep. While insomnia can increase with age, a good night's sleep during regularly scheduled times helps memory and recall. If you're struggling with sleep, skip afternoon naps, stay away from electronics an hour before bed, avoid late meals, keep your bedroom cool and watch alcohol and caffeine, as both steal sleep.

Socialize. Loneliness takes a toll. Spending time with others has been shown to decrease the incidence of Alzheimer's.

Getting older does not have to mean sickness is inevitable. Many, if not most, of the illnesses people experience with aging are largely preventable. If the list above is news to you, it's not too late to start incorporating all of the above into your daily routine. Health is a natural state of being. If we give our body more of what creates health, our bodies will move toward greater health.

BIRTHDAYS PHILOSOPHY

At first, we count life in months and movements: "He's six months old" and "She just rolled over." As toddlers, we declare age in years, months and achievements, proudly announcing we're "two and a half" and we can "go to the potty by ourselves." Crossing into our teens, our right to party rules along with angst and confusion thanks to hormones and teenage-ness. By 18, age triggers twinges of anxiety as we contemplate adulthood responsibilities. We're counting opportunities as we wonder how we'll handle growing up and venturing out on our own. Work or college years are marked by various tests of independence. In our 20s, we're working and beginning to understand the challenges our parents had, as we struggle to take full responsibility for our choices, lifestyle and financial situations. In our 20s to 30s and beyond, we're considering partners and filled with mating hopes. These years may or may not introduce parenting into the mix, and a whole new reality of life with the endless challenges and responsibilities that accompany raising another and coping with daily living.

Life continues to roll on if we're lucky. For better or for worse, in sickness and in health. Work, friends, family, homes, locations: all changing. Never predictable. Filled with static, high fidelity, noise and distortion and wrinkles. Nothing digital about it. We can't plug, play and do a quick edit. Our lives get recorded like an old vinyl record for posterity. By our 50s, we're realizing the truth in adages like: "If we knew how long we'd live, we'd have taken better care of ourselves." But we also start to realize that our hopes are still possible because we did not "die before we got old."

We're not dead. We can still change, live and love: Doing what we can to leave our marks on the world and the hearts of others. Life's not over until it's over. Age is a beautiful thing. Each birthday is a gift. Birthday or not, celebrate today.

SELECTIVE MEMORY

Forgiving and forgetting are the two best strategies I can think of for having a good day and an overall pleasant life.

I've been in business, self-employed, for more than 40 years. I've dealt with all kinds of people on my entrepreneurial up-and-down journey. Those who know me well, marvel that through it all I've maintained a pretty good attitude toward others and life.

Of course, I've been screwed many times and always by someone I really liked at first; otherwise, I'd have protected myself better. Friends and coworkers often remind me of those times. But the irony is, I have what I can only label "selective senility."

While we all could collect an arsenal of reasons for bitterness, I genuinely don't remember most negative incidents. I made the decision that certain things were just not worth remembering. Another way to look at it is this: Imagine our heads have only x number of storage compartments: Why would we want to fill them with junk?

Selective memory is a choice. While some might think this is a weakness, I believe it is a strength. In fact, I'd say it's the root of power, not stupidity. It's an empowering choice to forgive others, forget them and move on. This becomes their loss instead of ours because we choose to think enough of ourselves, knowing that smarter folks will value our association. The best revenge we can ever have against being done wrong, is to make the entire event irrelevant by forgetting it. Not allowing anything to hold power over us in a way that constrains our happiness is how we own our own strength.

BEING DETERMINED

Did you ever have something happen that just completely infuriated you? You know, something that really knocked you over and filled you with anger or intolerance?

Of course you have! We all have! Nobody gets to our age without having gotten really livid with another person or toward a situation. On those bitter days, we're filled with resentments of all sorts. On the flip side, what about those days when we feel like the world is ours? Everything is great! We're filled with love and everything feels extra bright and cheery. Love is in the air and possibility is everywhere!

Does the world change that much from day to day? Yes and no. While certainly there are events that are shocking to us on many levels, most of the turmoil or joy we feel on a daily basis is within us. When we lose sight of light within ourselves and others, allowing negativity and darkness to dwell, daily life can feel insurmountable. When we stay positive about ourselves, our lives, situations and humanity—the light shines on all that is wonderful and our perspectives related to possibility reign. It's like we have a flashlight in our minds and we can zoom in on whatever it is we want to see most clearly.

We yield the power over these emotional swings. As long as we keep our faith that kindliness, good will and love are possible, we will be psychically, mentally and physically stronger. Turmoil rises if we fall back on suspicion, fear, anger and hatred, which are closely tied to our sense of pain and suffering.

Be determined to live a happy life filled with light.

DAYDREAM BELIEVER

Whenever we are not sure what we want to do next in our lives, we need to look to where our mind wanders for answers.

Daydreaming is a powerful messenger for relaying our hearts' desires. The more we find ourselves daydreaming about something, the more we are getting great information about what we really want to be doing. Daydreaming is an important way that our minds work out solutions to problems and refresh. Daring to daydream is often the first step to accepting the dare to live our lives a bit differently.

Go after your dreams no matter how others might try to discourage you. Be courageous and make those daydreams your realities. You might have to listen very closely to hear the inner voice that is pushing you to make those dreams real. But I'll tell you what it's saying in case you can't hear it yet. It quietly whispers, "Try again tomorrow."

URGENCY VERSUS IMPORTANCE

The best part of getting older may just be the sense of patience we develop toward the goals we set: Where we want to go with our lives becomes much more important than how fast we get there. How we prioritize our time seems to be aligning with what we know is important to be doing with it.

Stress levels rise when we somehow disconnect with this innate wisdom—namely, knowing the difference between what is urgent, and what (or whom) is more important to be spending time on (or with, including yourself). Satisfaction, health and well-being improve when we spend time on things that might be less urgent but are really more important to us.

We all deal with being chained to the seemingly urgent "must-dos": mail, bills, work, those we care for and zillions of other responsibilities. I won't list the "important" things because those are highly personal to every individual. Yet prioritizing—between what is urgent versus important—absolutely raises life satisfaction. Acting on our important but not necessarily urgent choices raises our spirits. With each passing year, regardless of our responsibilities, prioritizing our vision, values, principles, conscience, focus and plans is at the root of the sense of peace we feel through each passing year.

Now is the time to be sure that our daily choices and actions are prioritizing the genuinely important over what is seemingly urgent but might not be truly so. This can result in greater peace, progress and harmony within ourselves—so we are living the life we want to know we lived.

Owning Pride

Pride is the pleasurable feeling of satisfaction derived from owning our achievements, qualities or skills (note no mention of "things"). Pride shouldn't be confused with conceit, egotism or vanity. It's earned. Pride develops from doing things right.

Society often frowns on those expressing pride in their achievements. This is sad and a limiting way to view another.

If someone has put in effort to accomplish something, whatever that is, why should they not feel proud of their accomplishments?

If we feel jealous, annoyed or irritated by observing another's pride from their work or achievements, perhaps we need to think about what we might need to do to feel proud ourselves. Feeling irked really turns the mirror on ourselves and what we were not willing to try, risk, do, restrict or attempt.

For example, when observing someone who's really gotten themselves into great physical shape, there's a tendency to rationalize: "It's easy for them." This is rarely true. Rather, being in shape is a choice. Those with the toned, shapely physiques—at any age, but even more so as we pass 30—are exercising, making healthy food choices and skipping a lot of foods that they love as much as we do. I am a model, and when I go to a casting and see another model do a one-hand handstand, I don't say, "Oh well, she's younger than me!" Rather, I say, "Can you imagine the hours of training it took to achieve such a goal—and all the ice cream and French fries she skipped?" I feel the same when I watch any professional athlete.

The awe extends further to all forms of excellence: Like parents and teachers who have patience. Skilled laborers with technical expertise. Musicians practicing endless hours alone. Mathematicians and scientists developing formulas and therapeutics. Nurses, doctors, firemen, policemen and other caregivers helping others. Artists and writers who've inspired our imaginations. Electricians who get us lit-up again after a storm destroys infrastructure.

The list goes on. Each of us has invested time and effort in accomplishing something. So, I ask: What are you personally proud of having achieved? Please allow yourself to own it and share it—with pride.

How to Ruin a Day

There's a high probability that if we have too much stress in our lives, it's time to look in the mirror! Usually it is our own responses that contribute the most to our stress levels. Here are some examples:

Demanding perfectionism. If we want everything to be perfect all the time, we're making a deal with misery because we'll be focused far too much on what's going wrong versus what's going right.

Rigidity—that "my way or the highway" attitude—works very well for ruining a day. Not only will others feel the pressure of your demands, your own blood pressure will skyrocket also.

Worry about what you can't control. Traffic, others, store lines—complain about them, get wound up, rant—and you'll win the prize for ruining the mood.

Overbook. On any day, be sure to add more to the agenda than can possibly be completed! This will add stress and agitation and likely help others feel the same way, too.

Take everything you hear personally. Let yourself be super-sensitive. Assume that every frown, delay and remark is somehow directed at you.

Forget your sense of humor. Treat everything that happens as a matter of life and death. Be sure to let everyone know what you think is not funny. Including this article—which is written tongue-in-cheek! Because I know for sure we are too smart to want to ruin our days!

Let's release the desire to be perfect; practice flexibility; stop worrying about what we can't control; respect the hours in a day; understand that sometimes others just can't get out of their own ways and things happen in life that are not intended to be personal affronts to us—and most importantly: Allow yourself to smile and laugh!

THE DIFFERENCE BETWEEN SELF-ESTEEM VERSUS SELF-CONFIDENCE

There's a lot of talk these days about building self-esteem. We worry if we've hurt it in our kids or if ours has been damaged. Frankly, be more concerned about self-confidence.

Here's the difference: Self-esteem is how positive we feel about ourselves or our self-love. Self-confidence is built by our actions: Our willingness to test our abilities to handle life, people and the situations that come at us day after day—pushing forward knowing that we cannot necessarily predict the outcome.

Self-confidence is a verb, not static like a noun. It develops from our choices and actions in situations involving ourselves and others. Self-confidence is the foundation necessary for building self-esteem.

By our age, we've had countless challenges that have tested our abilities to cope, overcome, surmount and thrive. If we allow ourselves to see our past history kindly and clearly, we'd see mountains of proof confirming that we've gotten stronger every year and honed immense capabilities for navigating life's challenges.

Self-esteem follows self-confidence. It results from knowing that each challenge tested the strength of our self-confidence. The more we are challenged and are able to confirm that we have the ability to handle a myriad of experiences, self-confidence builds. Self-esteem grows when we can reflect on how we managed those challenges and accept the proof that we "passed those tests."

Self-confidence should not be confused with being egotistical. Rather, it's a subtle confidence that grows from understanding our abilities; realizing we have the potential to use our talents and improve upon them; and knowing we're OK because we'll be learning along the way no matter what happens. Our self-confidence, and ultimately our self-esteem, builds on the personal acknowledgment that we've accumulated lots of experience worthy of our esteem.

IS YOUTH THE PINNACLE OF LIFE?

We often hear people pining for their younger days as if they represent a golden time of life that has passed. While observing children, it is certainly easy to envy how they seem to be overflowing with energy. Teens and young adults are often also full of ideas about changing the world. Our younger years were a time when we might have had certain physical advantages that were instantly accessed—without aches and pains. In our younger days, we likely had certain mental advantages too; for most of us, our earlier years didn't include any stress about work or worries about paying rent and bills. If we compared our life today to the life of a child or teen (and comparing is usually not a great idea), one might think our days of youth have gone for good.

But the real thing we're observing—or maybe pining for—when we contemplate "youth" is the energy to explore.

Youthfulness is not merely a physical state. We all know plenty of teens and even some in their 20s who act pretty stodgy—because they either think they know it all or they are wasting their ability to move by sitting around, hour after hour, texting and playing video games.

Youth—in my humble opinion—is a state of mind that can be owned by anyone at any age. Youth is the urge to explore every curious idea that comes to mind; the desire to learn anything and everything we can about whatever we want to know to the fullest. With this definition, yes, I do believe that youth—the desire for, and energy put toward, continual learning—is the pinnacle of life. So how are you enjoying your youth?

BELIEVE IN OTHERS

When we think of youth, we often connect it to a time of innocence—that era in our lives when we believed whatever we were told. Children tend to approach others with openness and trust. This frightens parents and others who love us and worry that we'll get hurt in some way or another.

Sadly, at some point in life, due to socialization and various other factors circulating within families and communities, many of us stop believing in others. We censor our judgment. We start to wonder why others would do certain things. We doubt the goodness of their intentions. We worry they might be trying to trick us into doing something that benefits them, not us.

For most of my life, I've been a believer in others. Yes, I've been brutally disappointed, wounded and hurt; I've cried and wondered why I didn't protect my heart from the pain that I should have seen coming. I admit it. To this day, there are still those who will tell me to my face that they think I'm a complete sucker for deceptions and lies.

I don't think I'm gullible. I enter every relationship—both personal and work-related— eyes wide open. I do my homework if necessary. I walk away from glaring red flags. But still, I choose to believe in people and possibilities. And I believe it is people who help make possibilities realities. I think we're all trying to make our way in life.

By believing in others, I find I'm disappointed much less than others might expect. I can't think of anything I feel truly bitter about. More so, by believing in the goodness and good intentions of others, I think that my expectations have been positively fulfilled. I believe that by choosing to believe in both others and what may be possible, I've become a happier and more energetically spirited person. This is a good thing.

SAME TIME, DIFFERENT CHOICES

Suppose that if you drove to an appointment 100 miles away from your home, you'd be assured of greater happiness, health and prosperity. You have the time to get there. But instead, you decide it would be more fun to drive 25 miles in the opposite direction. Seems ludicrous, right?

Yet often when it comes to going straight to the appointments we make with ourselves for our own fulfillment, we decide to go with momentary fun instead—and drive the wrong way. Spending the same time and energy, we fail where we might have succeeded. And believe me, it does take energy to fail.

It takes energy to resist motion. Powerful struggles are waged against the forces of life to keep us inert—although these struggles sometimes take place far beneath the surface of our consciousness, so we're not always aware of this happening.

When we fail to choose happiness, health and prosperity by devoting precious hours to time-wasting activities, it is more obvious that energy is being diverted. For example, instead of taking a walk, which would be using our energy to improve our moods and health, we might choose to sit on the couch. We made a choice to do something that is counter to strengthening our bodies. As in the opening example, we drove in the wrong direction.

Considering that everything we do requires energy, what if we opted to use our energy as often as possible in ways that propelled us forward into a better state of being? We might be living healthier, happier, more prosperous lives like the ones we hope to live until age 100+.

Those who make positive choices see the same sunsets, breathe the same air, love and are loved no less than any of us—and they have something more: The satisfaction of knowing they have chosen to go in in the direction of a life of health and growth.

P.S.: I don't know about you…but just reading this makes me pretty inspired to go take a walk!

BUCKET LISTS

The idea behind bucket lists is this: They're all about doing what we really want to do instead of what everyone else thinks we should be doing. Because I've always been self-employed, my work has always fulfilled my bucket list. I've been fortunate in this way; working has always felt more like a game than a job I had to do. This said, we can all acknowledge times when we suspect there's more out there than whatever we've been able to experience thus far—and maybe we want to try to turn those dreams into realities.

I've seen all kinds of bucket list ideas, from jumping out of planes and trips to exotic places to learning to play an instrument or a solo in the church choir. Your list is your list. That's the point of it. Actualizing it is all about you as well. As a result of some online research, I've assembled a plan for moving your dreams over to the "been there and done that" column:

* Think about realistic and achievable goals.
* Make a written list. Keep it in a prominent place and review it regularly.
* Don't stress if you change your mind and want to modify it. It's yours and yours alone. Change it up all you want.
* Don't feel a need to share it with others. The naysayers will be naysayers.
* Planning isn't optional. Pick one or two items from the list and start to plan your road map for making the dream come true. Set a timeline with a due date and try to stick to that.
* Cross off each achievement as you fulfill it.
* Assuming you lived through your goal—and unless it was ridiculously dangerous, you probably will—repeat, starting from step one.

REACTION

The dictionary defines "reaction" as: 1) an action performed or a feeling experienced in response to a situation or event; 2) a person's ability to respond physically and mentally to external stimuli; 3) an adverse physiological response to a substance that has been breathed in, ingested or touched.

Overall in daily life, I'd define most of my reactions as mental "re-actions" (read that kind of like a mental repeat). Somehow, when I react to people or circumstances, I realize I have mentally stepped out of the present. I have moved into my immense head-case filing system (yes, pun intended) and I've pulled out some old files. In nanoseconds, the result is that I am trying to connect unrelated memories or feelings about a past moment to the present situation. So instead of staying present and assessing the current circumstance or person, in my mind I am "re-acting" some other moment and trying to tie it to the present one. I'm in a state of "re-call" and response.

Since this current moment has never happened to any of us before, whether alone or with others, unless it is one where we are in danger (which is rarely the case), we don't want to be "re-acting." We want to be wholly present to the individual and moment at hand.

Not "re-acting" is the only way we can really see and try to understand another person or live fully.

COOL

Being cool means our unconditioned self is attuned and we're keeping our groove on. Instead of being reactive, we're chill and observant. Watchful in the moment, doing our own thing, our intuition sharpens.

The closer we get to seeing all life from a neutral, balanced, calm and impersonal perspective, the cooler we are. "Cool" is a synonym for all those words as they share similar definitions. Cool means we're good if something happens and good if it does not.

You were born cool. You may have even been cool before Elvis. Now's a good time to get in touch with our inner sense of cool. We know it when we see it. Find yours and wear it. Nothing looks and feels better.

MAY THE FORCE BE WITH YOU

Everything in the material universe holds the dual forces of attraction and repulsion. People magnetically draw fondness and sympathies as well as polar opposites such as animosity, aversion, distaste and repulsion. With magnetism, there is always some likeness in atomic structure that causes the effects of attraction; otherwise there is no attraction. For example, a magnet will not pull glass toward it, only iron particles. People are similar. We sense attraction and repulsion based on who we are.

We determine the type of magnet we become. Just like the physics of magnets, the stronger the magnet, the more powerful the force. Our magnetism may be physical, mental, spiritual—or ideally a bit of all three. We can learn to strengthen our physical magnetic forces by exercising and eating well; concentration and focus on any task will get it done more quickly and build our mental magnetism for future benefit; and keeping our minds tuned into the moment enhances spiritual magnetism and brings a greater sense of peace to our lives.

While magnetic power is inherently within each of us, our actions and choices determine what kind of magnet we become and what we shall attract. However, we cannot choose one magnetism over another: Our magnetism is symbiotic. If we choose to focus solely on material magnetism such as increasing our wealth, unless we are also focusing somehow on our spiritual magnetism (as in providing value of some kind), the wealth is less likely. If we think we can go to the gym to increase our physical magnetism but drink too much alcohol or smoke, our magnetism will be weak. Likewise, we can't say: Today I'm going to become more spiritual, so I won't work because that is too materialistic.

As my favorite line in the entire Star Wars series says: May the Force be with you.

A PEACEFUL MIND

A peaceful mind is an ultimate life goal. Peace does not mean living in a place with no disruptions, troubles, hard work or struggles. Peace means that regardless of what is happening around you, you can hang on to your inner sense of calm. Having a peaceful mind is the greatest goal any of us can seek and also possibly the hardest feat to achieve. Yet the only way we can ever have peace in our homes, at work or in the world is if we each seek to have peace begin in ourselves. I'm not saying it's easy, nor am I claiming to have achieved it. Peace is my daily personal goal. It is my wish for today and every day that I will make my heart the ruler of my reactions to others instead of my mind. If I allow my heart to lead the way, I will improve control over my thoughts and choices in more positive ways.

To find our personal pathway to peace, we must each look deep within our hearts to find the barriers we have built against others, against ideas, against anything we are at odds with. Only by breaking down our personal walls and seeing others as one with us—struggling for peace themselves—can we have love and peace in our lives.

This is my wish for myself and for everyone today and every day. Let there be peace on Earth and let it begin with me.

LIFE IS CHANGE. GROWTH IS OPTIONAL. CHOOSE WISELY.

Changing anything is never easy, yet change is a constant factor in our lives. Although there are certainly moments when we'd all like to freeze time: our work lives change; daily routines change; family and friends move, get sick or die. We're changing—aging from the moment we are born. We're always getting older. It's a fact of life that comes with birth.

Change is always accompanied by a period of discomfort and/or stress—even when it's a change for the better.

Growth is optional during any experience that might be considered a change. We have the option to resist growing through our circumstances. But it's our ignorance that would choose resistance. Ignorance is really defined as unawareness or unfamiliarity with an experience.

When we are ignorant, we are choosing to ignore. But we have the opportunity to choose growth by educating ourselves with new knowledge and information about the newest change. This is how growth flourishes, how we empower ourselves, how we win the fight against resistance and how we reduce our stress, thereby improving our physical health and mental well-being. Resist or grow. How are you growing today?

Don't Wait for a Pat on the Back

Sometimes we do, do and do, expecting that we're going to get a reward. A great parenting blog I once read by James Lehman really resonated with me. Writing about living with teenagers, Lehman said: "Don't expect a pat on the back (for all you do)." That statement hit me and it's become something I still remind myself of regularly—in all aspects of my life.

Resentment builds if we do for others expecting accolades or trophies or compliments. It is an expenditure of negative energy to keep track of what we do for others or to think our actions somehow oblige another. When we give, we must do it freely. When we're being kind, loving and generous, it is a no-obligation gift that we choose to give. In that moment, it's a one-way transaction. When we get love, generosity or kindness in return, it's a bonus. While we might feel that certain people drain our energy with their ongoing needs, it helps to remember times of fulfillment that you received in the past and what may be coming from others in unrelated ways. Strive to be grateful for these people—sometimes random strangers (like those who let you have the parking spot when you're in a rush)—and remember those moments.

There is balance in the world—if we choose to see it. The people you give to might or might not be the ones who return generosity to you—but others will. It's how good will works. Try thinking of good actions as if they were currency for a universal bank. We all make deposits and we all make withdrawals. When we're worried about whether we're getting our fair share of good will, it's time to make more deposits.

Sunshine

Like rays of sunshine, we each have powerful illuminating capabilities that can brighten our days. Our attention and focus work as transmitters and receivers of powerful light that is within ourselves and that is also radiating from those around us. We can cast our glow onto others and they can light up our worlds as well. Together we can all create magical moments of light.

The Importance of Sleep at Every Age

There was a time sleep was determined by sun cycles. We awoke at sunrise and went to bed shortly after sunset. Candles extended evenings a bit for a few remaining household activities, family time and reading. The electric light altered sleep patterns forever. It became possible to stay up all night. Technology—televisions, computers and smartphones—have drastically changed sleep even more so. We're compelled to "check in on what's happening." But technology's impact on sleep goes deeper: the blue light emitted by cell phone screens, computers, TVs, etc. all restrain the production of melatonin, the hormone that controls our sleep/wake cycle or circadian rhythm. Reducing melatonin makes it harder to fall and stay asleep.

Benefits of a good sleep are well documented. Research shows seven to eight consecutive hours of restful sleep are crucial for life quality as we age. Besides keeping under-eye circles away, sleep makes us feel better. If memory is slipping, sleep may be missing. Sleep keeps our memory cells firing. Too little and too much sleep can shorten lifespan. Why? Bodies need recovery time for digestion, memory-filing and "housekeeping." Lack of rest causes waste buildup, illness and accidents. Tired people shouldn't operate machinery—including cars. Diabetes, arthritis, autoimmune diseases, heart disease and stroke have many causes, but inflammation is at the root. Cells inflame and begin malfunctioning when they are unable to clean out toxic waste from normal life processes, foods, drink, stress and the environment.

Creativity juices and emotional stability are positively impacted by adequate sleep, as are all aspects of physical performance, attention, learning, impulsiveness, stress, likelihood of depression and weight gains. Making seven to eight hours of sleep a priority, as often as possible during normal nighttime hours, is a must for our health and longevity.

PURPOSE

When we commit to a purpose, the mountains and valleys of life begin to reverberate energy toward our goals. If we choose to go for broke—not merely wishing but really implementing action in a step-by step way, thinking of everything we can possibly do to move ourselves toward what we want—totally awesome things seem to start happening miraculously. Little signs pop up: help is offered, doors open, opportunities suddenly present themselves, people reappear and we notice things we never saw before.

Each new dawn presents opportunities that come into our lives once we make a commitment to whatever it is we want to achieve. What we desire could be anything: better relationships with ourselves or others, different work opportunities or a new career, a healthier life, enriching friendships. These signs of synchronicity aren't uncanny although they might feel that way. They are confirmation that you've set your mind to achieve a goal—and the life forces that connect with our hearts and minds are helping us fulfill our vision if we are open to accepting assistance.

Each morning, I awaken at least 30 minutes before anyone else in my home. I drink one to two big glasses of water at room temperature. Then I immediately sit in my favorite chair with my eyes closed for five to 10 minutes. This is my time of the day. I allow myself to think only about what I want in life. I use my best imagination. I see myself happier with my family and think about my part. I think about everything I want to achieve. How I want my life to evolve. I envision big things. What I think about is private. I don't share it, except for those ideas that arise and make me want to start writing. In those quiet moments, all things are mine: peace, resolution, commitment, optimism and faith. My plan for the day has been set. It's now up to me to do the work that's necessary to make it real.

SHORTCOMINGS AS ADVANTAGES

Whatever we believe to be a personal or physical shortcoming or weakness may actually be a source of strength. A simple example of this: When health problems arise, we all tend to improve our actions, trying to figure out what we need to do to get better. (When I get sick, I swear I'll never eat another cookie or miss a workout again!) Conversely, when we're feeling healthy, we might be more inclined to burn the proverbial candle thinking that we can handle anything, when maybe we need to consider a little more balance.

Awareness of any weaknesses is the first step to becoming stronger. Simply being aware of a shortcoming is great because it can serve as a way we whisper to ourselves: "I can work to improve this somehow."

I know many people in their 70s, 80s and 90s who are still mulling over what they need to learn about themselves or something that they still want to accomplish or improve at. They're educating themselves to overcome weaknesses they think they have. Seen in the right perspective, it's our awareness that can trigger the urge for self-education and new efforts that result in our growth and improvement. Each time we challenge ourselves, we've assured our growth.

While youth might come with stronger bodies, it lacks the experience and knowledge that is accrued year over year through daily life, experiences and all of the lessons learned through trial and error. As we age, we may forget a few things and possibly be a bit physically weaker—but we've become more aware and flexible about changing. We've gained life experience and consequently a special wisdom that is absent in youth. While certain elements for success may seem inclined toward youth (and its naivete), age proves that it is among our weaknesses where we find our strengths.

Yesterday's Chains

If you've lived long enough, you're likely to feel you've been screwed over in one way or another at some point—possibly at many points.

A normal reaction to feeling wronged is to start building up defenses and walls to prevent it from ever happening again. Consciously or not, we decide we need to protect ourselves against such perceived violations in the future. Apprehension builds against things that might or might not ever happen again. The proverbial baggage gets packed and carried. If we can't put our offended, pained and angry feelings about the situation (or person) behind us and move on, we become harder and jaded. We actually relive the pain, re-hurting ourselves. We begin to become rigid. Not only do our perspectives become more rigid, our bodies stiffen and become less flexible as tension is held onto. This affects our mental health and our physical health as well. Arteries, so essential to having blood flow freely and flexibly through our bodies, harden.

Aging begins when anything gets stiff and rigid and starts to lose its inherent flexibility. Youth is associated with flexibility, possibility, unfolding and stretching. Flexibility is a trait of life, rigidity a trait of death. The more flexible we can remain, the more we can move on, living. Life is challenges and adversity. To believe otherwise is naive. Working to maintain our flexibility in body, mind and soul, the greater our physical and mental health will be. Release the chains that bind you. They're yesterday's news. Embrace today.

Rocking Energy

Everything has either kinetic or potential energy. Moving objects are said to have kinetic energy (KE). Stored energy is referred to as potential energy (PE).

Stored energy is released via work. For example, although a rock on the ground seems harmless, it still holds PE. Once we apply our own KE, or work to lift it, the energy of the rock increases because it has been elevated. It went from PE to KE because it can now be thrown and break a window. By applying some heavy lifting—work—that rock is no longer a lump on a log but rather a powerful force in motion.

This example applies to every aspect of life because we are each either a mass of PE or KE. The question becomes: What work do we have to do to move our PE into powerful KE that propels us forward toward whatever we want to achieve?

QUESTIONS ONLY

Even though I've been self-employed my whole life, having teenage children in my late 50s is forcing me to try a new form of communication. I'm trying very hard when speaking with my kids to listen without saying anything except in answer to direct questions. I'll be real: I fail at this a lot. Yet when I succeed, I usually get a hug. So if Pavlov was right, someday I'm going to improve at this practice.

If you want to try this in any of your relationships, the goal of this listening exercise is to be pleasant while practicing it. Don't let anyone know you're doing this. Just practice it. Don't give the impression that you're suffering and deserve a reward or that all your listening is causing you a bad headache. Be as ordinary as possible; just do not speak. Answer any questions with as few words as possible and do not attempt to get the other person to ask you a question.

Doing this helps me realize that I often rush into speech, because I've sometimes seen an expression on another's face that I interpret as misunderstanding or confusion. The impulse then is to keep talking and try again. Yet continuing to speak usually does not resolve the supposed misunderstanding. My attempts likely linger in the listeners' minds, further clouding the issue, making me ineffectual at best.

When I make my silence last, I feel stronger. Others feel heard. The longer I make my silences last, the more thoughtful and purposeful the conversation seems to be.

Try it to see how your communication with another can positively change.

TIDES

We all know that people react differently to the same things on different days. One day what we say and do doesn't bother others. Then on other days, it seems as if we inadvertently trigger an apocalypse. The same holds for our reactions to others: Some days we find what they are doing amusing and it's easy to roll with their antics. On other days? Their behaviors grate on our nerves—and we want to tell them, often with a flash of fury, exactly how we feel.

These up-and-down reactions to related situations are normal. High and low spirits can be counted upon with regularity as dependable as the ocean tides.

Various circumstances can hasten or delay our periods of elation and depression. When we're feeling like we're in a slump, good news gives our spirits a brief boost. Conversely, bad news is only mildly depressing when we're feeling emotionally high.

Some research confirms that these mood cycles coincide with moon cycles. In other words, our individual low or high periods are likely to develop a pattern—and our feeling will follow an up-and-down trajectory roughly every 33 days or so per cycle.

Then, for some of us, mood cycles are directly related to hormonal cycles.

Recognizing the normality of emotional cycles is very helpful. It helps us understand—particularly during the lows—that this too shall pass. There is nothing wrong with you—particularly as you are uniquely you. Try not to confuse your feelings for facts. Instead, be a little kinder and view your moods as your own personal lunar cycles that trigger fascinating emotional tides. This is a much kinder way to treat ourselves.

ON THE LOOKOUT

It's always a good idea to stay on the lookout for ways to increase the possibilities in our lives.

Possibility is anything that provides us with a chance to change our circumstances for the better. Unless your crystal ball is working better than mine, we can never predict the ways that life will present new exciting possibilities, prospects, opportunities, adventures and friendships. I'm a big believer in synchronicity—the concept of meaningful coincidences between two people that occur with no causal relationship yet that seem to be purposely related.

When I reflect on the trajectory of my life, which has moved more like a roller coaster than a rocket ship, the most outstanding aspect is how—through meetings of chance and synchronicity—door after door opened. As unprepared as I might have felt, as ill-suited to the opportunity as I might have been, I've entered every door. I'm grateful to every person who offered me an entryway, and to all those I meet on a daily basis who continue to do so. I'm convinced that my practice of daily meditation, which is often as unstructured as simply locking myself in the bathroom for five minutes of deep breathing and solitude, increases the probability that synchronicity will increase exponentially in my life. It is these chance meetings with other people that can change a life. Be on the lookout. Be open to the possibilities. Trust in the adventures of your experiences.

NOT OUR FIRST RODEO

Most things are possible if we've got enough nerve to buck up and throw ourselves fully into the challenge.

Thanks to the life lessons that come with age, much of our grit is based on a foundation of experience. Our self-assurance for many of our decisions is honed from our prior experiences both positive and negative. Our confidence reflects a mature temperament that either we can do it—or we can figure it out if it doesn't go according to plans. Although every day brings new tests that present themselves in any number of ways, this is not our first rodeo.

The pricelessness of all of our years of experience is what makes us incredibly valuable to any work, volunteer or other situation that requires critical thinking. Those who have hung on, been bucked and still taken the bull by the horns are more equipped to climb into the saddle.

Embrace your confidence and determination and be sure to share it with others in any situation. You're ready for the ride. As John Wayne famously said: "Courage is being scared to death and saddling up anyway!"

SOME KIND OF WONDERFUL

As we age, we often tell each other, "You're looking good…" with the subtext being: "…for your age." I propose we all start changing the phrase to: "You're looking wonderful." After all, "wonderful" is an adjective describing something that arouses wonder.

Don't other people regularly arouse wonder in you? I wonder what people are thinking. I wonder why we choose to do certain things. I wonder what others would be like if I really got to know them. I wonder how other people feel about so many things that happen in life. I wonder about the ways people choose to express themselves. Can you imagine how many smiles we could bring to the world if we started acknowledging our wonderment of others?

"Wonderful" is not a possession of the young nor old. Yes, I know there are some pretty wonderful pictures out in the world of models, celebrities and others—and that is wonderful! They add interesting color to the world. But seriously, I also know what I look like when I'm tired—and I certainly know the magic an amazing stylist, makeup and hair team can create, along with a great photographer who understands lighting. And of course, who can resist the remarkable effects possible with any number of filters—also known as the social media facelift?

Let's get back to recognizing the wonderful nature of individuality and start a new trend. Let's all cheer our wonder of others. Let's practice being "wonder-full" and full of wonder. What do you think?

FIRST AND LAST

Each moment is a first time. Each moment is a last time. We don't ever get the same moment twice in a lifetime. Each moment is a new, fresh clean slate. As such, each moment holds the potential for growth and new possibilities not just for ourselves but for everyone else as well. Really think about that.

KNOW THYSELF

My mother embroidered and framed a picture that said, "Know Thyself." We couldn't leave our house without seeing it. This sometimes really annoyed me, especially since it was also my mother's rejoinder whenever I blamed someone else for something troubling me.

"Know thyself" is one of those simple expressions that we really have to think about and work on understanding. Why do we have to work so hard to know ourselves? In part, it's because we've spent a lifetime constructing our self-image through the facial expressions of others—people who are often tired, overworked, overwhelmed and trying to do their best to deal with their own limitations. Their expressions weren't (and aren't) always happy, approving or embracing. Sadly, mixing up our true self-image with an image of ourselves perceived through others' moods or circumstances can result in misinterpretation. It can make us believe that the answer to finding and knowing ourselves is rooted in external factors.

This further triggers faulty thinking that goes deeper if and when we start to believe other people are the cause of our problems. While that may be the case under certain circumstances, more often it is our sense of self that needs to be embraced during problematic moments of discomfort.

We must develop a real sense of who we are—and own it. Our uniqueness is that inner voice that nobody else has. It empowers us, heals us, finds us, corrects us and makes it possible for us to love and respect ourselves. To find ourselves means we have to think for ourselves. We must pay attention to our intuition, not our rationalizing brains. We must follow our hearts, as that is where our wisdom resides.

GRATEFUL

Thank you (in no particular order) for: Health. Mind. Parents. Children. Brothers. Sisters. Family. Friends. Laughter. Work. Education. Peace. Love. Reading. Sleep. Process. Freedom. Mistakes. Relationships, Even When They Are Challenging. Food. Coffee. Clothing. Seasons. Beds. Wine. Safety. Security. Our Armed Forces. A Home. Medicine. Scientists. Jokes. Entrepreneurs. Sunshine. Musicians and Music. Artists and Art. Freedom of Speech. Tears and Pain. Philosophers. Wisdom. Age. Oceans. Mountains. Roads. Sunny Days. Rainy Days. Snow. Naps. Sex. Blue Jeans. Vision. Hearing. Exercise. Walking. Understanding. Sunrises. Sunsets. Clients/Customers. Plumbers and Plumbing. Showers and Baths. Electricity and Electricians. Garbagemen. Internet. Movies. Postal Delivery. Public Transportation. Movies. Holidays. Vacations. Travel. Books. Letters. Diversity. Voting. Challenges. Successes. Failures. Furniture. Animals. People I Don't Particularly Like. People Who Open Doors (Literally and Figuratively). Alone Time. Volunteers. Our Galaxy and the Universe. Everything I Missed.

AT ENOUGH, WE SHARE

At some point, while on our individual journeys, we realize that others really can't give us everything we think we want. When this realization dawns on us, the temptation arises to abandon that person (or situation) in search of someone or something different. The problem begins because we think that another's inability to fulfill our wants means that they are being selfish or holding back.

The reality is actually this: We need to look at ourselves and realize that none of us can give what we don't have. Until we can take care of our own needs in a way that nurtures our own hearts, it's very difficult and stressful to share and care for others. This applies to each of us from birth to death. To visualize the problem with being emotionally overwhelmed, imagine you asked a starving homeless person to share their food—and then made them feel guilty for not wanting to give up what might be their only meal.

We each must focus on giving ourselves enough of whatever it is that we need (healthy food for energy; sleep for recuperation; exercise for stress relief; quiet for thinking; times with friends and laughter; etc.) Through this self-care, we enhance our ability to share more freely while becoming better able to accept the limits of what others can give. At enough, we share.

Silly Is Serious Business

Whenever you have a moment to be silly—do it. Yes, if you have teenagers, they'll be mortified—but you'll be better for it. Being silly is serious business. It is good for everyone. Being silly has been proven to be healing in a variety of illnesses, particularly those involving autoimmunity.

Getting your silly on is more than goofing around. It's actually a part of how our brains are wired. The play impulse comes from our brain stem and limbic systems and is inherent in both humans and animals. This physicality makes us more flexible under stress and is essential to our adaptability in life. As such, it's to our benefit to stay in touch with this natural part of our nature.

Getting silly and playing around bolsters our immune system and reduces blood pressure: These two things make us more resilient. People who laugh regularly are likely to be more mentally and physically healthy.

When we're being silly, our minds tend to check out of the crowded thought-hotel we all stay in too often, and our minds are gently allowed to relax, wander and explore. Since our minds most effectively recall two extremes of memories—the very good and the very bad—building more great memories based on silliness is a good way to shore up against those days when we all feel a little sad.

Feeling Happy

Our feelings of happiness are in constant flux. We are all unique in what makes us feel happy. What makes us feel happy today will not necessarily have the same effect tomorrow. This goes for people, places and things. Our individual state of happiness requires introspection while doing things and moving forward with actions.

Things beyond a roof, food and clothing are only really accessories in life. I'm not saying things aren't fun and enjoyable; I like accessories of all kinds. But if we look at these things any other way, they tend to complicate and stress our lives. Our worlds are overloaded with stuff that is constantly vying for our attention, time and money. Most stuff rarely elevates our sense of happiness for any extended period of time.

INNER PEACE

Nobody can give us inner peace. It would be nice if we could buy it by going on a retreat or vacation, but this is not a reality. While we might enjoy a peaceful vacation with no arguments in a beautiful, peaceful setting—this doesn't mean that we experienced peace in our mind.

It's hard to shut down our inner clamoring. Researchers believe that we have anywhere from 50,000 to 70,000 thoughts per day, or 35 to 48 thoughts per minute. Not only do we have all of our own thoughts vying for attention; add interactions with family and friends, work environments and all other external stimuli, including television, radio, email and the internet. We live in a state of constant overload.

Our overall peace can be enhanced by learning to practice meditation or steady breathing. There's a reason the word "practice" is used: It takes lots of practice to quiet our minds. I've been practicing for more than 30 years and I'm still no expert. Sometimes I succeed beautifully; at other times, I feel like I'm failing miserably—yet I force myself to try again. This is because I figure the discipline might help make me stronger for another day, when hopefully the quiet will come more easily.

Learning to practice basic steady breathing is a perfect way to begin to feel more peaceful. You don't need to know any yoga-style positions or worry about taking deep breaths (although good deep breaths—in through the nose and out through the mouth—are stress-relievers). Research supports that just practicing steady breathing reduces stress and increases relaxation. This makes sense if we're aware of how often we inadvertently hold our breath—particularly when feeling mildly aggravated.

Closing our eyes in a quiet spot—a car, bathroom, bedroom or yard—all work. This shuts out visual stimuli. Next, focus on steady, in-and-out, even breathing—counting the ins and outs and keeping breathing even. Just a few minutes at a time is all that's necessary. The only thought process is: "I'm breathing in and out." If you notice a different type of thought pop up, gently remind yourself: "Later. Now I'm breathing in and out."

As a Taoist proverb says: "We cannot see our reflection in running water. It is only in still water that we can see."

SEEK THE SILVER LINING

When life gets tangled up and messy, we need to seek our personal silver lining. It's an ongoing mental exercise to seek the positive when it seems like we're mired in negativity. But if we start to change the way we look at people or situations, everything we are looking at begins to change as well.

Choosing to see the silver lining in any situation or person is a first step to a better outcome. Sometimes the easiest way to recognize the positive is to ask ourselves, "What is this teaching me?"

If we're not looking at the bright side, giving others the benefit of the doubt when it involves people, it's too hard to read the situation accurately. Our situations at any moment may not be what we'd choose, if we had been offered a choice—but this does not mean all aspects of any situation must remain the same. A bend in the road is not the end of the road unless we fail to make the turns.

As Elvis Presley said: "When things go wrong, don't go with them." Seek your own silver lining.

BLOSSOM

All life goes through phases. From tiny little seeds, plants take root, grow, bud, blossom, pollinate, wither, fruit, fall, change colors, lose their leaves and crumble back to the earth. A tight bud is distinct in its own right yet it must open and flower to share its inner beauty with the world. It is only through flowering that the butterflies come along with the bees that sip the sweet nectar. Like plants, we change throughout our lives as well. We grow. Our beauty, just like the energy contained in a flower, comes from within.

Let yourself blossom knowing that no two flowers are alike, nor are any two seasons. Would anyone argue that the fiery oranges and reds of fall are less beautiful than the bright greens of spring? Each phase is distinctly beautiful and incomparable to another. No stage of life is less stunning, less remarkable or filled with less fabulosity than another. Each phase of growth for every flowering being is beautiful.

IT'S NOT ALL BLACK AND WHITE

Someone once said, "What I like about black-and-white photographs is that they're more like reading the book than seeing the movie."

Now, let's talk about the idea of a "black and white" world.

When we really study a black-and-white photograph, we realize it's really not just black and white at all! It is the many gray and silver tones between the extremes of black and white that captivate our attention. There is so much hiding in the grays. It is these nuances that create the depth and capture our wonder. The silver tones are what make us linger a bit longer, wanting to explore the image further.

While we're certainly a colorful bunch at our ages due to the years behind us, we also carry those dimensions that are so unique to a beautiful black-and-white photo. And as fashion icon Karl Lagerfeld said: "Black and white always looks modern, whatever that word means."

Today, I cheer the beautiful magnitude of our range including all the silvers and grays we've developed between the extremes of our black and white.

SELF-PERCEPTIONS

Did you know that positive self-perceptions about aging can increase longevity? A study of 660 people ages 50+ found that older individuals who perceived aging positively lived 7.5 years longer than those with less positive self-perceptions about age. The advantage remained after age, gender, socioeconomic status, loneliness and functional heath were included as predictive aging variables.

So if you needed a reason to get your Silver Disobedience mojo on, there you have it! Remember: It's all good! Now how can you start pumping up your perceptions and increasing your lifespan?!

MAKE THE LIST

Here's a helpful exercise. Make a list of all your good points. Type it or write it on paper. Be generous. Pretend you're someone you really like ;-) Then, start adding all the things that people have told you they liked about you over the years. Think about compliments you received. Add everything you can think of that you've been praised for since the day you were born.

Everybody has good points. They aren't always acknowledged by others but that's no reason not to acknowledge them yourself. We can easily forget all the things we've done right and do right—and the things about us that are right. Sometimes we wish others would just notice and understand—but we can each be our own "someone" who notices.

The reasoning behind this exercise is that as we get older, we tend to become more self-reflective. Unfortunately, we often magnify the times when we were criticized or embarrassed along with the times we think we did something wrong and wish we could do over. Too often, we tend to forget the times we were praised and did things right. Carrying that load of criticism, while forgetting to pack the good stuff, doesn't just feel bad; it can make us think negatively about ourselves, our lives, our circumstances and our abilities for future possibilities.

Reminding yourself of your positive traits won't make you too full of yourself. It won't make you an egomaniac. It will just help you recognize your good characteristics and actions, of which there are many. Making a list helps you remember things you might not otherwise take the time to acknowledge. Get to it!

REFLECTIONS

Of all the things we wear, our expression is the most important. All of us spend at least some time during our days looking in the mirror. We check out our hair, makeup and clothing. As we pass glass windows, our image catches our attention.

The most important thing to check out when we see our reflection is really not whether our accoutrements are in place. More importantly, it is our expression that should be our focus. Are we frowning too much from worry? Bunching up our face with stress? Looking tired from lack of sleep or drawn from some excesses? Is the reflection looking back at us someone we'd like to know? Or would their expression make us turn away because they look angry?

I once read that everything in our lives reflects the choices we've made. So if we want to change the image we see looking back at us for the better, we may need to make some different choices.

OPTIMISTIC

Optimistic people live longer. Researchers at Harvard University published a study a few years back that concluded that optimistic people not only enjoyed the benefit of better moods, they also had a significantly lower risk of dying from major diseases like cancer, heart disease, stroke and respiratory disease compared to those with less positive outlooks.

Optimism appears to directly impact our biological functioning in beneficial ways that relate to longevity. Optimistic attitudes reduce inflammation and improve biomarkers and lipid levels.

The researchers concluded that in order to feel more optimistic, it is helpful to imagine our "best self" succeeding and achieving the best possible outcomes in a variety of life domains, such as personal relationships, careers and friendships. The researchers further determined that recalling things we are grateful for, in addition to things that make us happy and what we're looking forward to, add up to an optimistic outlook that contributes to a longer, healthier life.

Not sure how to define an optimistic attitude? An optimist wakes up and says, "Good morning, God!", not "Good God, it's morning."

Today's a good day to start looking up! I want your company for the next hundred years!

STEP OUT OF THE SHADOW

Have you ever wondered if it's time to step out of the shadow of your comfort zones?

So much of our lives are routine-oriented. These "patterns"—including all that's involved in raising children, working and other responsibilities—typically have us set in pattern-mode. Psychologists believe that patterns tend to minimize stress. Now, I don't think anyone is claiming that kids or work are stress-free—but knowing there's a routine to the day seems to be perceived by some as less stressful. Perhaps this is because we think we know what is happening from one day to the next.

When people begin contemplating any change—work, moving, etc.—the change in routine can be paralyzing. Even if we don't like a particular pattern, we know it, we know what to expect to some degree and we are used to it. Therefore, we worry and resist change because we can become afraid contemplating what might happen if things get changed up.

THIS is all delusional thinking.

Every day we are alive, the risk is omnipresent that life as we know it will change in moments. Illness, accidents, loss of work, divorce, death, empty nests, retirement, starting a new career, marriages, new kids, blended families—the list goes on and on. Silver Disobedience® is a state of mind whereby we opt to gently push the boundaries of our comfort zones by doing things a bit differently. Getting more comfortable with accepting the inevitable changes of daily living makes it easier to deal with new and unanticipated changes. We can learn to brainstorm new ideas and solutions, channeling our creativity and arriving at new heights of satisfaction. How do we do this? We choose to do something different every day.

Whether it's a big or little change is irrelevant: Saying hi to someone we pass regularly but usually don't acknowledge. Taking a class. Going for a walk in a new direction. The differences we add to our daily routines recalibrate our thinking.

The Silver Disobedience® mindset knows that "new" can be difficult, uncomfortable, a challenge or—just plain new and different. Yet we do it anyway.

How can you find new ways to step out of your comfort zones?

FLYING NOT ALWAYS ACCORDING TO PLAN

Plans don't always go the way we plan. On October 10, 1981, I went flying in a small plane for the first time in my life. Our flight plan was to take off from the airport and fly only about 73 land miles to have breakfast in Montauk, New York on a sunny morning. While enjoying the views from the sky of the Westhampton shoreline, it suddenly got very quiet. The pilot who was the only other person in the plane besides me very softly said, sh-t. (You can guess the letter in the blank.) By the time he calmly said it the third time, I understood the sudden silence was not due to peaceful skies. The engine had failed.

Keeping his cool, the pilot quickly gave me a job to do with some simple instructions to follow. I followed his directions as I thought about the moments of my life in rapid succession. I also remember thinking that dying wouldn't be so bad. I didn't owe any big apologies—but I wished I could have told some people I loved them, particularly my parents. I felt peaceful as the pilot was searching for a place to land, ultimately aiming for an airstrip at Westhampton Air Force Base.

The pilot actually made an amazing emergency landing—yet the front wheel caved and the propeller got tangled in plant brush so we flipped upside down. But we both walked away, thanks to staying calm under pressure and to a very responsive U.S. Air Force crew that came to our rescue.

So why am I telling you this? Life doesn't always go according to plan. Sometimes you can have whopping crashes. Hopefully we still get to live. Carpe diem.

Self-Reflection in Small Doses

Self-reflection is either great motivation for assessing ways to make positive changes or a form of self-torture that keeps us mired in unproductive thinking.

Being self-reflective might be a good thing—in small doses.

Take peeks into those windows but don't linger. Hanging out in the past takes us out of the moment and brings out our best dramatic creativity as we rewrite the scripts for what we or others coulda, shoulda, woulda done.

Thinking about how we reacted, what we did or could have done, rehashing the words expressed by those involved, revisualizing what we or someone else did, removes us from what is happening now and what we can do today.

Our pasts have included wonderful and painful memories, and everything in between. But yesterday is past. Last year is even older. Reflect briefly but avoid moving in for extended stays of reflection. There are far better hotels and places to inhabit. Benefit comes only from quick glances—like catching a reflection in a window. Then move forward with conviction and trust.

Know that the path we each walk is shaped from those experiences. This is how we become grateful and have all our future actions reflect what we have learned along the way.

Doing 'It' Again

Recognizing we're "doing 'it' again" is helpful whenever normal, repetitive, unproductive thoughts get stuck on mental replay. Whether "it" is a thought about an emotion, person, place, situation or thing, trying to push these thoughts out of our minds doesn't work because (as I believe) we can't actually get rid of thoughts—but we can help them fade away.

By busting or calling out a thought that isn't real in the first place, via conscious recognition of it, we can reduce its power over our emotional state. Then we can begin to see it for what it is: an illusory form of self-protection.

Acknowledging repetitive thoughts in a nonjudgmental way—whether it takes 100 or 10,000 practice tries—eventually makes these thoughts sound as boring as a broken record stuck on replay. Ultimately, we become ready to act by moving our needle to a new tune that's more present-day.

AGE IS NOT A ROADBLOCK

Don't be afraid when life seems to be moving forward more slowly than you would like. Be afraid of standing still and not growing. Don't worry if you stumble, fall or even have to crawl to get to where you want to go when you try something new. Age is not a roadblock.

We can still achieve many of the things we want to achieve. We can push ourselves a little harder no matter what is happening. We can choose to do something that will move us forward right now. But we won't get anywhere we want to go if we opt to stand still.

Stagnating is a great drain on our energy and it is also a form of depression, because we are really depressing what we want to do.

Instead—if we visualize first and then put action behind our thoughts—we become invigorated. Anticipation and excitement build up in the form of a special kind of energy, even if we're not 100 percent sure where we're going.

We must decide on our direction and go. We're in the driver's seat. Keep moving down the road. Don't worry about going in the wrong direction. We know how to shift. Wherever we're going, there will be forks in the road. Whether we take the right turn or left, it will be all right and we will have left behind indecision. Do it. Get moving.

PORING OVER BEAUTY

I remember watching my mother while she would put on her makeup and set her hair. Every day—no matter what she had been doing to care for her five children, our home and yard— at 5:00 PM, like clockwork, she would get dolled up for our father's arrival home from work.

One day, as she was preparing to be her most beautiful self to greet her husband, I asked her: "What are all those holes on your face?" Her skin didn't look like my 11-year-old skin.

I'll never forget her expression as she looked at me and said: "Pores: It happens." I'll also likely never forget the shame I felt for maybe making her feel less beautiful.

If we're lucky, aging happens. We all get larger pores as our bodies strive to grasp as much oxygen as possible to keep us alive and well.

Interestingly, today my mother is more alive than ever. Honestly, I think she's the most beautiful woman I've ever met. I hope I'll be lucky enough to look half as wonderfully beautiful as she does. In her 90s, my Mother is an ultimate poster girl for Silver Disobedience®.

INTENTIONS

Outward goals tend to fall into categories such as the desire for wealth, obsession with physical beauty, fame, accrual of possessions and certain relationships. These goals can be fleeting, coming and going due to a variety of factors including our commitment—but also factors like time, illness and choices that others make. Events beyond our control can also impact outward goals.

In contrast, inner intentions are individual goals. They are focused on desires such as greater peace, balance and maturity in how we approach situations in our lives. They include things like improving our responses, patience, feelings like love toward others and kindness—regardless of the moment or situation. Inner intentions are goals whereby we choose to take full responsibility and exert our influence to achieve a desired outcome. These form the foundation for outward goals and often trigger unanticipated, positive life events that many would otherwise strive for as goals.

Let me use basketball legend Michael Jordan as an example. He is wealthy, embodies peak physical fitness, is a household name and can likely purchase whatever possessions he might desire. However, it was his inner intentions and goals to practice, grow and mature as a basketball player and leader that made him achieve success—and that enabled him to exert his influence on a world of sneaker buyers.

By letting go of expectations associated with outward goals, but holding firm to our inner intentions, life gains wholly new potential. Think carefully about what you choose to make your intentions.

EVERYBODY HURTS...

We all have those times when we feel alone, overwhelmed and tired. Life can feel insurmountable, as if the pileup of crap on our plate is never ending. Time after time. More, more, more. One thing after another. Where the heck are the instructions, right? We would all follow directions if only we could all get the same book. But that's just not how it is though, is it?

Life happens. While there are certainly factors we can influence, like looking both ways when we cross the street, there are no ironclad guarantees that we will get through life unscathed no matter what we do or how we plan. We can exercise every day but we can still have a heart attack. We can do amazing work on the job but we can still get fired. We can do the best we can for our kids and it may still result in a lifetime of therapy. For greater peace, we must accept things for what and how they are. We have to trust that we are doing our best in the moment—and our best is good enough.

Life is challenging and so are the people we meet along the way. We're all on our own journeys. Somehow, sometimes, our roads seem to intersect marvelously or, conversely, collide horribly. Children, family, work, money, bills and other responsibilities, whatever—the endless stream of demands on our time, attention, financials and energy is formidable.

But you know what? Hang on. A new day will dawn. You can rally. Stay in the moment, focus on what you can do to manage and cope. Each new moment is a new possibility. Breathe. Don't quit. Hang on. We are not alone. (R.E.M. inspired)

Starring in a World Production

Did you ever consider the fact that each of us is an important character charged with giving our best performance in the great play called "Life?" Isn't that cool? We each get a role as an actor in the biggest production in the world! Not only that, but because of free will, we get to write the script, select our lines and choose exactly how we want to act, move and respond.

We're in charge of our performance each day. We have the ability to sway moods and emotions based on our actions. The rewards from our performance, our efforts invested in our multitude of relationships and daily scenarios, will unfold from the choices, judgments and actions we decide to take. As actors we're emotional beings. Driving energy. We choose the vibe of the show (or our day).

While others can critique the show—positively or negatively, because we each get to exercise free will—it is our individual decision to choose happiness or unhappiness with our performance at the end of each day.

Wind

Pablo Picasso said, "The older you get the stronger the wind gets—and it's always in your face." Stephen King mused, "I like to hang out clothes on windy days. Sometimes that's all I feel like. A sheet on a line." Charles Schultz, creator of Charlie Brown, reminded us that "Faith is holding on tight when the going gets windy."

Whether the wind is at your back, helping you get to your next destination in life—or in your face, so that you want to tuck down and hide—the fact is that there will always be wind.

Winds are characterized according to their force, strength and direction: Gusts, squalls, breezes, gales, storms and hurricanes. Wind is a cause of erosion and extraordinary destruction in the event of a wildfire. But wind also aids in the pollination of flowers and planting of seeds, while providing cooling relief on a hot summer day.

When facing a cold front, when life feels like a tornado is stirring up a ruckus on every front, remember it will pass. Weather situations are always temporary. A satisfying, balmy, refreshing breeze will come. This is life.

LOOKING BACK

Throughout life, it's normal to reflect on past situations and interactions. This is partly how we change and improve ourselves.

As we age and reflect on our lives and choices, there can be a tendency to think too negatively about what we did or didn't do, could have done, wanted to do, or would have done differently. We may be thinking this way about ourselves and others.

There are really only two reasons we ever want to look back in life: 1) If we are reflecting on a wonderful memory that puts a smile on our face while warming our hearts, or 2) If we want to offer a sincere apology to someone we feel we wronged. Otherwise, no looking back.

Looking back in any way that falls into that "if only..." category is abusive to ourselves and possibly others. Our choices and mistakes didn't make us failures, but they sure can make us feel like that if we don't decide to let them go. When we find ourselves looking back, we may stumble and struggle because we're supposed to be looking ahead toward where we're going. A far more productive approach is to talk to ourselves as we would to encourage another. We can do this by shifting our focus and spending a few moments recalling and celebrating those times we did things right. The moments we lifted another by saying the right words at the right time; offered our help; shared our compassion and understanding. Consciously directing this kindness toward ourselves can work miracles. It can heal us on countless levels. It might take practice getting used to the idea of looking back on our lives only with compassion or to reflect on wonderful moments, but it's important to start practicing this to enhance health and longevity.

STRATEGIC WORRYING

Worry occurs when we obsess over negative thoughts or images, fueled by emotions that seem to get stuck in repeat mode. When we're worrying about something, it usually indicates that we're feeling inadequate to deal with the real or imagined risk, threat or potential consequences.

Regardless of our age or stage in life, we can get stuck in worry and it can be triggered by very real issues such as health, relationships (personal or otherwise) and finances. Do you worry about worrying too much? A little worrying is OK, but when it gets excessive, you are stealing your own happiness in the moment.

Here are four strategies to get a grip on worrying:

1. Set a mental time limit. Whenever your mind starts to wander in a negative direction, if you can't stop it right away, play a game by setting a time limit. Tell yourself, "OK, I've got 10 minutes to worry about this. Then it's time to move on." Surprisingly, this often ends the worry more quickly.

2. Ask yourself if it will it matter a year from now. Often, whatever we're stuck on is temporary. It really won't matter in the long term; it is just sidetracking us in the moment. So we want to ask, "Will this matter next week? Next year? In three years?" Our answer will usually add perspective and balance regarding whatever we're obsessing on.

3. No "What ifs..." I learned this from my son. He skateboards and does really crazy tricks that sane people would not try without a skateboard. When I would say, "Why are you trying that? What if you get hurt?" He'd look at me and say: "I focus on landing the trick, Mom, not what can go wrong. I'll never get the trick if I'm thinking about getting hurt." While I often wish he'd chosen ping-pong as his sport, I can't argue with his "No what ifs..." lesson.

4. Lastly, remind yourself that you've managed to handle all that life has thrown in your direction in the past. The odds are in your favor that you can deal with whatever is happening in the moment—which is all you have.

While none of us can expect to become completely worry-free because we all face daily unknowns, the impact of worry can be dealt with much more easily by adopting a strategic worrying strategy!

CURIOSITY

When envisioning the quintessential image of curiosity, it is quite possible that a child—one with all the time in the world, one who is asking a zillion questions—comes to mind. Juxtaposed against this might be a tired adult, stressed with responsibilities and lack of time.

Curiosity is a youthful trait. Yet in an effort to socialize us, society often frowns on too many questions in an effort to keep "education" progressing and the classroom orderly. Add too much imagination to our questions and suddenly labels such as "attention deficit" or "hyperactive" start to be used. "Why can't they just stick to the topic and stop all the mental meandering?"

This is ironic, because when we recall the genuinely fascinating people we've met in life, it is likely their curiosity that caught our attention—along with their lust for life and a deep desire to learn on their own and from others. Curious people are in a high self-education mode and enthusiastic about enhancing their knowledge. Knowing this, why is the value of curiosity diminished or, worse, claimed to have killed cats?

Curiosity threatens the status quo. It insists that we reassess those areas in our minds that we've closed. Curious people ask questions that sometimes require us to acknowledge that we don't know everything. How uncomfortable to admit we might not have all the answers! Curiosity demands that questions be answered and unknowns explored when really sometimes all we want is certainty. Why can't some people "just leave it alone?"

Curiosity is a wonderful trait. It's the most alive, youthful trait we can have. Don't worry if you think you've lost your curiosity. It can be practiced. It's all about being willing to listen and ask questions. Taking the risk to try something new. Asking opinions of others and trying to understand their perspective instead of getting them to understand ours. Changing up a routine to take a new route to just see what's around the corner.

We can be curious at any age. It's never too late to develop our curiosity, going boldly to explore new possible ways of thinking and seeing. What can you be curious about today?

12 Ways to Train Your Brain

A lot of new science supports a variety of simple ways we can keep our brains healthy for greater creativity, focus and quick wit. Here are some easy-to-try favorites to stimulate our brains for better cognition and memory for our second acts:

1. Brush your teeth or eat a meal with the opposite hand.
2. Try to recall five things that are the exact same color in your wardrobe or in a room.
3. Yawn. Allow a yawn when you feel it coming. It adds oxygen, wards off sleepiness, helps focus and regulates metabolism by cooling down your brain.
4. Study a foreign culture. Pick a place you've always wondered about. Read and try to learn as much about that land and its people as possible.
5. Watch your weight. Excess fat releases cytokines that can produce hormones harmful to your neurons.
6. Stop multitasking. Although it might seem uber-efficient, our prefrontal cortex is designed to perform one task at a time. When trying to master anything, silence your digital technology, close the door and focus.
7. Breathe. Long, deep breaths lower blood pressure and can reduce anxiety, pain, asthma, stress, anger, cramps and more. The exchange of carbon dioxide and oxygen releases tension and creates a calming effect on the entire body.
8. Blink. Laptops and mobile devices cause us to blink less. This causes strained blurry vision and mental strain. For every 20 minutes on a computer, spend 20 seconds in a blinking break.
9. Improve your posture. Standing as if you have a plate on your head isn't such a silly idea. Hunching down over tech devices crunches our necks, causing muscle strain, fatigue and pain.
10. Walk and stretch. Both lower bad cholesterol and stress hormones that reduce immunity.
11. Drink water. If you're dehydrated, toxic cellular waste is building up in your brain and body.
12. Laugh. Laughing at life, like exercise, strengthens us. It also ups dopamine, which is the chemical that activates the brain's pleasure center.

GETTING HAPPY

Did you know one of the primary reasons people worry is that they are afraid to be too happy? People actually worry that if they allow themselves to be too happy, others might think they're selfish and insensitive.

Suppressing happiness is a terrible thing to do to ourselves. It won't save anyone from their misery. In fact, it could possibly compound theirs and our own!

Restraining happiness becomes a very serious issue if it is the surviving partner's response when a spouse dies. Far too often, the surviving partner worries that they might be perceived as "happy too soon." The result is that they live "dead-like," afraid of what their children might feel or how others will judge them.

Consider me your cheerleader for getting happy in any and all circumstances. The only thing being happy will prevent is being sad! Nobody gets a medal for allowing sadness to linger the longest. There's no virtue in it.

If you think I'm wrong, try this: Use your imagination to visualize your own personal tragic fate—because you decided to be happy. Like a Shakespeare tragedy—only it's a comedy! Define your character. Build out the absolute worst-case scenario, like any disaster scene from a Michael Bay movie—with a "must save the world" element from the disaster you've created via your happiness. Think *Armageddon* or *Transformers*. Add explosions and floods. The end of humanity is coming because you're allowing yourself to be happy—and it's being delivered by a hockey helmet-wearing, chainsaw-carrying, mutant amphibian. Go large in your mental production; spend billions!

Hopefully, when you realize how getting happy cannot possibly be worse than the movie you've just imagined—chillax and get happy. Cast yourself in your own really-in-love-with-life romance movie.

And with that, I'll close with a popular quote often (mis)attributed to Willy Shakespeare: "Love me or hate me, both are in my favor…If you love me, I'll always be in your heart…If you hate me, I'll always be in your mind."

It's time to get with the program of today—and get happy! Life is for the living.

LED ZEPPELINS

Legend has it that the name for Led Zeppelin, the British rock band, resulted from a quip about the likelihood of its music—along with the band—going down like a lead balloon.

Giving the world its first taste of heavy metal rock, Led Zeppelin did the contrary: Rising, breaking countless "records" including for "Stairway to Heaven"—reputedly the most-played song of all time on radio, even though it was never released as a single.

When introducing an idea that suggests an alternative direction or different way of thinking in a business meeting, I find it helpful to start with: "This may go down like a Led Zeppelin…" It's not original but it sure is visual for those who know either music or aviation history. The smiles it triggers usually makes the introduction of my contrarian thinking go over more smoothly, enhancing my audience's receptiveness.

There's always a degree of risk that trying something new won't work out. Will the direction we choose be the right one?

Here's the thing: When traveling the road of life, whichever direction we choose is the right one at the right time. We can't second-guess this. Too often there's the temptation to play the game, "What if I made X choice instead?"

Such silly thinking! It carries the humongous, fantasy assumption that a wonderful and glorious series of events would have unfolded with less adversity than the path we actually traveled. Life doesn't work this way.

The *Hindenburg* was developed over countless hours of engineering and aeronautical research by arguably some of the best minds, but a docking error sealed its fate. While Led Zeppelin—with a name that implied imminent failure—went on to create music history, combining perseverance, talent and practice plus luck, they didn't crash (although they came close on countless occasions).

We make choices daily. Each will unfold as it will. No guarantees. Just life unfolding in any number of directions. Keep going, knowing you're going in the right direction no matter what you've chosen in the past and what you'll choose today.

CHROME

Chrome sparkles and captures attention. It's a distinctive material that draws our eyes—like when we see it glistening on a Harley-Davidson motorcycle. Chrome reminds us of sleekness, speed and power. Google liked the word "chrome" so much it used it as the name for its browser.

Chromium, which became known as "chrome," derives from the Greek word "chroma" or "color." It was thus named due to the colorful nature of the chromium compounds and the popularity of their pigments, which are found in yellow, red, orange, green, purple and black. Chromium is a hard, corrosion-resistant transition metal. It can withstand tarnishing and has a very high boiling point. Its steely, blue-gray, lustrous tone can be highly polished, and so it is used as a very identifiable decorative trim for cars, motorcycles and industrial tools.

What if we began referring to our random gray hairs as they popped up as captivating chrome highlights? Can you imagine? Not that we'd have to stop or start coloring them—but regardless that we would see our chromie strands in terms of sparkle, light, power, speed, energy: Wow! That would give the idea of going gray a whole new meaning!

Today, whether we're showing off our "chromies" or not, let's start owning the implied energy, strength and beauty of our chrome!

ORDINARY VERSUS EXTRA-ORDINARY

Ordinary: Plain; undistinguished; of no special quality; common; average.

Extraordinary: Beyond what is usual; strange; exceptional; noteworthy; phenomenal; amazing; curious; fantastic; marvelous; odd; outstanding; particular; rare; singular; special; surprising; terrific.

Want to know what the biggest difference is in who we are at this stage of our lives versus years ago? It's the little "extra" (also known as experience) that we developed year after year by overcoming, managing, moving on, learning and growing stronger from the endless challenges presented by people and situations. Through this thing called life, something intangible and priceless developed: Experience. Each year our countless experiences keep adding up, helping to make us uniquely extra-ordinary.

Allow yourself to think about all the "extra" you've accrued over the years, including what you've learned, what you've overcome, how you've grown and why you're a better, more experienced person today than ever before!

LEARNING TO THINK

I'm often asked by Silver Disobedients how I learned to think. My parents restricted TV to Walt Disney once a week. To entertain myself, I read. Anything. Like the *Encyclopedia Britannica* from A to Z. I listened to radio. I loved broadcasts of *Mystery Theater*. It's funny, because it sounds like I grew up in the '40s, but this was during the '60s and '70s. My father said little but had lots of facial expressions that I constantly tried to "read" to interpret the family mood. While in high school, with babysitting money, I bought a cheap plastic stereo and a pair of good headphones. I put it in our living room so my mom could listen to music during the day. At night, I'd finish homework, read and then put on my headphones to rock myself into a meditative state, drifting in semi-sleep until around 2:00 AM, when I'd go up to bed, waking at 6:00 AM for school.

Today, every morning, I wake an hour before anyone else in my house to spend a half hour (with a cup of coffee!) thinking exclusively about one subject. While it seems simple, it's sometimes ridiculously hard. I recommend everyone try it. Start with five minutes. Really think about something you find interesting. A flower, a book you want to write, the window you're looking out of, a newspaper article or book you just read. The meaning of a word.

The subject of your focus isn't important—but I usually try to focus on something I think I want to do. You don't need to actually see anything; it's more important that in your mind you visualize or imagine something. In your mind, describe it in full detail. How you see it expanding. Senses you feel. What it symbolizes. What uses could be made of it. From this simple beginning, work up to contemplating a problem. If you like to draw, or think you like to draw, do this exercise with a pencil and paper. Randomly sketch words, lines, images of whatever you're thinking.

The goal of this is to practice concentration. Once you master it, the benefits are immense. My favorite benefit? It helps me read faster with better recall. It also sharpens thinking.

GRATITUDE VERSUS APPRECIATION

Gratitude is the quality of being aware and thankful of the good things we have. Appreciation may be more important, as it is the recognition and enjoyment of the good qualities of someone or something besides ourselves.

Appreciation takes gratitude up a notch—because to be appreciative, we are actively looking for what is good, even when it might feel particularly challenging.

Let's look at the difference: When we want everyone to follow our rules and they're not, there's not much to feel grateful about. However, we can appreciate that others have opinions, that they are entitled to them and if we choose to listen, maybe we can learn something from their opinions.

More so, noticing that not everyone follows our rules can make us appreciate those who seem to be connecting more with what we are thinking or feeling. This might ultimately make us feel more grateful and also make the other person feel more appreciated, especially if we told them that we recognized and appreciated them.

While the dictionary says "gratitude" and "appreciation" are nouns, somehow appreciation seems more verb-like and action-oriented. We have to seek things to appreciate and can feel it more if we somehow choose to share our appreciation.

Practicing appreciation helps improve relationships because if we're paying attention to what we value in others, their behaviors that bug us may become less bothersome. Practicing appreciation also gives us a chance to be more real. We are not only grateful for help from others, for example; we also feel happy that they shared their time and energy or lent an ear to hear us.

Think about those times you felt appreciated. Didn't they make you feel like you wanted to do even more? While someone might know we're grateful to have them in our lives, that is kind of more about us than them. But, if we show genuine appreciation, the focus is on the other—and the attention is off us.

MISUNDERSTOOD

Do you feel misunderstood? Do you wonder what life would be like if people could really understand who you are deep down inside? If yes, let me tell you this: If everyone intuitively understood everyone else, life would be Boring with a capital "B."

A life reality is that if we were all completely understandable, we wouldn't be that attractive to anyone nor would any of us want to spend much time conversing to try to discover the nuances of each other because we'd already know them.

A large part of what makes us attractive is the compelling nature of our complicated and incomprehensible personalities. Little things are comprehensible. Big events —and you are a very big event — are rarely understood. Rather, it's more likely said: "There's no explaining her or him or it"

Nobody fully understands another, nor oneself. Don't worry about it. Instead, view this as a never-ending opportunity for self-exploration and reinvigoration of our most important relationships.

OPPOSING THOUGHTS

Did you know it's impossible to hold opposing thoughts in your mind at the exact same time? You can't be angry at someone and feel lovingly connected to them simultaneously. You can't feel sadness when you are telling a happy story, nor can you laugh when you're thinking about something sad. Humans cannot think contradictory thoughts simultaneously.

This is why learning to refocus the thousands of thoughts that fill our minds daily is so important. It's also why we want to think of ourselves and those we love in the most positive ways possible.

Trying hard not to think of something pretty much assures that it will remain top of mind. All research studies confirm this. But let's look at a constructive example for restructuring our thinking: Suppose you were meeting someone for the first time, workwise or personally. It would be natural to start wondering: How will it go? Will they like me? Will I say the right things?

The only way we can eradicate these worries is by thinking the opposite: Imagining a fantastic meeting! Seeing ourselves laughing, visualizing the exchange of a constructive conversation, imagining ourselves really relating and connecting to the other party, picturing ourselves confident and relaxed.

Trying to control our thoughts doesn't work. Refocusing them does. Give it a try!

FREEDOM

Freedom is defined as the power or right to act, speak or think as one wants without hindrance or restraint. But freedom is not without responsibility. To be truly free in life, means we must learn to put restraints on ourselves. For example, if we say or do whatever we want, we may end up in jail or broke. Both could result from expressing our "right to be free."

Real personal freedom often requires delayed gratification, willingness to settle for less, understanding there are things we can do without—or as the expression goes: Getting what we get and we don't get upset. Choosing to be highly materialistic, keeping up with the proverbial Joneses, is one of the fastest ways to lose our freedom. Living on the edge and worrying about payments is not fun. Most of us have likely experienced this and some may be in financial straits today. Eating or drinking excessively are freedoms, but neither works out so well if our health fails as a result. When that urge to splurge strikes and we mistakenly think we are exercising our freedom, think about these points.

It's human nature to desire, win and improve our circumstances. Otherwise, our ancestors wouldn't have survived, as they'd have been eaten by wild beasts. Yet there are things we want for our survival and things we think we want but are really not necessary, don't improve anything for us and are usually not appreciated once we get them.

Social status is elusive; someone will always have something we don't. Aiming for experiences and making memories will always be uniquely ours, no matter how simple they are. Striving to win approval from others is a losing game. Give yourself permission to be the approval.

Being free also means learning to accept the axiom: "You do you; I'll do me." Assuming the arbiter position and declaring how everyone should act in our lives is confining for ourselves and others. Practice appreciation for what we have already—particularly health. If we're healthy, we're really very lucky. From health comes the greatest possibility to exercise our freedom: to move, to speak, to dance, to be and to choose to live.

BALANCE

Physical balance is one of the most important things to keep steadily improving upon as we age. The ability to stay firmly planted on our feet, walking a straight line, avoiding falls and holding a firm position while standing or getting up are essential. Falls come with any number of complications and surgery is ideally to be avoided at any time—but particularly in our later years.

Maintaining our ability to stay balanced and strong is the number one reason we all want to be exercising. We fall because the muscles in our hips and legs are not quite as strong as they once might have been. Our joints are shifting. Changes in vision compound the issue. Our reaction times slow down, so when we're stumbling, the realization we need to stop the fall can come too late. Then there are medications that might alter our balance along with our blood pressure. Also, many of us are hunching over computers all day— which is certainly not helping our posture and balance. While some of us are yogis, most of us are not.

For those who need assistance, here are some simple things most can do to work on improving balance:

1. Hold onto the back of a steady chair and try balancing on just one leg. Lift the other in whatever way you can. Hold a few seconds, then switch to the other foot.
2. While holding onto the back of the chair, lift one leg to the side, holding your body upright and steady. Switch to other leg. Repeat.
3. Try walking heel to toe. Consciously step down with your heel and roll your foot to your toes. Repeat with other foot.
4. Sit or try standing with a book balanced on your head. See how long you can hold it.
5. Try balance walking. See if you can take a few steps keeping that book on your head.
6. Try squatting down and getting back up again. Find something for balance to hold onto if you're afraid you'll tip.

Check out the news section on the Silver Disobedience website (https://silverdisobedience.rocks/). I'll be adding articles about balance and how you can improve yours!

POSITIVELY ACCEPTING

Most emotional issues arise from the fact that there's something within us that we cannot accept. We resent our limitations and want to be someone else. We daydream about what we'd do if we had another chance or if we could change something about our bodies, our relationships or current life as it is. As a result, we disregard our own possibilities and those in the moment—and we don't do what we can do, get what we want or become who we'd like to be.

We can all find plenty of reasons to dislike our current life, whatever state it's in. But this really isn't beneficial, either to ourselves or to those with whom we live. Some of the most stimulating examples of success have come from people who have faced some kind of challenge, yet opted to play the game of life splendidly.

As soon as we begin to accept what we might perceive as limitations, they can be viewed as fascinating, challenging opportunities. Rebelling against our limitations gets us nowhere. Instead, we must summon our most adventurous, daring selves to accept ourselves as a bundle of possibilities, the likes of which have never been assembled in any other body in the past (nor will they be again in the future). This lets us undertake the most interesting game in the world: Making the most of our best.

NOTHING

Since everyday life is life, if we want to say sane and healthy (and we do!), we need to learn how to enhance our observation skills. Practicing observation is the best way to maintain peace, our minds and a piece of our minds.

"Observing" isn't doing nothing. It's a very active process of choosing to watch (keyword: "watch"—not "feel" or "internalize") the chaos around us: to observe (notice) the rapidity, rigidity, frustrations, emotions, tensions and bouts of anger—internal and external—that take us out of the center zone.

The more we choose to try observing again (and again and again!)—instead of reacting, commenting, getting upset and all those other responses that take us away from peace—the better we become at maintaining balance, peace, love and understanding.

While we each might fail often, the secret is to keep trying. Why? Because when we succeed, nothing feels better. There's a lot of peace in nothing.

ACHIEVING THE UNACHIEVABLE

You can achieve the unachievable. Here's proof: Mick Jagger, Billy Joel and Bruce Springsteen were not born with microphones in their mouths. Neil Armstrong crawled on a floor way before walking on the Moon. Coco Chanel was the child of an unmarried laundress. Wayne Gretzky, Michael Jordan, Willie Mays, Joe Montana, Lionel Messi, Billie Jean King, Peggy Fleming—and the thousands of other athletes who have awed us—practiced their ways to greatness. Born blind, Helen Keller changed the way we view disabilities, along with her teacher Anne Sullivan, who introduced the world to sign language. The founder of Apple was put up for adoption at birth: The Jobses gave him a name and home that did not have a computer in it upon his arrival. Dyslexic Richard Branson began his business foray at 17 in a church, writing a magazine called Student. Howard Schultz drank milk like the rest of us long before holding his first Starbucks coffee. Sidney Sheldon dropped out of school during the Depression—yet went on to write *I Dream of Jeannie*, *The Patty Duke Show* and countless bestselling books like *The Other Side of Midnight*. He wasn't born with a pen in his hand, nor was Jane Austen, whose books are still the storylines of Hollywood blockbusters. Likewise, J.K. Rowling invented Harry Potter and she wasn't born magically at Hogwarts. John Wayne wasn't born riding a horse into the sunset. Marie Curie wasn't born in a lab discovering radium and polonium—both of which continue to impact modern medicine and science. Sojourner Truth escaped slavery and went on to preach about abolition and the right for women to vote. George Washington Carver, also born into slavery, invented alternatives to cotton crops and ways to prevent the depletion of nutrients in soil.

Every day, people prove we can achieve the unachievable. Our military forces rebuild towns after natural disasters. Brave firefighters enter burning buildings to save strangers. Teachers work all day, giving up evenings to correct essays so we can learn to better express ourselves. And think of all the parents, caregivers, relatives, grandparents and others who raise thoughtful, caring, confident people while coping with the challenges of daily living.

We can each achieve what we might initially consider unachievable at any age. Opportunities present themselves every day. Keep on the lookout in this world of opportunity.

HEARTFELT COMMUNICATION

We all think of ourselves as being a certain kind of person, so it hurts when someone points out how their perception of us differs from our own. While haters will be haters, let's focus for the moment on those assessments that come from significant others—whether they are our partners, children or close friends.

Such revelations feel like a bomb dropped. We're shocked, want to run for cover or fight to defend ourselves. Yet when those bombs land, listening and quiet self-reflection is required. This is particularly so if the message has been delivered with tears—maybe even anger or heartfelt pain—from someone we love.

We tend to hurt those we love. Not because we are mean people but because we are "works in progress." Close relationships allow us to observe aspects of others that we might think need our assistance to improve. Sometimes we're not even aware of how we might be criticizing others.

The ways we show disapproval are as varied as what was foisted upon us throughout our lives. In turn, whether we're aware of it or not, we tend to impose the same learned behaviors and responses on others. A facial expression; not listening with our full attention; a quick, poorly considered response; an unwitting sign of displeasure; jests or attempts at humor with a subtext; sarcastic replies and standards we apply consciously or unwittingly—these can shake others to their core, chiseling away and destroying intimacy we crave.

Good communication takes heart, time and commitment. It's hard, hurts and will require genuine apologies and forgiveness. But the results of not choosing to listen and undertake self-assessment can be far more painful if important relationships deteriorate. Nobody really likes hearing what they're doing wrong. But it's only by accepting this fact—that perhaps our ways of communicating might benefit from some improvements—that we can achieve more loving, peaceful and constructive relationships.

EASY PEASY FITNESS

You might not be a "workout" kind of person. But here's a list that removes excuses. Let's start with science. Walking, water and natural foods are essential for health and we must stay active. Calories are the energy (heat) created by a body "burning up" foods eaten, or the energy required to perform activity. We need energy/calories to live. But if we consume more calories in a day than we burn, the excess is stored as body fat.

On average, we burn 15 calories per pound of body weight (your weight x 15 = calories necessary to maintain current weight). About 3,500 calories equal one pound. So if someone wanted to lose excess fat, it requires figuring out how to burn or cut those calories that are above their ideal daily caloric consumption based on that 15 x their desired weight. Each activity below is grouped by the number of calories (C) burned by that activity in one minute (CpM). Multiply this number by the number of minutes (M) being active and you'll know what you're burning. Here goes:

1.5CpM: Resting, sleeping, sitting, reading, kneeling

2CpM: Eating, playing cards, sewing, typing on a keyboard, dusting

3CpM: Squatting without weights, standing, hand-mixing a batter of ingredients, hand-peeling veggies/fruits, birdwatching, cleaning gutters, hand-washing clothes, carrying laundry to the washing machine, carrying an infant, coaching

3.6CpM: Walking around your house, showering

4.5CpM: Hanging laundry to dry, bathing a dog, ironing, housecleaning, electrical work, plumbing, gardening, carrying tools

5.1CpM: Making beds, mopping floors, pushing a wheelbarrow, chopping, yard work, bagging leaves

6CpM: Walking outdoors, walking downstairs, scrubbing floors, active housecleaning, shaking out rugs, drilling

7.5CpM: Walking upstairs, sawing wood, shoveling dirt or snow, stacking

10CpM: Carrying heavy loads, carrying an average two-year-old, most farming activities

Bottom line: Whole foods, moving our bodies as often as possible, managing stress and healthy relationships all strengthen our lifelines. Hopefully this list helps clarify "activity!"

EPIPHANY

Have you had an epiphany yet? Maybe you've had many. Epiphanies are those surprising insights, awarenesses, realizations, inspirations and eye-openers that suddenly make us see the world, another or a situation differently. It's kind of like a lightning-bolt strike that gives us new clues that unearth different, fresh perspectives.

Epiphanies can be triggered by momentous life events, whether perceived as positive or negative. Yet they can also arise from something as simple as a passage read in a book or even from lyrics in a song that resonate with us for some reason.

Like the expression that you can't put a square peg into a round hole, the fascinating thing about an epiphany is that it's as if our minds reshape with these new realizations as well. We have a sudden, intuitive perception and insight into different realities or essential meanings relating to whatever it is we're having that epiphany about.

While epiphanies can be triggered by big things, I believe our years make us more open-minded to the possibilities of daily epiphanies, which can arise in the most unexpected yet also all-quite-common circumstances. It could be an expression we catch on our own face or another that suddenly grants deeper understanding; a phrase uttered in passing that takes on a new meaning; an unfiltered thought from a child that delivers a new truth; the sight of a stranger's plight that changes our perspectives; help offered to us or by us that opens our hearts. Anything, really, that triggers a change. Our thinking gets revised in a way that helps us grow into kinder, more open and welcoming people.

GETTING EXPERIENTIAL

Lots of research reports that experiences provide greater satisfaction than accumulating yet another thing.

Basically, getting experiential is doing anything that you've thought about and wanted to do, but just never did—or never did enough of.

Experiential living doesn't have to be expensive: There is a great deal to see and do in this life that can be new, different and inexpensive. However, without action, the opportunity to do so may fade away.

What are the experiences you'd like to try? Think about how you feel about the idea of experiences versus things. And if experiences are what you crave, how will you start to make those plans become experiential realities?

THOUGHT-AUDIT

What we expect to happen more often than not will. This applies to ourselves and our relationships with others, as well as to work and other situational outcomes.

It's quite fascinating that once we develop a strong opinion about whether someone or something is good or bad, life seems to line up and get into place to make that opinion our new reality.

Consciously or subconsciously, our thoughts result in actions and responses that assure our beliefs and expectations will materialize. The catch is, this happens both positively and negatively.

In light of this, it pays to notice how you are speaking about yourself, others and situations. For example: If someone is speaking and they say, "This situation is killing me," that thought—that statement—needs to be corrected and nullified. Nothing is killing you. The situation may be really crappy, challenging, adversarial, difficult, whatever—but it is not killing you and you cannot allow your words or thoughts to state otherwise.

Today is a good day to do a thought-audit. Are your thoughts constructively inclined toward a positive and healthy life, loving and supportive relationships, and rewarding work experiences? If life doesn't seem to be going as well as we might like, the first place to start changing things for the better is with how we're thinking about it. And let me close with this: I'm not getting old—I'm getting better! How about you?

SOMEDAY

Someday I'd like to evolve to the point where I see anger as the purest display of another's hurt and pain. Instead of fighting against anger or seeking refuge far from whatever is being hurled, I want to learn to stay with that person and watch their anger flow like water. To respect the flow so I can show the other that they don't have to feel alone when they are feeling so bad. To stay because I know they feel awfully miserable and lonely—and by staying I'm able to show that I still care. To listen without reaction because I love the person even when I'm being tested through their hardest times. To demonstrate I can support their existence as another struggling human being—and that by staying I am showing I love them even when they might not love themselves.

I think this would be the ultimate achievement.

NO PARKING

Taking calculated risks and pushing oneself into uncharted territory is healthy. Stagnating is not. Exposure to situations (and people) that might involve risk and uncertainty can help us to confront and release our fears of failure and of success.

When we decide to make a move out of our parking zone, it's normal and wise to consider the downside. It's equally normal to fear "what ifs" as well as changes that might occur if we were to actually succeed.

The problem is when paralysis by overanalysis hits.

As you consider your options without the benefit of a crystal ball, know that if you feel you need to change something in your life, more comfort lies in action—and few actions are set in stone. While we might make mistakes (and learn from them!), it's a bigger mistake if we think we can get a guarantee for a particular outcome. No guarantees are ever assured, except taxes and death.

Life is far more satisfying (I didn't say easy...) if we risk reaching for our very own personal definition of "the fullest life" at every age. Go for the gusto! Regardless of the ultimate outcome, there's no shame in taking a risk. Don't worry about what others say or how they might try to discourage you. Don't wait. Find the time. Never allow waiting to become a habit. No parking. Life is happening now.

WORRY

We all have moments when we worry about what the future holds. Aging brings a whole new set of uncertainties. Still, worrying about tomorrow steals the joy from today.

Here are two important things to remember whenever we start to worry:

1. If and when we are thinking, we are not fully present. (Before moving on, really think about that a moment...)
    So...
2. Whatever we're worrying about is not worthy of our time, because the present is a gift that is all about what is happening now. We always want to embrace the moment because it is only in the moment where everything is really happening.

PLACEBO EFFECT

Scientists know the mind has immense power to trigger healing and recovery. While research might not be able to explain the whys and hows, the impact that faith and spiritual beliefs have on healing cannot be denied. Anyone who's ever been involved with a clinical trial for a new drug knows that belief can impact the success or failure of the trial.

Here's why.

Placebos are inactive drugs with no therapeutic benefit. Depending upon the illness being researched, placebos are usually administered in lieu of the drug being studied or in combination with another drug for more serious illnesses. The power of the mind and spirit is demonstrated by what is known as the "placebo effect," a physical benefit that may occur and can't be attributed to the treatment itself. Placebos have been investigated for years. A 1955 American Medical Association article reported that during World War II, when morphine was unavailable, soldiers who received a saltwater solution for their pain still experienced pain relief. Ample research confirms the placebo effect impacts a variety of clinical trials for psychiatric illness, including those involving antidepressants, and pretty much every other type of drug trial that I can recall.

I share this because I occasionally receive comments on my blogs that question my beliefs, imply I need a reality check and tell me to stop being so rosy.

I've studied spirituality, religion, nutrition and hypnosis for 30 years because of my personal interests. Professionally, for the past 25 years, I've analyzed data from pharmaceutical and biotech clinical trials. My beliefs and science are now merged— because when trial data miss the endpoint, it's often due to the placebo effect or the nocebo effect, which involves imagined negative responses from a non-therapeutic placebo.

So here's why I write my sunshiny posts: I always want my mind thinking about health and well-being. Our powerful minds will go in the direction of what we focus on— whether good or bad. Silver Disobedience® is a place for positive thinking with a strong dose of direction to keep our ideas real and actionable.

LEGACY

Have you ever thought about what you'd like to leave to future generations? Money, art, a business—or something else? Maybe something far more important, yet less tangible? After all, most people who inherit money spend it far too quickly. Financial gifts, while welcome, don't necessarily come with an appreciation of the effort it took to make and save that money.

Shakespeare proposed honesty to be the best gift; Kanye West suggests betterment for all based on how and what we can give to each other to support their growth; Billy Graham said character; Taylor Swift proposes examples of how to be good people; George Foreman is quoted as saying, "I want to leave the legacy that being nice is the treasure"; Michael Bloomberg speaks about better education for all; Richard Branson's legacy wish is not wealth or fame but happiness in choosing and following one's own path; Peyton Manning said respect; George H.W. Bush wanted a day when the legacy of 1600 Pennsylvania Avenue would be that man or woman, regardless of race or creed, could run our country; Barack Obama furthered that sentiment by achieving it; Stella McCartney noted not just the importance of family but not taking that lightly; and Andy Warhol proposed that the idea in life was not to live forever but to create something that will.

The best legacies are what we leave *in* people, not for them. Heart, spirit, determination, will, kindness, spirituality, peace, love, willingness, desire…

We each get to decide the legacy that we will leave. Each day we're alive, we're building our legacy. How will you define yours?

VARIATIONS ON OLD

Growing old and being old are not the same. It's a privilege to grow old as each moment, day and year holds untold potential until our last breath. Growing older is a result of the passage of time.

Getting older does not mean our joy for the light of each moment has to diminish. The moment might even become more vibrant. My mom is in her 90s, her husband is seven years younger and I've got a lot of friends in their late-70s. I can honestly say none of them are old. However, becoming old can happen at any age, at any time of life.

Becoming old is "living-dead," which likely originates from despair and a sense of hopelessness. If we are alive, we can choose hope and possibility exists. Believe in the magic of each new day at every stage of life. Age does not have to be the brake of life and living.

EYES

Have you ever noticed how, when we're angry at someone, it's so hard to look at them? Or maybe you're the opposite: When you're angry, you stare the other person down. Then there are the times when we're hurt and we just want to look past another person—in an attempt to ignore their existence while we reconcile our emotions. Yet again, when we feel in love, we get googly eyes!

It's said that our eyes are the windows to our souls, so when we're angry, venting or raging, maybe looking away is how we hide any shame we might feel about releasing those emotions.

But even sometimes when we're feeling love and affection toward another, it can be hard to maintain eye contact. Is it embarrassment? Fear of having our feelings exposed and possibly not welcomed as we might prefer?

Gazing into another's eyes brings reaction and emotion to the surface. It creates vulnerability.

Sometimes we avoid the eyes of another because we're feeling insecure, submissive, less than, unprepared, nervous, uncomfortable, disinterested, hiding, having a bad day—but sometimes it's because of love.

Eye contact is where our power lies. It is our connection to another. It's not just what we see, but how we see and feel.

If you notice yourself or another avoiding eye contact, you've received an important message worth deciphering. Trust, confidence and openness are missing. There is something causing inhibition. While eye contact is associated with social connection, it's also a balance. And in an era when so much time is spent looking at a screen, maybe we need to focus on getting back to looking deep into the eyes of others and experiencing connection in the old-fashioned sense of the word.

IMAGE

We all seek to convey a certain image of who we are. All of us have individual needs and they materialize for the world to see based on the images we feel a need to project. Culture, family and the media in its many forms add pressure and influence many of our decisions. In some ways, our responses to these outside forces imply a subconscious belief that "one size fits all," so we strive to fit in.

Meaningful living is grounded in recognizing our strengths and weaknesses, and accepting who we are by nature, while changing and learning more of what we need to know so that it might better us and improve our circumstances. The end goal is to accept that it's OK to do what we're doing for ourselves rather than to impress others.

Accepting this "self-ishness," for lack of a better word, is a good thing. Owning who we are and fulfilling what we believe is our destiny benefits not only us, but also those we love and even the world. The more we accept that our life goals are unique to ourselves, the more opportunities appear to help us achieve those goals. Taking advantage of these opportunities is not selfish. It is how life is supposed to work if we're open to letting it deliver its miraculous power to us.

And here's the big thing: Taking advantage of what comes our way—when we act in a way to inspire abundance—is fantastic, right and healthy for us. It's not something to be embarrassed about as we feel more exposed and open to the world. It's time to share the secret parts of ourselves. Have the courage to let your inner self loose! It won't betray you. Rather, it might help rid you of superficiality and superficial needs that weren't quite fulfilling in the first place. When we act not to impress but to express our essence, amazing forces come to help us go in the directions of our dreams.

CRITICISM

It takes a lot of soul-searching to stop taking personally what others say and do. Major self-awareness and understanding of the human condition are essential. Of course, we are well-meaning and care about others. However, most of our perspectives, comments, ideas, thoughts and criticisms about others are reflections of ourselves, not necessarily accurate ideas about another.

Hugh Prather's brief essay in his book *Notes to Myself* made a big impact on my memory. He wrote something along the lines of this: When we are criticized by another, we don't suddenly become less than we were prior to the critique. Rather, we've just received information for us to consider.

A criticism—whether we are the critic or receiving information from another—is nothing more than insight into someone's critical thinking.

If the critique was expressed at work about a situation or problem versus our being, we'd debate it and decide if we agreed or not. However, when criticism is directed at us from another, reasoning tends to halt as emotions rise.

But we do need to step back and be reasonable when we are on the receiving end of criticism. Is there merit in the criticism? In other words, do we agree that the comment reflects some work we need to do? Maybe or maybe not. Either way, criticisms do not reflect our value or worth. As criticisms reflect the thoughts of another, it's up to us to decide their relevancy, or not, regarding our behavior.

And regarding sharing our criticism with others: It pays to remember there is a big difference between constructive and destructive criticism. Think long and hard before sharing either.

INTERNAL AFFAIRS

Bad drivers, annoying people on the grocery store line, whining children, unappreciative or insensitive others, demanding bosses and customers, richer people, differences in perspectives—along with more serious things like environmental disasters, tragedies, sickness and death—are part of life and always will be. But how day-to-day stuff impacts our sense of happiness is an internal matter of perception.

For example: Imagine driving and getting cut off. One choice is to get all worked up and have a screaming match. Another option? Just let them in. Maybe they're oblivious or in a rush or just a bad driver. Whatever. Their action need not impact our happiness even for a moment.

Happiness is not something we need to "get." We don't "deserve" to be happy (which well-meaning friends are quick to tell us), nor will it come by "working harder." In fact, sometimes people find the opposite to be true. Too much "working" to get happy can make happiness feel elusive. Also, contrary to any belief we may have, money won't buy us happiness: The amount of money we need to feel happy and secure is more likely correlated to how much we spend.

Being happy is not a selfish act. Achieving a happy state is generous and a gift we offer to all humankind. Happiness results from choosing to focus more on the good that's happening around us versus the bad.

We're all walking a tightrope in life: Focusing forward, not looking down, doing our best to maintain balance with our emotions. By choosing to notice positives in the world, we all feel happier, and think and perform better. Physical health improves as well as our sense of well-being. Our relationships improve, as does communication. Our experience of life gets better. Happiness improves by choosing to see good, which is everywhere, if we choose to see it. None of this implies putting our heads in the sand: Instead, it is about viewing solutions by realizing most people are good and that together we can make things good and right. Imagine a world where we could each spend more time noticing "good": Complimenting the good in others and rejoicing about good whenever we observe it.

TIME MACHINE

To stay as mentally sharp as possible, we need to keep our minds toned by exercising our brain cells daily. This is essential if we want to avoid mental decline.

There's a lot of research that confirms the harder we make our brains work, the better our brains will serve us for the long haul. Not only that, it is also quite possible to regain some of the mental abilities we may have lost.

Here's a game that's scientifically proven to improve brain power and reaction time. Think of the year you graduated from high school. Visualize the town your school was in. Try to recall as many things as you can about your hometown. Mentally or on paper, start naming streets. Next, begin to recall everything you can from that year in "collections"— like the friends you hung out with, then the cars each friend drove. Who was who's first girlfriend or boyfriend? Then move to the school. Who were your teachers your senior year? What subjects did you take? Do you remember the grades you got? What else can you recall? Then, sticking with that same year: Who was president of the U.S. and vice president? What was the hit movie that year? The song at the top of the charts? Who was your favorite radio DJ, movie star or band? Was there a hit TV show? Add any questions you want to add to the list and your answers. If this is easy, pick another year. Go back to sixth grade when you graduated from elementary school. Really imagine what the year was like: what you thought was cool. Think, talk, write and visualize it.

The deeper and longer you can keep this exercise going, the more it benefits your brain. By entering our own personal mental time machines, we can strengthen our brains. Try doing this with a friend, too. Start with recalling everything you both can about the year you met. See if you can do this exercise for five minutes a day. Keep building on your recollections. Then start working through every other year.

UNCERTAINTIES

Uncertainties are life constants and we are regularly faced with the need to make decisions. As we get older, many of those decisions become more complicated. They may involve changes within our families and other relationships; moves to new towns, leaving homes we've been in for years; work changes like retirement by choice, force or downsizing; and health—our own and others.

When faced with the need to decide, try this strategy series for better decision-making:

- Have a good cry if you need one. Allowing yourself this release can clear a lot of emotions so you can then get down to the business of decision-making.
- Make a list of your priorities and brainstorm ideas until you find one that starts to feel good or least unobjectionable. This could include writing down what is most important to you, whose opinion you might like to seek and why.
- Focus your energy on thinking about these things, as it will help you come to your decisions and possibly relieve stress.
- Accept the challenge as not just a new reality but an opportunity to grow. Sleep on it. Most major decisions are best made after adequate sleep.
- Search online. There is a massive amount of information on line about jobs, health, towns and more. Do your research. Informed decisions are better decisions.
- Ask and reach out to others. If you're moving, see whom you can speak with who's lived where you're thinking about going. If it's health, speak with those who've gone through something similar.
- Keep your sense of humor. No matter what is happening, really no matter what, there is something to laugh about.

Lastly, remember you've made decisions your entire life. So far, you've done just fine.

MANTRAS

Finding a mantra is one of the best ways to start a day off on the right note and keep us singing when moods start to dip from any number of life's zingers. A mantra is a phrase that we relate to, that helps define our life philosophy and might aid in keeping us going in whatever direction we want to go in life.

The idea is to choose a phrase that inspires and comforts. It could be a line we read, a proverb, something we heard or even lyrics from a song.

My favorites vary depending upon the day or moment. My kids find me very annoying because I've used affirmative mantras my entire life, so I seem to have a one-liner collection that I use for every situation that arises. I like to keep them simple so I can get back to basics as quickly as possible.

Here are a few of my favorites in no particular order: It's all good…Choose peace… Get over it…Life goes on…It's a long way to the top if you want to rock and roll…To everything, there is a season…I say to myself, it's a wonderful world…I'm choosing love…Breathe…

When you pick a favorite—repeat it often. The more you do, the more likely it will become automatic when you need it, and it will provide quick comfort.

TOGETHER PEOPLE

"Together" people have "not so together" moments. Everybody has those times when the stress of day-to-day life makes us feel like we're about to crack, blow a gasket, explode, collapse, fall, unravel, lose it and erupt. To assume others don't is a really good way to beat ourselves up. Why would we ever want to do that?! Answer: We wouldn't. The goal is to accept that stress, anger, frustration and anxiety are energies that build yet can be transformed like every other form of energy. So this is why we breathe.

It's always good to recognize the signs of tension building.

Tension usually starts in our minds with a conversation that feels like we can't shut it off. We all know how it goes: We're thinking about what we should have said or done, could have or would have. Then it moves to our chest, triggering shallow breathing and breath-holding. Before long, we're filled with tension and our fuse is very short. It won't take much to light us up. Watch out—we're ready to let it rip.

Observe the mental conversation. Stop. Take a breath. Then repeat again and again. Find a private space. Even a public bathroom stall works.

SUNNY SIDE UP

How would you define your outlook on life? A) Sunny for the foreseeable future; B) Partly cloudy; or C) Rainy and likely to thunder.

I hope you got an A on the quiz—or at least a B, which holds the next-best potential for improvement. Why? Because optimists have fewer health problems and have a reduced risk of dying prematurely. A plethora of research proves that cardiovascular health, postsurgical complications, blood pressure, mental health and even basic survival are all significantly better for those with a positive attitude. It seems that finding ways to sustain positivity in our daily lives improves our health.

And here's a chicken-versus-egg benefit of positivity: The more positive we work on becoming, the more resourceful characteristics we build. Or maybe it's really that by working to recognize and use resources around us—within our families, friends and communities—we become more positive! Either way, working on our positivity and resourcefulness is a win-win.

If you find your thoughts taking a negative turn, focus on what is happening in the exact moment. Decide what you can do right then and there to change your thinking. Take action.

P.S.: There is always something you can do then and there at every moment to take action! You just have to decide to do it. Remember: When it rains, look for rainbows. When it's dark, look for stars.

FINE PRINT

Hope is like putting on eyeglasses if you need them. Without my reading glasses, words on a page are a blurry mess. For someone who loves to read, when I can't find my glasses, this is stressful. But when I put glasses on, I can see! I feel alive and excited.

Hope is the same way. When we have hope, we are open to seeing opportunity. Hope is like putting on your glasses and looking into the mirror within your heart.

Sometimes when we need it, hope might not be so easy to find. Maybe it's wherever we left our glasses, or written in the really fine print that sometimes seems to be getting smaller and smaller in our Contract with Life. But hope is always there, waiting to be seen and ready to provide a way if we choose to find it.

Hope kicks into action when we are willing to trust that our right actions will bring us the most positive possibilities. Choose hope and thoughtful action; then, anything is possible.

PERSEVERING

In many ways, life is one big perseverance test—starting with things as basic as walking and, for many, ending with walking difficulties. In the middle, we face off against life, going up against whatever comes our way as we try again and again, with hopes of improving our lives for the better. Defined as a steady persistence in a course of action, in spite of difficulty, obstacles or discouragement, our strength shines when—with tenacity and purpose—we commit to persevering versus quitting.

While not always easy, surmounting whatever challenges we undertake or are confronted with throughout our lives, builds our sense of self-esteem. Self-esteem does not come from others. It comes from within our hearts, from knowing we persevered, giving our best whenever necessary.

If we look around, inspiring examples of perseverance can be found everywhere—undertaken by people of all ages.

Go after whatever is important to you: Expect to stumble as you try and maybe even crash. Get back up. Don't linger on yesterday, because whatever you did then is already old news. Today's a new day to get out there, persevere and move yourself one step closer to whatever you want to be doing differently. Your future starts now.

DREAM ON

The more we allow ourselves to dream, the more reality intersects. Dreams are basically a road map to our heart's desires. If we open our hearts to dreams, hope is alive. When we're feeling hopeful, we're excited and pumped up about living.

The biggest risk in life is usually not taking the risk of pursuing our dreams because this involves the chance of failure.

Fear of actualizing our dreams mostly arises because we're afraid others will scoff at us.

Toughen up. Ignore the chiming. I've been laughed at my whole life. But when I die, the only thing I intend to regret is that I couldn't manage to function on less sleep so I could have crammed in more dream chasing.

More dream chasing leads to dream actualization—also known as new, exciting realities. Dream on. Dreaming is real.

NEW MODELS

Want to shape your body into a slightly new "model?" Keep reading. Overeating and eating junk starts in our heads when we think we "deserve" or "need" something. Despite best intentions, our mind doesn't hear our body saying, "No thanks! I'm full." Re-modeling our thinking starts with modeling behaviors we know will get us to a leaner, healthier body.

Here are my favorite tips:

If you think you're hungry, rinse your mouth with a minty mouthwash, with sorbitol as one of the ingredients. Sorbitol is a sweet sugar alcohol that sends a message to your brain that it's not starving.

If you're still hungry after rinsing, eat—but at least you will have extended the time between meals because nothing tastes tempting right after mouthwash!

Chew! Simple idea but missed by most. Chewing takes time, allows the body to register that it's getting fed and tires out your jaw!

No shoveling food into your mouth until you have thoroughly chewed and swallowed the prior one.

Bring your mind and body together. If you're thinking about eating, rest your hands on your stomach, close your eyes and ask if you're really hungry. Practicing this gets you in touch with real hunger versus emotional hunger and helps us realize that maybe we need to call a friend, walk, exercise or do something else besides eat.

If you can't understand why you are gaining weight or can't lose excess fat, keep a food log. Writing down everything we eat makes us aware of what's junk or healthy, as well as volumes of good or not-so-good choices.

Remember, maximum nutrition per calorie is the secret to a lean, healthy body.

Think: Fruits and vegetables for every meal so you get your nutrient load filled. This naturally results in hunger reduction. If your diet is low on nutritionally rich foods, you are always going to be hungry. The solution is simple: Eat more whole foods!

If the meal is not fruits or veggies, think in terms of handfuls. If you could put all of the food on your plate into two handfuls, that's about all a stomach can comfortably hold per meal. More is too much.

Before grabbing food, have two glasses of water. Most often we are thirsty, not hungry. If you're still hungry after drinking the H_2O, choose something healthy.

Own your bones! Bodies come in all different shapes and sizes based on bone structure and muscularity. Strut whatever is yours! Make yourself your own personal version of a lean and healthy model of the human body!

PUMP UP THE VOLUME

Doing something that pumps up our volume is vital to healthy, energized living.

The first time I recall observing the effects of pumping up energy was years ago when a girlfriend and I committed to taking a flamenco dance class. Every Monday night, we showed up in our new dancing shoes. Neither of us was good (in fact, that's an understatement) but we went, tried, learned, moved, loved it and laughed. To this day, we still burst into laughter as we think of the male teacher, who was about 65, wearing a pirate shirt unbuttoned to his navel, telling us to raise our right arm, stepping forward with our left while pushing out our chests with attitude. Usually we had the arms wrong, but the mere act of being told to jut out our breasts was hilarious, harmless and invigorating.

Too often, we don't take the time to pump up our energy. We all know the reasons: I can't dance, can't play, no time, too busy, tired, didn't work the last time I tried, afraid, don't know anybody, don't want to do it alone. Think of each of these as excuses you're making for not wanting to have fun. Why would you not want to make sure you laughed and got more energy?

Pump up activities can take many forms—whether you are already accomplished in the underlying skills or not. Dancing, playing music, jamming with others, painting, mixing, sketching, hammering, molding, bending, folding, stretching…

The goal is to choose something that will get your blood flowing because it's "you time" that makes you feel alive and energized. Taking the time to pump up our volume is what gives us the energy we need to help us through the rest of day-to-day living—also known as normal life.

TALENT

Studies show 99.9 percent of people worry about their lack of intelligence. If you happen to be in that 99.9 percent, remember it's only one point that makes the difference on an exam between mediocrity and genius. We're all intelligent and the most important aspect of our intelligence is learning to find, nurture and use our talents. Talent is our natural aptitude and skill. Talent will always rule over intelligence, assuming we learn how to harness it.

We've all got equal rations of talent, albeit in many different areas. Life satisfaction is about uncovering our unique talents and using each to our advantage.

Often, people who focused for years on formal studying don't comprehend how others who seemed to goof off can end up prospering. The reality is that life experience is a great teacher and most of what we have learned from our individual day-to-day experiences, year after year, is not covered in any university lecture. In actuality, our times of play are more likely than not, the times we started to notice what we were good at—the times when we started to notice our talents.

At any stage of life, it is immensely important to nurture our talents. Building, repairing, conversing, teaching, caring, creating, imagineering, coaching, time-managing, troubleshooting, cleaning, organizing, typing, woodworking, computing, decision-making, doing math, critical thinking, focusing, trend-setting, friend-making, adapting, designing, selling, conflict resolving, detail orienting, drawing, painting, dancing, encouraging, asking questions, writing, future thinking, high-energy having, juggling, leading, engaging in routine tasks, persuading, observing with a keen eye, planning, problem solving, being reliable, researching—the list is endless.

What are your talents? How are you nurturing them? Do you use them for work, play or both? Celebrate them all!

GETTIN' ALONG

Most of us really want to get along with others. It is human nature to prefer peaceful, constructive conversation. Communication breakdowns are frustrating and painful. Often, they leave one, both or all parties angry, confused and hurt.

We've been trying to get across our messages since the day we were born. So why does it sometimes still feel so difficult? Whether partners, kids, work or anybody else—communication challenges are inevitable and as unique as each of us. However, this does not mean they must be divisive.

Here's how to improve communication breakthroughs:

1. We really need to know who we are in our hearts, which is more than some mental image of who we are. Hearts are not tough, right or firm. Conversely, hearts aren't a pushover or too flexible, either.
2. Our pulsating hearts are knowing and loving. Our hearts have to become the guiding force of our thoughts. This means we have to risk vulnerability, because...
3. We must be willing to allow "us" as a possibility—to coexist. This means we must be open to adjust, reverse, switch, shift, transition, about-face, change or advance our thinking to be open to "us" thinking, which comes from the heart.

While in our heads we can script out all that we need to say to get our point across, if we're not willing to allow others to do the same—and then are not willing to risk "us" thinking—the problem remains and the relationship falters.

Exchange, liaison and rapport can only happen when we choose to embrace the possibilities of unity versus antagonism and division. Communication cannot move forward with mental rigidity. This does not mean we must always concede: Rather, it means that we must be willing to be flexible versus inflexible—much like a beating heart.

OFFENSE

We are as much of a pain in the arse when we take offense as when we give it. Every offense is tied to perspectives. And no matter how aware or enlightened we become through our years, we will never be able to control another's perspective regarding the offenses they perceive we have given. We never become perfect people who never offend.

So if we believe we might have offended another—or if someone tells us we've offended them—try apologizing sincerely. Agreeing the apology is warranted? That's irrelevant. The purpose of the apology is to help restore balance within the relationship: Not with elaborate justifications and explanations, just a sincere "sorry" and letting it go.

The only thing we lose with each apology—what we give to others—is our defensive ego. And I can assure you this: Egos are very strong, so we should have no worries about losing ours when we strive for greater peace by releasing our resentment and anger.

PADDLING OUT

Isn't it interesting that the word "retire" can mean 1) to withdraw or go away; 2) go to bed; 3) withdraw from office, business or active life due to age; or 4) retreat from battle according to plan?

Talk about a sweeping definition with broad room for personal interpretation!

Why doesn't it say: "Retirement means that it is time for a new adventure?"

How we each view retirement is very personal. It's connected to individual factors such as the characteristics of our current employment and daily activities, family dynamics, health, income, savings, locale and more.

Let's look at some aging statistics: As of 2017, 50 percent of the United States population was over age 50. About 10,000 people in the U.S. continue to reach retirement age every day, although most of us actually plan to work well past age 65. Forty-five percent of the Silver Disobedience® population says they are entrepreneurial and are considering starting new businesses in their "retirement." Others are opting for travel and other forms of recreation. Then there are those who believe they've created a life whereby work never really felt like "work," so work and retirement are already blurred together; not much would change regardless of their age as long as health isn't adversely impacted.

So much to consider with all these opportunities! Whether it's a present-day reality or looking out into the future, today is a good day to think of all the ways you can paddle out to your "retirement" adventures!

SERIOUSLY

While it's important to take what we do seriously, what we do is not who we are—and we can't take ourselves too seriously.

Life is one gigantic spectacle and no matter how we see ourselves in the cosmic mix, we're only a speck in a massive universe.

When we get stuck taking ourselves too seriously, our ability to progress is hindered because we become too worried thinking about what everybody else is thinking about us, our choices and our actions. Our naturally creative selves suffer. Instead of glowing and flowing, we start getting sticky—unable to extricate ourselves from excessive self-examination. We question our instincts. Artistic flair falters. Humor dulls. Excitement fades. Life ebbs.

Our wrinkles run deep from laughter—except those between our eyebrows, which are often our "Did I *really* just do that?" or "What the heck?" wrinkles. Regardless, they're a part of us— little carvings in our face of all the experiences and challenges we've surmounted.

Enjoy the day! Don't take life too seriously!

ENERGY

We all want more energy. Nobody likes to feel tired and drained. So how do we get more energy? Two ways:

1. Reduce time spent on those things that drain us; and
2. Increase time doing those things that invigorate us.

So how do we do #1 and #2?

Trust your instincts. There's a little voice in your head that's telling you exactly how you want to be spending your finite time on Planet Earth.

GOOD FOR YOU

There was a time when I believed that the expression: "Good for you!" sounded like a total diss. A way of blowing off recognition of the accomplishments of myself or another. Upon reflection, "Feeling a bit sensitive and insecure?" is what I would ask my younger self if I had the opportunity to coach her. Let me tell you why.

Age has taught me that what is good for you may not be good for me and vice versa. That's a fact.

Choices that are good for us individually, may at times have nothing to do with what might be good for another. This doesn't make them good or bad, right or wrong. It simply means they are indications of preferences of what one might like versus what another might like. What we want might not appeal to others at all. What we feel may be feelings that others do not understand nor relate to. Directions we want to move in might be incomprehensible to another. Desires to learn something in particular, may be of zero interest to another.

"Good for you" is simply that. What is good for you, is good for you. No awestruck adulation or validation is necessary from others when we share our ideas, accomplishments, thoughts or plans.

Be honest: We don't always relate personally to what others share or are excited about. But we can sincerely respond: Good for you. I'm happy this is making you happy.

Genuinely feeling this way is good for you.

OLDER, NOT IRRELEVANT

Years do not make anyone less relevant; nor does losing a job, retiring, divorce, empty nests, illness or other life events. Although we may be less-important to certain people, you are never less relevant in your own life regardless of age or circumstances.

To the contrary, even if we're still working by choice or circumstance, our Silver Disobedience® years bring freedom: the opportunity to reframe our identities, purpose and authenticity.

We can choose to release ourselves from being defined by what we do. Instead, we can focus on being who we are, doing things we like! We can work on being present in an entirely different way. The amazing thing? The more we embrace any given moment as a treasure, the more surprising new outcomes seem to present themselves. The gifts in the present become abundant.

UNSTUCK

We do what we want to do.

The only way we can make a change is if we find the benefit that we will reap for ourselves by making a change.

Suppose we want to drop some excess weight and get ourselves in shape for the benefit of greater energy and health. We are going to have to recognize our conditioned choices (behaviors) that are preventing this and take actions to change them.

Here's how:

1. We are going to eat more fruits and veggies, and start walking and moving more.
2. We will eliminate the junk that keeps us from our goal.
   Sounds easy, right? Here's what else will be necessary to reach our goals:
3. List the triggers that break our resolve, such as the rationalizing voices in our heads (I deserve an ice cream sundae; I earned this pizza after my hard day). Junk "food" in the house. Building stress. Afternoon energy dips. Tiredness at night.
4. Define alternative actions. What are you going to do when you're stressed and tired? You could take a walk. Read a book. Crunch carrots. Stretch. Take a shower. Get into bed. Paint. Draw. Write letters. Woodwork. Plant. Something that otherwise occupies our hands and minds.
   Next…
5. Become aware in the moment. We must keep telling ourselves it's time to wake up our consciousness. Awareness is how we plant change. When we really think about an action, we can become aware of its benefits—and its disadvantages to us. Then we can choose new behaviors like those we outlined above.

When we choose to become aware of what we're doing—not rationalizing that we're doing it because we've been triggered by some external force—we can become unstuck.

This is not to say we won't still eat junk occasionally—but we'll be doing it with awareness of our actions, which are choices. It's not about "trying" to change. Change happens when we become fully aware: We wake up, recognizing that we do what we want to do. When we're fully aware, it's very hard to act counter to our awareness. Suddenly, we find ourselves doing more of what would be more beneficial and less of what is counter to our physical, mental and emotional wellness.

FORGET YOURSELF

This is indeed a comically ironic headline from someone who models and posts photos of herself daily on a blog—but really, it's the big secret behind my smile in every one of these photos. When I'm not smiling (read that as "frowning and hoping nobody sees"), it's because I forgot to practice this.

If we want to feel better mood-wise and improve relationships—a win-win for all parties involved—the goal is to forget about ourselves and start recognizing that others see almost every aspect of life differently than we do.

We each tend to view life from our exclusive perspective because we think it makes things easier. But does it? It might be temporarily convenient, but also possibly alienating and isolating. For example: If punctuality is important to us because we're on a tight schedule, our anger is likely to arise the minute others are late. Suddenly, the fact that they may be an otherwise great person is obliterated due to their lateness—because we're taking it personally and deeming this action inexcusable by our standards. Now they are "rude and selfish" instead of just late.

Punctuality is important. But annihilating positive feelings about another due to our frustration with whatever behavior is irking us won't resolve the punctuality issue.

Rather, at times like this, we need to pause and reflect: "Great person, lots of fun, but just seems to regularly miss the bus."

Point being: Relationships with other humans are inconvenient. Opting to let others "in" means accepting that they will regularly bring other ways of thinking and doing things that will require more open-mindedness on our part before we reject it.

And a newsflash from those married 50+ years: This fact doesn't change. But their responses to each other do—if they want to stay married.

Our perspectives on life and others reflect our likes, dislikes and experiences. It gets down to this: To allow ourselves to practice forgetting ourselves is asking, "Is the relationship more important than being right?" Only you can decide.

A LETTER

Letter-writing is an underrated form of communication. Many prefer to write in texting shorthand, which includes easily misinterpreted acronyms, incomplete thoughts, ridiculous expressions requiring us to consult Urban Dictionary and annoying abbreviations (like leaving out the "a" in "Thanks" because it's just too much effort to spell it out). Not everyone does this but it's a growing trend.

Long form, well-thought-out writing, along with beautiful handwritten letters, seem to be going out of style. I love getting letters. I can also say that there were at least four very memorable times in my life when taking the time to write a thank-you note changed the direction of my life for the better. Way, way better.

Writing a letter, even if it is never sent, is a fantastic meditative exercise. It's especially challenging to try to write a genuine "thank you" that never uses the words "I," "me," "my" or "mine." It's not easy, as it forces our minds outward to the world around us and others. Try doing it. We all know someone who would appreciate receiving a genuine, handwritten thank you, 100 percent focused on them.

P.S.: The same exercise works with trying to speak for five, 10 or even 15 minutes without using "I," "me," "my" or "mine." Trust me on this: It's really hard! Or maybe it is just for me!

P.P.S.: My mother is a wonderful letter writer and her exquisite script —another thing sadly going out of style—is as beautiful as her words. Thanks, Mom, for instilling in us kids the importance of handwritten thank-you notes.

TAKE THE BEAT

Telling ourselves to "Just be calm" doesn't work. But taking a beat, stopping and remembering to breathe *does* work. That's it. Now breathe! Again and again. Take the beat.

Anchors Away

When we think of an anchor, it's usually as a massive piece of iron designed to hold a ship steady and prevent it from floating away. Keep that visual in mind while we consider the benefits of creating mental anchors.

Mental anchoring involves creating an association between an external stimulus and an internal experience to create a more favorable response, greater comfort and better learning. Mental anchors can be effectively used to reinforce confidence in any situation. This could be a job interview, a date, engaging in a difficult conversation, committing to healthier eating or exercise, or just about anything.

Let's say you'd like to feel more confident. Follow these steps:

1. Recall a time when you did feel confident. Run a movie in your mind about that moment. Try to really see it, and remember how you felt at that time, making the memory as vivid as possible. If there is music or a smell you can associate with it—add that into your mental movie as well. Use Technicolor! Keep the imagery bright and vibrant. Go ahead and smile as you recall the wonderful moment.

2. Now that you've got the imagery going strong, choose a part of your body or an action that will serve as your physical "anchor" that you will use when you need some stability and strength to conquer what might be perceived as threatening waves. My favorite is making a small, tight fist that says, "Yeah!" (Like a fist-pump!) You can also do this with a mental image, visualizing yourself standing in the victory stance with your hands held over your head like the champion you are.

3. Next, get back to that happy moment movie and add your physical anchor to the memory.

4. Take a momentary break, then repeat this process to get used to the power of anchoring your memories with a physical gesture for greater recall when you need it. Remember to add all your senses to the picture while adding your physical action.

5. Drop your anchor regularly. Anytime you need positive reinforcement before a confrontation, situation, new meeting or a potential moment of insecurity, take a minute to recall and activate your anchor. Practice doing this enough times so that initiating the physical action triggers a positive emotional response and a flow of endorphins, which are your feel-good hormones.

6. Repeat until you can get this desirable feeling on demand.
    Anchors away!

SELF-ISH

Getting a bit "self-ish" isn't such a bad idea.

Have you ever noticed and really listened to what your "self" is telling you? Does your "self" need more relaxation, peace, self-love, exercise, fun—or something else it's not getting?

Although you might not realize it yet, getting a bit self-ish is good not only for you but others around you will benefit as well.

If you're not sure how to practice a little self-ishness, try these ideas:

- Speak up! People can't read your mind. You need to tell others what you need. Don't be a martyr expecting those with whom you interact to know your wants. You have to tell them.
- Start doing what you want to do! Yes, you might have to work (as I do) but that's about 40 hours out of 168 in a week. What could you do that would be more fulfilling during the other 128 hours and ultimately equate to creating more energy?
- Notice your micro-achievements! Sometimes we ignore the small steps we're making because we live in a world where everything done by others seems so stupendous. (Don't believe it.) Give yourself credit for every step moving forward.
- As per above, do something every day that feels really good! Why? This will increase your energy.

Accept that *you* are the manager of your life! You're the boss! Own it! Make some decisions that are invigorating!

Are you charged up? Envision how you can harness your energy!

BRAIN POWER

Did you know the brain is as individualized as our fingertips? No two brains act alike— even those of identical twins. What's even cooler, brains are in a constant state of change. And here's why this is important: How our brains change is directly impacted by daily challenges and experiences throughout our lives. The brain is so supple and responsive to what we think that it is in a constant state of reorganization. Thoughts, emotions and memory can actually be self-regulated for the most part, and our ability to recollect past events can be sharpened.

Stress without the counterbalance of relaxation, along with inadequate use of our brains, is what starts the deterioration process. These are the effects we're noticing when we're getting moody, forgetting things or making questionable decisions.

Dementia is not predestined. While we're all going to get wrinkles if we live long enough, we can avoid senility and retain strong brain power right to 120 years and beyond.

Three main factors trigger mental decline: Poor diet and lack of exercise, which cause preventable diseases like heart disease, high blood pressure and strokes; and third, lack of curiosity or no longer being interested in living. While poor diet and no exercise are obvious causes due to lack of nutrition and inadequate oxygenation, disinterest in living is surprisingly underestimated. Disinterest in living is most noticeable when a long-time partner dies or leaves and the other person retreats. Other factors that can trigger disinterest include moving, job changes and lack of companionship.

But the good news is: We can stay sharp. Due to the malleable nature of our brains, any declines we may have noticed can be stalled and possibly even reversed.

How? Start problem solving: With work, reading (especially mystery books), brain games, writing, self-education or class learning and staying fit—because a fit body builds a strong mind. Start socializing and figure out how you're going to relax. Breathing with eyes closed—even for a minute—helps. And last but not least, never forget the Silver Disobedience® theme: Age is an attitude, not a number.

WANTS VERSUS NEEDS

Society values bigger, better, more—particularly when it comes to material things: the house, car, gadget, vacation and so on. The selfies that are really "wealthies" (images of possessions) bombard us consciously and unconsciously daily. A significant consequence is that it's easy to overlook what we have.

Attitudes of gratitude can make the difference between a good day and a bad one.

Problems begin when we start to mix up our wants and needs. Envy, depression and jealousy are rooted in the confusion between necessity and desire. Very few of us have everything we want, and just because it seems others have more, it shouldn't be assumed that having more correlates to greater happiness. In fact, there are any number of studies confirming that "more" does not equal "happier." There's a point where enough is enough, and having more than that becomes comparable to a rat running on a wheel.

When we want something, the Law of Awareness kicks in. We suddenly seem to notice whatever it is everywhere—except in our own possession, of course. We become hooked into feelings of lack.

To stay on track for happy lives—with enough money for retirement and the real needs that will invariably arise—distinguishing our wants versus our needs is paramount. This starts with recognizing what we have, and asking if the latest and greatest version of whatever will really make us happier or financially crunched or, worse, put us in debt.

A good way to assess wants versus needs is by asking: If my home was burning down, would I run in and grab this? Yes, it's an extreme question, but it does get to the difference between a want and a need pretty quickly. None of this is to say that we shouldn't buy and have what we want. But if it's something that means we'll have to work too much, take time away from loved ones, skip exercising or get more stressed because we need more moolah to get it—maybe something else is what we really need.

Only you can answer this question—but it starts with prioritizing our wants versus needs.

IMAGINE

"Logic will get you from A to B. Imagination will take you everywhere," said Einstein. What we can imagine is exclusively ours. We can choose to make our imaginings as public or private as we want them to be.

Imagination is the sign that our minds are operating on all cylinders, sparking with creativity that is just waiting to explode into a blaze of glory. Based in curiosity, the only limits to making our imaginings real is our commitment to working to bring them to light.

Some of us have vivid imaginations that are just waiting to be unleashed. Others are more comfortable with allowing imagination to direct our actions and move us forward. Picasso believed that everything we can imagine is real. Our actions will either materialize what we imagine or not. Of course, these could be good things that propel us forward—or those that keep us stuck if we allow fear to rule our imaginations while visualizing doom or gloom.

Imagination is power. It gives us our answers to new possibilities. It is the basis for all personal and societal advances. Add faith to imagination and anything is possible. Everything starts with imagination. Imagination converts ideas to reality because we believe it can, and are willing to make it so. Where can your imagination take you? Paraphrasing Norman Vincent Peale, imagination can deliver the ultimate magic carpet ride.

FORGET "IF ONLY"

The greatest dissatisfactions in life come from the phrase, "If only…"

Whatever the "if only" is—is irrelevant. You didn't. They didn't. It didn't. It wasn't.

"If only" implies we retrospectively believe we had fairly good reasons to do otherwise at the time. Maybe we did, maybe we didn't. Regardless, "if only" keeps us stuck in wishes, the past and dreaming of another life instead of the one we have.

The life we have is what we make of it—today. And you know what? That is enough. In fact, it's wonderful.

FOR THE HEALTH OF IT

Just for the health of it, here's how to stay lean and healthy:

- Lots of water. At least two eight-ounce glasses before any caffeine. More all day.
- If imbibing alcohol: Two glasses of water per glass of wine or cocktail. Dehydration ages skin: Nobody looks good puffy!
- Lots of fruits and veggies: 75 percent of every meal. Imagine a plate three-quarters filled with vegetables you like—no oily sauces or dressings. Whether you also eat grains, meats, fish or dairy products, limit them to no more than 25 percent per meal.
- Walk. Wear a pedometer. Count your daily steps for a week. Add up the total of all the days and divide by seven. Then add 3,500 more steps than this every day— which amounts to about an additional mile (or seven miles more per week!).
- Prepare simple, home-cooked meals. Buy fresh foods using as few ingredients as possible—but as many spices as you like, which will add new intriguing flavors.
- Don't bring junk foods home. We all crave a variety of junk. I don't bring it into my house—except for small amounts of dark chocolate (one ounce per day). If I were to buy junk, by 8:00 PM my willpower is weak and it's too much temptation. If it's not there, I can't eat it, so instead I'll reach for a piece of fruit and have an "I'm glad I did" moment.
- On that note, keep fruit on a counter within reach. What you see, you eat.
- Join a gym and go. Some form of weight resistance is important. When I can't go to the gym, I do planks or push-ups on the floor or against a counter. I do 30 of them three to five times, dispersed throughout the day. If you want to try this, begin with 10 pushups or a plank, counting as long as you can. Do it again, three to five times a day. These are full-body motions that will get you in touch with all of your muscles.
- Get sleep. While I might get by with a six-hour night, two of these in a row leads to serious grumpiness. Seven to nine hours of sleep each evening in a cool, dark room is ideal for physical, emotional and cognitive health.
- Breathing breaks. Throughout the day, try to stop and take deep breaths for a minute. It's so easy to fall into a habit of slouching and not fully expanding our chests for a deep breath. Even just a minute with closed eyes is a rapid mood elevator.

This sums up an easy-yet-healthy-to-do routine.
Simple, right?
Just have to do it.

ICEBERGS

The expression about how we've only seen "the tip of the iceberg" is really one of the best descriptors of people. While most think this phrase is a warning about how a problem or difficulty is only a small part of a bigger issue, I actually visualize icebergs quite differently. Let me explain:

Ninety percent of an iceberg is below the water's surface. What is below the surface is very difficult to judge—but it runs deep out of necessity. It is the large foundation that allows the iceberg to maintain its stability. Instead of being wholly exposed, we only see a tip of it, while the rest remains deep in the ocean. The generation of a powerful upward buoyant force enables icebergs to stay afloat. The bigger the mass below the surface, the more stable the iceberg.

Why icebergs analogize so beautifully to people is this: Those who develop their inner sense of self have greater stability in life. Further, those with a strong comprehension of who they are and where they've been are more likely to hold a lot under their surface that is not visible to other people. They don't need to brag about their power, nor be critical of others. They're more likely to laugh at themselves and be kind to others.

Experiences form a strong foundation for greater buoyancy, which serves to make us lighter, whether we are facing troubled waters or calm seas. Assurance of who we are need not be announced. Our strength of character can be allowed to swell from deep below the surface. Hard-earned emotional stability is well-regarded as strength. As such, confidence radiates.

Character is dependent upon the degree to which we have created strong foundations for ourselves. Some of us had the benefit of being born into stable environments, others not. Either way, stability comes from growing through years of challenges, opportunities, people, situations and circumstances. It accumulates through living but can be chipped away, only to resurface yet again. Even though icebergs float upon the ocean waves, they remain stable, able to withstand the storms of life.

Icebergs remind me of healthy aging. With each year, the foundation that defines our spirits and character becomes more solid—better able to withstand the challenges, suffering and setbacks that come with the tides of life. Moving, ebbing and flowing but remaining steady and strong.

I far prefer this view of "the tip of the iceberg." How about you?

TIED UP

Does an age arrive when suddenly we have lots of free time and don't know what to do with it? Having read thousands of responses to my blog posts, I can say this: Most are loving the lives they've created—but life is busy in our 50s and beyond! Maybe the expression should be: "Retirement years abhor a vacuum!"

For most of our lives, we've operated in two modes: work and rest. Free time may have been, and may still appear to be, something that we get after everything else is done. Time seems tied up as we keep performing to maximum overload. There is nothing wrong with this if we like it—but everyone benefits from "me time." It's OK to slow down regularly and make yourself a life priority. Here are a few areas where we can set some new grays in our schedules versus the black and white of work/rest:

- Exercise is not another job. It is how we clear our heads, increase motivation, build energy and improve our likelihood of a longer, healthier life so we can better enjoy our time. Whether a walk, a class or a visit to a gym, exercise is just as important as any work task.
- If we're being enlisted to help others, which could involve homework or other tasks, declare a deadline. For example: I've always said my homework help stops at 8:00 PM. Setting time limits works with many other demands, too.
- Playtime is not just for kids. Setting dates with ourselves and others helps everyone plan. My parents went out every Friday night for pizza and beer. When they came home, they went straight to their bedroom and none of us five kids bothered them. This showed us all how they prioritized alone time. We learned that this was the night to feed ourselves and make our own plans. Whether it's seeing a friend, having a dinner date, taking a stroll through a park, enjoying a massage, attending music events, going on a museum trip—whatever. Setting a time to do whatever you want and planning it as a priority is important.

Define life-work boundaries, including when you will or won't check emails and take calls. Not sure how? Imagine you're passionately making love. Would you stop to check your email? Doubtful. Take the visual further. Is it OK to interrupt your meals? Take time away from family? We all need to define our home boundaries or life gets too crowded.

Free time isn't a leftover that we possibly get after everyone else has had their fill. We're entitled to a healthy piece of our pie of life!

A Series of Nows

How did we get to this age? Where did the time go? At this stage, we either feel we've had a long life or it's been the blink of an eye. Universally, we feel it isn't going to be long enough.

We can't reverse time. The sun sets each evening of our lives—and it won't turn backward. Pasts can be contemplated but not redone. Futures remain unknown. Life is just a series of "nows." Accepting life as a series of nows, makes us honor the value of moments. Whatever we're doing needs to be done with purpose, so we can enjoy little victories with the passing of time.

With only 24 hours in a day, making the right choices regarding how we spend our time is paramount.

Of course, many of us must work. To make work time more rewarding, it helps to remember that there are no "just" jobs. Each role, regardless of pay scale, is necessary for society to function. While working, we might as well get into being the best at whatever we're doing, with pride. This will make our days more rewarding and give us more energy to spend on other things we might like to do with our free time.

Also regarding working: It pays to remember that we can save up money but we can't save up time. We can borrow money but we can't borrow time. There's no carrying over the hours in today to tomorrow. Everything is contained in the moment of now.

As we can't stop time, we must maximize the quality of our time.

Experiences help us realize that clocks don't measure the quality of our time. Quality time can feel timeless. Think of an album you love to listen to. While it took weeks or months to record, the music now plays from start to finish in two hours or less. But assuming we like the music, we are transported into timelessness. Such is the experience whenever we do things we love.

So here's the thing: We are this age. How will you increase the quality of your time to enjoy it to the max?

Infinity and Beyond

Love is like infinity. A continuum, expanse, immensity, limitless, myriad of space. We can't have more or less infinity. It is endless in time and place. Likewise, no two things can be equal in their infinite nature.

We don't have to worry if we love—or are loved—more or less, as the boundaries of love cannot be measured due to its ubiquity.

We've likely done a lot of loving and caring for others. We might be doing these things now, and might be doing a lot more of them in our advancing years. This requires kindness, patience, tolerance, joy for another's successes, and lots of optimism about the wonderful things often hidden deep within others.

As well, to love requires the ability to keep giving without much thought about what we'll get in return for our time and energy.

More challenging is knowing that love and care will involve moments when nobody is kind, patience is short, tolerance is limited, doubt rises, disappointments happen and self-doubt about our choices crops up.

No single person could be the "be-all and end-all of love." This would contradict the infinite nature of love, which is all around us, coming from many sources if we choose to see it.

We may feel we have had a great love in our lives or even felt we had a few. This does not mean love for us cannot exist again. Also—if we feel we missed something or never had that great love—maybe we weren't seeing clearly what was around us and we need to open our hearts today, as love comes in many forms.

Love doesn't pass anyone by and it is always there to be embraced if we are open to allow its expansion. The possibility to love again and again always exists. As Buzz Lightyear says: To infinity and beyond.

I send love to you. Thank you for joining me on this journey by reading this book, reading my blog and sharing your thoughts. You fill my heart with infinite love and inspiration daily. Love and live.

SHIFTING FOCUS

Imagine for a moment entering a very dark room. If the first thing we can make out in the darkness is a beautiful doll that looks like a lovely fairy, we'd likely feel more secure. On the other hand, if the first thing we see is a broken doll or a creepy clown, it's quite likely we'd feel anxious or scared and start worrying how and when we're going to get out.

In either situation, nothing positive or negative has happened. But our minds shifted focus and began forming opinions—relaxing or getting defensive.

Our brains work by going to vast libraries of memories—real or imagined. The more vivid the memory, the more likely we are to recall it.

Suppressing thoughts doesn't work. In fact, there's plenty of research confirming if we're told to try to forget something, we're actually twice as likely to think about it. A great example is when we're in a public place and someone says: Don't look now…but…" And what happens? We look!

This same response is exactly what happens when we tell ourselves we have to go to sleep or we have to stop thinking about something.

So, what do we do? Find and focus on the positives.

By focusing on what we like, in ourselves, others or a situation, we are shifting our focus. We aren't pretending to like traits, behaviors or someone, or denying our feelings about a situation. Nor am I suggesting we repress or try to ignore anything that is bothering us. This is because trying to suppress a thought or feeling is like trying to cool a pot of water over a flame when what we really need to do is turn down the temperature.

Instead, the idea is that we shift the focus to try to find something positive about the situation or person. We can choose to be the ruler of our mental domains by shifting our focus to noticing what we do like. And here's a parting thought: If you're not the ruler of your thoughts, who is?

FOOD FOR THOUGHT

Our bodies are so amazingly tolerant and resilient that we may be guilty of taking them for granted. Since it's rare to get something for nothing, ignoring the basics of human existence will not work for the long haul. We must learn to give our body what it needs, so it can fulfill our expectations of a long and healthy life. It's up to each of us to maintain our health and keep it strong if we want to stay active and vital.

Maintaining health requires some discipline and acknowledgement of responsibility. Our minds must rule our actions. Our hands and mouth don't think—as much as we all might like to believe they operate with minds of their own! Every time we pick something up, put it in our mouth and swallow, we make a choice. So chew on that a moment…

Only conscious choices will control what gets into our stomachs, decide whether we exercise, determine how many hours we sleep and so on. In many ways, we choose our level of health. Yes, there are exceptions, but the majority of illnesses that come with age are triggered by poor health habits.

Our bodies are amazing, marvelous machines that are more efficient than the most exotic machines ever created. Years of abuse can be tolerated but eventually there's a payday. There is no "free lunch."

But here's the good news: Our bodies strive to be healthy. It's our natural state! So if we start adding more fruits and vegetables to our meals; drink eight to 10+ glasses of fresh water daily; reduce consumption of processed foods; limit alcohol and keep coffee to no more than one to two cups a day; eat more lean meats, natural grains and raw, unsalted nuts; start moving more and regularly, aiming to build our strength—our bodies will do their best to respond.

Today is a perfect day to consciously make healthier choices: To think before we put something in our mouths and before we sit on the couch. Little changes feel good—they're the catalyst for greater health and longevity.

WISHING OR DOING

There are two kinds of moments: "I wish I had" and "I'm glad I did." Each gets down to the choices we make in preparation for the inevitable surprises life will bring.

For example, if we plant bulbs in the chilly days of fall, beautiful flowers bloom in the early days of spring. In this case we can say, "I'm glad I did." If instead we chose to let weeds rule, not caring for the soil, maybe randomly throwing seeds, our garden likely will not look so great come spring—and we might have an "I wish I had" moment.

We make decisions daily. We can choose to eat well, exercise, educate ourselves, be creative, grow emotionally and spiritually, save money, find the best work, contribute to our communities and seek ways to nurture relationships with our family and friends—or not.

Whatever we choose, inevitably a time comes for taking responsibility and acknowledging that we made choices.

Even right now, on any number of fronts, there are choices that are ours to make. Each will largely determine how our lives will unfold now and in the days to come. As I've said, there are no guarantees in life. But I've also said it is never too late to start owning the "I'm glad I did" mindset instead of experiencing the regrets from "I wish I had."

Eating more fruits and vegetables, committing to strengthening our bodies, educating ourselves to increase our personal knowledge and options for work, saving money for our future, volunteering to help in our communities, spending quality time with family and friends, and more: All are choices that will reap rewards more often than not.

Every day, we decide how to spend our time. Today is a great day to begin doing, not wishing, so we can enjoy more moments saying: "I'm glad I did."

DIFFICULT TIMES

If pain and sorrow have any benefit, it might be that they show us the depth of our strength. While we'd all most likely prefer a pain-free life, compassion, patience and gentleness are admirable characteristics that tend to personify those who have lived through difficult times.

Sadly, when our lives are going smoothly, we can develop an invincible feeling about ourselves and a harsh view of others. When it comes to illness, we may even be so cold and ignorant to think that others may have done something to bring the sickness upon themselves—as if this is an excuse for a lack of understanding of another's pain. At best, such thinking is a poor attempt at rationalizing the incomprehensible nature of life and death.

Those who have been sick or made to suffer in some way gain a new sense of grace as they have learned the true essence of humility, often from having no choice but to relinquish their independence in reliance on others. It is deep pain that also creates empathy, which in turn makes greater compassion possible. Throughout our lives, our pain, losses and sorrows increased our capacity to forgive and love more deeply. Only by being forced to intimately understand grief, can we feel another's pain as if it were our own.

In times of pain and sorrow, we have no choice but to dig deep into our hearts. Know that during difficult times, we also reach new potential to awaken to deeper truths, understanding and growth. Our pains and sorrows make it possible for us to gaze more gently upon humanity. Patience develops that allows us to let others grow—and we seem to find a new willingness to let their growth and experience happen in due time.

Remember: When you break through the bottom of sorrow, the light floods out.

WRINKLES IN THE PLAN

Face it: No matter what we do, wrinkles happen—physical and otherwise. We can set schedules, timetables, calendars and plan—but try as we might, life will unfold with wrinkles. Take exercising and making healthier food choices: These are two smart things to do. But neither stops wrinkles—or getting hit by a bus if we don't look both ways!

So about life-plan wrinkles: They happen to us all. Yet our life force is fed by pushing forward, accepting the inevitability of wrinkles despite our insecurities about facing them.

Fears of failing can be as just as immobilizing as fears of succeeding. Yet the more we opt to accept that there are no guarantees of failure or success—no matter what choices we make— the easier pushing ourselves forward becomes, because we are accepting the inevitability of wrinkles from living life to the fullest.

Choosing to do the things that push our lives forward for the long haul (which is something we all want—a long haul!) is always better than doing nothing to fulfill our desires. Through action, while we will make errors (and certainly there will be wrinkles), it's a bigger mistake to allow our limited lifetimes to pass, waiting for a cosmic sign that guarantees some perceived "success."

Life is about living so that we reach our personal definitions of "the fullest life" at every age. Go for the gusto. There's no shame in taking a risk—or failing. Don't worry about what others might say as they try to discourage you. Don't wait. Find the time to do whatever is bubbling up inside of you, seeking expression.

Waiting can become a habit: Break it! Life is happening now. Embrace it, wrinkles and all.

FIDO

Once in a while, I see a bumper sticker that really captures my attention with its brevity and simplicity. Sometimes I have to be really careful not to hit the car in front of me when I'm trying to read those pithy little bits of wisdom. One of my favorites said "F.I.D.O." and in very tiny letters underneath was printed: "Forget It. Drive On." What great advice not just for calming road rage but for living a more peaceful life!

HOUSECLEANING

In spring, projects and plans that have been chilling in the recesses of our minds all winter start to come to the surface just like flowers. Many of us start housecleaning to clear out the old and prepare for new possibilities. We seek to eliminate what we no longer need: Shedding the things that have been crowding our homes that may be broken, no longer applicable, past their time and/or suitable for a donation or yard sale.

Spring is also a wonderful time to clear stuff stored in our minds and bodies.

Maybe we were less inspired to move our bodies because it was cold: Is the phrase "add a spring to our step" a coincidental double entendre or a reminder to get moving? It's time to reinvigorate our bodies with more activity: yard work, housecleaning, car washing, gardening, walking and exercising. No time is better than now to start a new routine that gets our gears in motion.

But how about the mental stuff that's been taking up space for too long? We've got a certain amount of room between our ears and no space to store junk. Spring is an excellent time to inventory our lives and desires. Have we always wanted to take a class? Start dancing, cooking, photographing, fixing engines, painting? Look for new work? Define new plans or trips? Figure out new ways to enjoy time with our significant others? Reconnect with friends and family? Maybe even reach out with an apology to someone? Offer a budding branch of peace that leaves the bitterness of winter behind us?

While we can't go back to redo our beginnings, today we can refresh our plans and take actions for new endings. We can choose to live like spring has blossomed—and so have we—with a fresh new perspective on how we're going to live this new season upon us.

JAILED BY COMPARISON

It is wholly possible to admire the strength, beauty, accomplishments and even possessions of others without diminishing or casting doubt on ourselves in any way. Comparison causes sadness and discontent. It's a prison of insecurity. We free ourselves by recognizing, appreciating and admiring our own unique physical, mental, emotional and spiritual characteristics—and those of others.

More of anything does not directly correlate to greater happiness. It is simply just more of something. Jealousy of what we perceive another to have over us, definitely doesn't feel good nor does it make us happy.

The happiness we feel, or not, at any moment is a topic for a whole other essay. Still, the only comparisons that may be helpful to us are those whereby we look at what we learned from our past experiences and how we are now better as a result of this knowledge today.

Life satisfaction has little to do with others. Rather, it is a personal reflection: Am I a better person today than yesterday?

It matters not what others are doing. What matters is what we each decide to act upon to increase our fulfillment throughout our life journeys. Our sense of freedom flourishes when we stop comparing ourselves to other people.

Today is a good day to use our personal "get out of jail" cards. We do this by developing a genuine "Good for you!" attitude when we hear about the good stuff that is happening in the lives of others. By flipping our switch to a sincere congratulatory perspective, we are better able to see possibilities for ourselves to reach our own unique accomplishments.

There's always room at the top for unique greatness to shine. Release your one-of-a-kind self today!

CONDITIONING

This is not about hair or our bodies—it's about mental conditioning.

All of us have been conditioned. It is a socialization process that starts soon after birth. As we arrived without instructions, those in charge of our care had to try to figure out something unknown: a human.

There were no directions and little guidance or understanding as to how their choices would impact us; when they'd need to release or tighten the reins; and how their choices might be diverging from the nature of who we are versus them. In an effort to cope with someone entirely unknown—while also coping with the unknowns within themselves, their mates and all of life's other stressors—these others sought to help us. They did this by consciously and unconsciously trying their best to show us the way; improve us; make our lives easier than theirs; and give direction. Yet this was all based on their perspectives, not necessarily ours—because how could they know? Daily, we internalized this education, setting the stage for the belief that others had the answers.

Since well-meaning people tried to show us the way from their perspectives, we learned to look externally, believing our worth revolved around being what others wanted. We learned that if we're not happy or things aren't going our way or we're not getting what we want in a relationship, it must be time to resort to what we learned. So we search our reference files, trying to figure out what's wrong so we can fix the problem.

Conditioning tells us we need to convince another we're right, even when we don't necessarily know why we think we are. Next, we push, pull, fight, cry, hurt—hoping. We double-down on efforts to make another understand. When our subtle attempts don't work, frustration builds: We start withholding, getting snappy, sarcastic, irritable, hardened. The root fear at the base of this all? Abandonment.

At some point, we all lost ourselves and started focusing on the responses of others as a sign of our worth. It's how we all cope. We began to believe others know what's right for us versus ourselves. Therefore, in relationships, we perpetuate this faulty thinking. Frustrations arise not by what someone might be doing, but what we think we have to do to get them to respond differently.

We want to be recognized. We fear abandonment and believe that to accept another as is, we leave ourselves—and worry that if we don't accept them, they might leave us.

We don't have to abandon ourselves or our needs. Nor do we have to ask others to do so with theirs. Rather, it's seeing the ways we've been conditioned, accepting the ways others have been conditioned—and coexisting. As someone very wise taught me: "You do you. I do me." Not to exclude the idea of compromise—but imagine life if only this were possible.

ANOTHER'S TRANCE

Stay out of other people's trances.

We all know someone who is stuck somewhere in their past. Maybe it's even you. Conversation with stuck people tends to go backward into how they grew up, the pain, suffering, cold or abusive parents, lack of love, missed opportunities, broken promises and more. We know it's all true. And our hearts feel compassion for this suffering. But here's the problem: They want us to join them in their trance because unconsciously and unintentionally, misery loves company. That person is waiting to hear: "What a horrible life. I have no idea how you survived."

Don't do it! Do not accept an invite to that party!

When a conversation gets stuck like this, it's time to change it up and try to transport the speaker into the present. To be clear, I'm not taking about issues that someone might be coping with requiring immediate attention, love, compassion and solutions—but rather when the person is stuck in a state of trance, recalling old memories and a bad situation over and over.

When I worked in private practice as card-carrying member of the Hypnotists Union, Local 472 (which I still am), I listened to many people who were seeking help to get out of their real live trance. But the time comes to stop listening and trigger change.

People can't go forward when stuck in a past trance state. They often say they want to change—but first they want to repeat and repeat, getting everyone in full agreement, in their trance, that life is miserable. They often need help from a friend (or a therapist) who can jolt them out of their trance with kindness and humor. This is not undermining another's pain. Instead, it is reminding everyone to stay present because this is where we can heal and find peace. It's taking a risk with love.

Whether for a friend or yourself, pay attention to the trances you choose to join.

FUHGETTABOUTIT

Why is it that when things are going wonderfully, we all like to take the credit, but when stuff seems to go down the crapper, somebody else must be responsible?

Here's the issue with this kind of thinking: It undermines the fact that each of us is a Co-Master of Our Own Fabulous Power-Full Universe.

Wonderful or not, we are each playing some kind of role and contributing to most of whatever is happening in our lives. "Most of," because sometimes really bad stuff happens, inflicted by circumstances or evil, and there's no explanation for it. But for the most part, we are orchestrating what happens in our daily lives through our choices and actions—whether we realize it (and want to accept responsibility) or not.

It's important to understand this because: If we don't like what's happening in our lives—how we're spending our time, the ways our relationships are relating, where we're living, whatever—it's time to figure out what we need to do to change it and act. If we can't control whatever is bugging us at the moment, we must move on and fuhgettaboutit, as they say in New York City.

Because we are each Co-Masters of the Universe, complaining, comparing or engaging in "what-ifs" is futile. We must each accept our roles, do the right things and not do anything purposely hurtful toward each other.

Co-Masters of the Universe have super-powerful consciouses, so breaking this rule, without immediately asking for forgiveness and making amends, tends to hurt our long-term health and well-being. (Note: It is never too late to use the superpower that is called "an apology.")

Further, as we are all Co-Masters, when we take revenge or an angry route, we only hurt ourselves in the process.

Upon accepting our strength and power, a greater capacity to be genuinely nicer to others activates. Why? Because the less threatened we are by the magnificence of others, the more good stuff boomerangs back to us. It's how the oh-so-powerful universe works. The more we freely give out lots of good, the more good comes our way.

And if it doesn't—fuhgettaboutit! Keep working on mastering your own superpowers, just as Luke Skywalker learned how to use the Force.

BIRTHRIGHT

Everyone begins life differently. Some are born into wealth, others into poverty, others in between. Some of us grew up in emotionally rich, loving and supportive homes. Others, in colder, emotionally vacant households. There's a range between these extremes as well. Lastly, there are physical health variables that arise, whether from birth or later in life, that further create challenges. The beginnings and obstacles we've confronted along the way vary widely.

What matters today is how we've moved ourselves forward from our respective starting points. Have we progressed? Overcome seemingly insurmountable difficulties? Kept trying to better our circumstances? Developed new, healthy relationships? Supported ourselves and families financially or otherwise? Grown emotionally?

As we age, it's helpful to recall how far we've come. No matter who we are, life to date has been a series of challenges and victories.

Adversity is the given that puts us in touch with our stamina, intellect, capabilities and will to live. Courage is built by overcoming and pushing ourselves forward each and every time we think we might be incapable. Struggles, both minor and significant, are exercises that build the strength we'll need tomorrow.

By focusing our energy and spirit on all that we've surmounted, channeling our power positively and taking actions in ways to improve our lives, we enrich each day moving forward.

People are incapable of thinking two contradictory thoughts at the same time. We cannot be saying: "I'm handling this well" and feel bad about that. The importance of this truth, the value of noticing the great things we've done to move ourselves forward versus dwelling on anything we think we may have missed, is something to take full advantage of—as it is key to greater peace at every age and stage of life.

Shift your thinking to seeing what's positive, better, improving—and it's nearly impossible to feel bad.

Stay in your line, keep smiling and actively seek the positive. You've come a long way. Focus on making this moment great while enjoying your triumphs to date, of which there have been many.

120 Years of Living

Many believe that while life ends somewhere in our 70s, 50 represents middle age or halfway through life. (Guess we all should have paid more attention in math!)

Let's create a new reality with this secret for a longer, happier life: Start imagining right now that we're all going to live to about 120—and when we do exit, it will be right smack in the middle of doing something we love.

The minute we shift our thinking to longevity—while understanding this is a goal, not a guarantee—we begin changing our behaviors: complaints and discontent start diminishing while decisions and action begin to rule each day.

Downhill life trends take root in our minds because we start believing that we don't have much longer to live. Conversely, if we believed we could live to a rockin' 120 years old—but accepted the fact that none of us know exactly which year marks our middle-age—we'd see we have more time to do a lot of more wonderful things. Likely we'd recognize that we'd want our bodies to be at their peak performance capacity to carry us through those extra years.

For example, let's imagine you're 60 now. What are you going to do for the next 60 years till you hit 120? That's a full lifetime ahead of you with no school rules—unless you decide you want to learn again on your own terms!

Recalibrating our thinking about lifespan starts us thinking that we have a lot of time left to live life! It's time to start planning, working, creating, saving, learning and doing!

I don't know your plan, but I've set my aging goal even further. I'm living to 137. When I kick it, it will be while doing an amazing lap in Monte Carlo driving my 1997 Honda del Sol. I'll have gone swimming early that morning before putting on a really cool racing suit. I'll set a new speed record but crash—off to the heavens in an instant blaze of glory. But it will be all OK, because after these next 80 years that started today, I'll be ready. What about you?

BECOME A HIT PRODUCER

Anytime we make someone else happy, it's not a simple equation of $1+1 = 2$ happy people; there's a ripple effect involved. Every act to make another person happy has two consequences: it inspires the recipient to return happiness to the giver and also to share it with others.

Love expands and spreads.

People tend to be happiest when they feel an abundance of love around them. Love makes us all feel alive and excited about living.

Love is hard to define in words but we all know the feeling. Likewise, we all know we don't feel it all the time, and when we're busy we might have to look really hard to find it.

The way to feel more love in our lives is by taking the risk to give more love to others. This includes the times when those others are being annoying and aggravating, and it's the last thing on the planet we want to do. (Consider it a personal cosmic test that you really want to pass!)

By becoming a "love producer"—one who intuitively knows we must keep charting new hits to stay relevant—whenever possible, we choose to record wonderful feelings of warmth in the minds and hearts of others.

Each time we share our love with another, we're scoring "hits" and making the world a better place for us all—just like all those love songs we love to sing along with on the radio. When we step away from love, it's helpful to remember this proverb: "You dig two graves when you hurt or curse another." This holds much truth: To keep holding onto negative emotions toward another might hurt them, but it will surely hurt ourselves as well.

Today's a good day to record some genuine chart-topping love songs, building fans while you're at it!

STEPPING OUT OF COMFORT ZONES

Much of the time, our lives are routine-oriented. The patterns—including all that's involved in raising children, working and other responsibilities—typically have us set in rote mode. Psychologists believe that patterns tend to minimize stress. Now, I don't think anyone is claiming that the daily requirements of family structure or work are stress-free: Rather, knowing there's a routine to the day seems to be perceived by some as less stressful. Perhaps this is because we think we actually know what is happening from one day to the next.

When people begin contemplating any change—work, moving, retirement, relationships, etc.— the idea of a change in routine can be paralyzing. Even if we don't like a particular pattern, we know it, we know what to expect to some degree and we are used to it.

Still, we worry and resist the idea of change because we fear what might happen if things get changed up.

This is delusional thinking. If we are alive, the risk is omnipresent that life as we know it will change in moments. Illness, accidents, loss of work, divorce, death, empty nests, retirement, starting a new career, marriages, new kids, blended families—the list goes on and on.

Silver Disobedience® is a state of mind whereby we opt to gently push the boundaries of our comfort zones, doing things a bit differently.

Getting more comfortable with accepting the inevitable changes of daily living makes it easier to deal with new and unanticipated circumstances.

We can learn to channel our talents and ideas to new heights of satisfaction no matter what changes we face. How? By choosing to do something different every day. Whether it's a big or little change is irrelevant. Saying "hi" to someone we pass regularly but don't typically acknowledge. Taking a class. Going for a walk in a new direction. Exercising. Eating better. The "differences" we add to daily routines recalibrate our thinking.

The Silver Disobedience® mindset knows that "new" can be difficult, uncomfortable, a challenge or just plain new and different. Yet we do it anyway.

SEASONING LIFE

It is the unanticipated little moments and conversations in life that add spice. Each helps us to realize that we are all connected in some mystical, magical, divine way.

Instinctively, we know this as children: We meet others at play and suddenly form "best" friendships. Sadly, some of this spontaneity to connect gets lost as we live our lives, as we become a bit more jaded, protecting ourselves and our emotions.

When we reach our Silver Disobedience® years, many of us begin to see time differently, and as a result, we become more open once again toward others. (If not, it's a goal!)

Moments become those we share with spontaneous "friends," like others in a coffee shop or the grocery store while waiting in line; sitting and talking with other adults while watching kids play sports; the server in a restaurant; chatting with the postman or clerks at a store; connecting with a long-lost friend in a social media conversation; observing and engaging with a child who seems excited about everything and asking them about their fresh perspectives; and sharing ideas with anyone and everyone who will converse.

Each of these interactions adds dimension to our lives as we recognize and value another's existence. Maybe the interaction allows us to feel just a bit less restricted, more open to joking and sharing. Saying silly things that others who "know" us might not expect.

These impromptu moments run parallel to our responsibility-filled lives. They energize us in different ways: Adding connectedness and reminders of the force of life within ourselves and others. Embracing these unplanned moments with others releases our spirits to soar to new heights.

MINDFUL GARDENING

Our minds are like gardens. They hold all kinds of seeds in the form of thoughts that have been planted and purposely tended to or inadvertently ignored over the years.

Let's consider a plant for a moment. We admire the green foliage and colorful flowers. Yet what we don't see is more important: The roots that go deep into the soil to make the beautiful plant possible.

Our thoughts are like seeds. We have to be careful with what we allow to take root because we can grow flowers or we can grow weeds. And remember, for plants to grow tall, they must grow tough, strong roots that can dig deep among the rocky soil—much like all of us who have truly experienced living, while growing and blossoming in the process.

HIT REFRESH

When we're children, quiet time is often viewed as a punishment. The idea of no talking, closing our eyes and sitting still, feels like we're in big trouble, guilty of something, and now we have to pay for it. Many of us still feel this way when contemplating taking a moment for ourselves to relax during our busy days. The result is that the peace we covet—which would be so health-promoting on countless levels—becomes ever more elusive.

Nothing will bring us the bountiful gifts of greater energy, clearer thinking and better health as much as giving ourselves quiet time daily.

Quiet is the key to releasing ourselves from knots (and nots) that tie up our lives and actions. Each time we allow ourselves to take a break, close our eyes and chill, we clear the lens through which we are seeing our lives. We get clarity and our thoughts are able to prioritize, focusing on what really matters.

All the hurrying and rushing around is energy-depleting, whereas moments of quiet—even just a solid minute—work miracles to reenergize our spirit while connecting us to our internal power source, without which there is no power or life.

Daily we give so much energy to those around us, fulfilling our responsibilities. The result is that we run low on the energy necessary to shape our lives as we'd prefer them to be: We keep getting pushed in haphazard ways.

Without much thought, we're fighting our way through, not even sure where we're headed, feeling like we're in survival mode.

When we're in this state, we intuitively know this isn't really living. Quiet time changes this. But until we agree to give ourselves a minute or more of peace on a regular basis, we can never realize how constantly running our engines has removed us from who we are in our hearts.

Stepping away from the rush of daily life—not just as we get ready for sleep but at random times throughout the day—is how, without even thinking, we can become better acquainted with who we are, what's missing and how we're feeling.

The best part? It's as if we hit refresh. When we resume thinking, speaking, loving, working and living, it is from our center.

ENTER STAGE RIGHT

Good entrances or exits in a show can define climactic moments. Done with passion, they can make supporting players new stars who are suddenly in demand for future productions.

While we're alive, it's our job to play our parts boldly. This often means we must adapt to new challenges that require us to dig deeply into our hearts to bring greater passion for each role we accept. All this, while also interacting with the characters we meet throughout every "stage" of life.

It is our unique responsibility to do whatever is necessary to play our roles with all the energy we can muster to make our "life show" a greater success. Adapting, ad-libbing, using prompts and retakes as necessary. This life is your show: The big show.

At the end of a lifetime, nobody will reflect with us on the tragedies, comedies, love stories, fantasies and dramas in the same way. The end story is ours. With this said, at any and every age we might as well write a good story and perform it well!

Whether our tales will be told as part smiles and laughter coupled with tears and heartache, season after season, it will all only be decided at our final cut. Until then, we must accept our part, playing each stage with the best and most passionate performance we can give. To do otherwise only shortchanges this gift we've been given of life.

While we don't always get to choose our entrances or exits, we are the writing team of our lines. We decide the plots, build the dialogue, determine the conflicts, overcome the complications and decide the climaxes—of which there may be many.

The stage is ours. How will you recall your performance? Remember, at any point (as Hollywood knows) prior to airtime, there are plenty of opportunities for all kinds of changes, rewrites, new settings, new characters, evolving personalities, special music and more.

Direct as you see fit. The show is yours.

DECISIONS

Sometimes the very idea of having to make a decision can be immobilizing, even though we've all been making decisions throughout our entire lives.

At this stage of life, many of us are considering retirement; second (or third or fourth!) careers; downsizing and apartments versus houses; new cities; facing health realities, choices and operations; teenagers, empty nests or adult children living back home; all while weighing the financial viability of any and every decision we'll make from here on out—and more.

While certain decisions are no-brainers, others can make us feel like we're stuck in the quicksand of indecision.

Sometimes our emotions feel like they are the beacon guiding us, yet at other times we're making lists of pros and cons, being far more methodical. We continue day-by-day until we reach a point whereby our comfort or tolerance for a situation reaches its limit. We know it is time for change.

When our intuition pushes us toward a decision, this is a surefire indicator it should be made. Opinion-seeking is no longer necessary. We have our answer. It's time to trust our gut and do whatever is necessary to make the change with confidence: Acting boldly, without hesitation or guilt.

It is during these moments that our instincts are serving as our wake-up call to take action. Our gut is pushing us toward something new that we should prepare for and act upon. Don't fret if your decision doesn't present itself with a straight course of action; it does not matter. I don't know how you ski, or even if you do—but I am the annoying person who goes from side to side, left to right, traversing down a mountain: 40 feet across, one foot down. But you know what? I still get to the same bottom as the racers—just more slowly!

Whether it's time to make better choices for your health, move, seek a new livelihood, be open to new relationships or whatever—go forward.

REVITALIZATION

Did you know that every three months, all your blood has been replenished by new cells? Every 11 months, all of your cells have self-renewed as well. And it takes about two years for your body to create an entirely new set of bone cells. Isn't this amazing? In other words, no matter how we might have abused our bodies in the past, if we begin healthier habits, within three to four years we can have a new, revitalized body at the cellular level! How fantastic is that?

While no change comes with an absolute guarantee of longevity nor total repair, any change toward healthier living is an assurance of more energy in the here and now.

Just because we're getting older doesn't mean we have to accept worsening health and physical decline.

Here's a review of basics any of us can start today:

Upon awakening, before coffee, tea or food—drink two to four big glasses of water.

Increase fruit and vegetable consumption to 50 percent of your diet. Need a visual? Simply imagine each plate of every meal half-filled with fruits or veggies. Raw, frozen and canned are all fine (ideally no sugar or salt added).

On the other 50 percent of the plate? Leaner meats, fish, whole grains, beans—limiting heavily processed, packaged, salty, prepared foods. Simple foods are best.

Eat regularly: When blood sugar drops, arteries are stiffening.

Get 15 minutes of sunshine daily. This naturally strengthens bones and improves mood.

Stretch. It feels good and increases flexibility.

Walk. To keep legs strong, we have to get up and move.

Be social. Connect with at least one person every day whom you really like.

Don't underestimate the impact of housecleaning, lawn mowing, car washing, gardening, etc. They're all exercise!

Don't smoke or vape.

If you drink alcohol, be moderate.

Get seven hours of sleep in a dark, quiet room.

Laugh and cry. Both strengthen the immune system.

And my personal favorite: Eat an ounce of dark chocolate every day—which is about a thin one-inch-by-one-inch square. Chocolate stimulates endorphins and contains serotonin, a natural mood elevator.

CHANGING ANOTHER'S BEHAVIOR

By our 50s, we've learned to cope with all kinds of personalities. Divorce, death and retirements further alter relationship dynamics and new communication skills are required.

Most advice says we can only change ourselves but this isn't 100 percent true. This technique can alter another's behavior without confrontation:

Imagine the behavior you want another to change. Examples could be to drive slower; help with housework; be more attentive; increase intimacy; give you more space—whatever.

To begin the transformation, start complimenting the other person sincerely for what they aren't doing. Here's how it will unfold.

Suppose you want someone to listen more closely when you're speaking but they're not. So you start visualizing that they are. When you're together, you start peppering the conversation with compliments about their behavior and say, "I just want you to know how much I appreciate that you've really been listening to me. It makes me feel really good. Thanks."

The other looks at you and wonders: "What are they talking about?" They might say: "I didn't do anything." But at this point you say, "You've really been great. I used to think that what I said wasn't important to you because you didn't seem to be interested—but lately I feel like you've really been listening. I just want you to know I've noticed."

The other will likely shrug or say thanks. But then, things start to change because conflicting thoughts cannot exist simultaneously. The other is now considering what they may have been doing that you favorably noticed! They'll start wondering: "What could I have been doing that made him/her think I was listening better?" Now they're engaged in thinking about changing.

The more we find ways to compliment a behavior we want to positively reinforce, the more we get results we want, which benefits our relationships!

MOMENTS OF A LIFETIME

Life is made up of moments. There are 1,440 of them in a day. Life isn't perfect but it has perfect moments. As children, we intuitively knew this, never wanting the moment to end.

Lives pass moment-by-moment: with ourselves, family, neighbors, coworkers, friends and strangers. We each have moments when we are open to others, open to our growth. Likewise, we have moments we're closed off due to past hurts, unable to allow others to penetrate the walls we've built over passing time, soon to become years.

The interesting aspect of life is the curious random quality of certain moments. The chance that becomes an opportunity. Some believe in the order of life. Perhaps randomness is actually order. One day, while shooting photographs on the street, a group of strangers asked if I'd like to borrow their balloons for some photos. It was a random moment, lasting less than a minute. There was no benefit to them; they didn't even ask when or where the photographs might appear. It was just a generous, spontaneous gesture in a moment, which became cemented in a smiling photograph for eternity.

Life cycles of moments turn into the seasons of our years. Springs come after winters, then summers turn into falls. There's no stopping time; it is a continuum. But it is those moments, the spontaneous gestures of generosity, given to others and received by us that make our days special and living spectacular.

While there's no denying there are moments we'd all like to have missed, it is the collective of moments that become the timestamps of our lives—each necessary while hopefully reminding us of possibility in the next moment. As we age, we become more aware of the finite nature of a lifetime. Today is a great day to smile and be open to play in the moment; pause briefly to reflect; and rewind only if it brings us happiness.

MOVE:
Maintain Optimum Vitality and Energy

While there's no surefire way to prevent aging, the wrath of years hits those hardest who've had a lifetime of non-movement or little movement. Movement is the bottom line in all discussions about well-being and life enhancement: Moving more, regularly and constructively. Movement to increase flexibility; movement to improve cardiovascular capacity; movement to improve digestion; movement to build strength. People who move a lot, live better—with more breath, strength and energy.

We don't age all at once. Squint lines appear at one point; gray hairs at another. But the age we feel—the age our bodies feel—has little to do with the passing years. What actually passes for aging isn't aging at all. It's the effect of disuse. Activity maintains vitality, while inactivity dramatically accelerates all the things we associate with age: stiffness, lack of mobility, creaks, decline and illness. Virtually every system—heart, lungs, muscles, bones, digestive, nerves—will degenerate from lack of physical movement.

Introduce more movement at any age and reap the benefits. Movement makes bodies quicker and steadier, bringing greater certainty to every step. Our cardiovascular capacity will improve, which translates into more stamina and vigor. Our sleep and nerves will be more restful because we will have constructively vented our stress.

The difference between what we all perceive as youthful versus old bodies is most apparent in the amounts of muscle and fat we observe. We all envy older people with physiques that seem to have found the fountain of youth—defined by shapely, defined, leaner bodies.

Stretch, walk, dance, flex, squeeze, carry your groceries, take the stairs, park farther away, join a gym, clean your own house, wash your own car: Move! Maintain Optimum Vitality and Energy.

LESSONS FROM ALL

Every person we meet and each situation we encounter throughout our lives can teach us more about who we are. Those people and things we find wonderful, loving, exciting, annoying, selfish, nagging, sweet, charming, arrogant, clever, fun, aggravating or whatever—present both challenges and clear mirrors into ourselves if we can reflect on the person or situation with love.

Reflection is key, because in the moment, we might not see things so clearly—although this is certainly the goal.

Understanding that what we are seeing in others is an innermost reflection of something within ourselves that needs to be acknowledged and accepted, is important to becoming kinder, gentler and wiser.

To get to know ourselves better, so we can all relate to others and situations more positively, here's an exercise: Imagine what might happen if we each began giving ourselves the gifts we were hoping someone would give us. Would it be something material that we'd buy for ourselves? A gesture showing utmost generosity of spirit? Greater kindness and compassion toward our faults and errors? Genuine enthusiasm for our achievements? Focus and attention to what is being said and felt so that understanding within our relationships grows deeper? What would it be?

If we can each start giving ourselves the things we need first, we can then be less judgmental and harsh in how we see others and what we expect from them. It's a process, but today is a good day for all of us to keep giving it a try.

Mental Photography

All day long, throughout our entire lives, our minds snap multidimensional images of everything we see, hear and feel. Sometimes, smells and tastes are also mentally recorded right into the pictures we're taking. This is why a smell or a song reminds us of a moment in our pasts and gives us a warm or cold feeling.

Our conscious mind "talks" to our preconscious through the series of "pictures" we've taken throughout the course of our lifetimes. This can be advantageous to us—or not. Mark Twain said: "When a cat steps on a hot stove, he'll never do that again. But neither will he step on a cold stove." This quote pretty much defines our challenge when we get stuck and resistant to moving forward in life.

Pulling out photo albums can be a wonderful way to recollect (or recollect) pleasant memories, but it can also be how we remove ourselves from what is happening now. If we start picturing, "This is me crying when I fell off my bike... This is me when the kindergarten teacher punished me... This is me ashamed when my parents caught me doing X... This is me when I was in shape..."—our shutters are stuck and we're not seeing the setting nor ourselves as we are today.

To move forward in life, we need to learn that those pictures we've snapped—no matter how vivid they might be—are nothing but an old photo album. And believe me, no two photographers ever see a scene the same way. One hundred photographers would interpret the exact same session differently with their unique perspectives!

It's time to put the albums away. If we start bringing these past pictures into the present, it's like watching an old movie yet again. Although we might be captivated by the storyline and actors, it had an entirely different cast, director and crew than the ones we're working with today.

Old films have nothing to do with today. What photographs will you take today? Will you stay in the moment or slip away to past images? Will you see only black and white? Or allow yourself to see all the grays and silvers of a situation in between the extremes? How about trying to see the present moment using a rose-colored lens?

RECONNECTING

While many of us are married, there are others who are single by choice or circumstance or from being widowed or divorced. Some of us are no longer sure about how to get out, meet and connect with others after all these years.

Here are some universal ideas for speaking with others that can help anyone break the conversation-ice to start new friendships or improve work relationships as well.

Smile! Nothing shows that you are open to a conversation like a smile. Out of practice? Pretend you're a model: Stand in front of a mirror and smile while moving your body. Practice regularly until you get comfortable with doing it naturally.

Compliment. Find something about another that you can genuinely compliment. Whether a jacket, scarf, hairstyle—certainly you can find something that deserves a compliment toward another. This is likely the second-fastest way to melt ice. Everyone likes to hear a sincere compliment.

Name it! After you meet someone, use their name. First off, this forces you to be very present, because you have to remember names! Second, saying another's name is personal and will make them feel more special.

Use your body. Lean toward those you are speaking with. No wall-hanging. If you must cross your arms to be comfortable, cross them behind your back—not in front of you, creating a barricade.

Focus. Bring your eyes into the conversation. Look at the other's eyes. Eye contact creates an extremely powerful connection.

Wear an article of clothing that is a bright, vibrant color. Color draws people and it's often a conversation-starter in itself. Another may come up to you to compliment you on your bold selection.

Start near the food—but move away! Food tends to keep conversations stationary.

To meet people, you'll need to get comfortable with at least a few of the tips above—so you can get out and mingle! As I've said before, life is for the living and connecting with other people is one of the best aspects of life. Today is a good day to restart connecting!

PERHAPS

Sometimes we all think our lives should be unfolding differently. Possibly we believe that the plans we imagine in our heads would be better than what is actually happening in the moment. Maybe we think life would be better if we could only direct those events we cannot seem to control. To rethink this, here's one of my favorite parables:

There was a farmer who worked long but peaceful days on his farm, never complaining, harvesting just enough to feed his family. One day, the only horse the farmer had for plowing his fields and harvesting his crops ran away. His neighbors all came to console him, saying that they knew he must be terribly upset. The farmer simply smiled and replied, "Perhaps." The next day, the horse returned and brought with it a group of wild horses. The jealous neighbors all came and told the farmer how lucky he was. The farmer only said, "Perhaps." Later that day, the farmer's son tried riding one of the horses, got bucked and his leg was badly broken. The neighbors thought this was a terrible fate. The farmer simply responded: "Perhaps." The next day, a military officer came through the area, drafting all the young men to fight in a war. Upon seeing that the farmer's son couldn't walk on his broken leg, the official left him behind. Distressed over the loss of their own sons, the neighbors cried, telling the farmer he was very fortunate. The farmer again replied, "Perhaps."

Life as it is—maybe, perhaps, for all one knows—is happening now.

RESISTANCE TO CHANGE

Every year of life brings change.

As we get older, we reflect on the changes we initiated; the physical developments that occurred due to aging and nature; and other modifications arising from external forces and events.

Sometimes we've embraced the changes. Sometimes we've been the catalyst for them. Sometimes the changes forced us to face our fears. The impact and types of changes are far too extensive to list.

There is an entire gamut of emotions related to change: sadness, happiness, fear, worry, anger, joy, exhilaration and more. Our feelings largely depend or depended upon how the change unfolded and if we felt as if we were in control of the change.

Whether or not we liked a particular change, in retrospect most will believe that it truly represented the way life had to unfold; or that it was something we survived and felt stronger and grateful about as a result; or that it resulted in a lot being learned about personal fortitude and life.

Interestingly, for many, a huge challenge is the resistance of others to accept a change when we individually felt that change was the best choice for ourselves. Such lack of acceptance might make us feel abandoned by others because of their resistance—or feel that we have to fight and pay a price for what we want.

Every decision involving change comes with possibilities and responsibilities. When we make choices, it pays to spend ample time thinking about how far we want to wander from our current life path to explore new views and experiences.

Each of us individually decides how we want to live our lives. When deciding, it's important to apply the wisdom we've learned from past lessons as we make our choices and determine which roads to travel. Do your research—and trust your judgment.

UNKNOWNS

We usually know exactly what we don't want to do. But knowing what we want to do—and acting on it—can be trickier. Why? Fear of it not working out? This is certainly a possibility, but if we don't try going forward, we stay exactly as we've been—yet possibly less happy for not trying.

Is it worry that others will throw shame at us? Trying to make us feel we're being too egotistical or grandiose? Yes, there will be haters and those who feel our desires threaten theirs. Of course, this is ridiculous thinking—but it doesn't change the fact that we may regularly need to recite: "Sticks and stones can break my bones, but words will never hurt me."

Uncertainty of the unknown? This is illusory, because whether we act on what we want to do or not, nobody has a better crystal ball for tomorrow. Only experience tells us it likely won't be linear and direct.

Finances certainly factor in: Changing may require sacrifices that may be uncomfortable. Time? We all get 1440 moments each day. From prophets to inventors and everyone in between: Everybody gets the same amount of time in a day; it gets down to how we choose to use it.

Lack of confidence? Accept we all suffer from this, even if it doesn't look that way. The only way to build confidence is challenging ourselves over and over again. Complacency? Possibly, because when we're comfy we are rarely in reinvention mode—and for the record, we don't ever have to be! But things we can do—like learning a new skill, instrument, language, etc.—will keep our brains sharper.

Life history is a big factor against changing: We've likely experienced enough life-altering experiences, so we really need to ask: Do we want another? Maybe, maybe not. Lack of belief? This is where we need to have some faith in God, the universe or the cosmic forces of life— believing that something bigger than us wants our one-of-a-kind, unique self to wholly manifest.

It's our life to choose. We can create ourselves however we want to be. All we need is a little umph and imagination.

CURMUDGEON

I vote to eliminate the word "toxic" as a definition or reference to people.

Oil and water don't mix yet neither are toxic. Chemistry comes in all forms and creates all kinds of end products, both healthy and not-so-healthy. However, it's all about the mix, not necessarily the ingredients.

How about we just start leaving it as: "We just don't get along." Period. The labels are unnecessary.

Just a thought. But if you really need a label? Call 'em a curmudgeon. At least you'll laugh when you say the word.

SECRET TO LONGEVITY

The oldest man in the world revealed the secret to longevity at a press conference. For years, everyone had been asking him to share his secret for living 120 years while looking so good and being very healthy. He used no cane, had no illness or surgeries and used no medications.

On the day his secret was to be revealed, people came from all over the world to listen. They paid big money to be the first to learn this priceless information. The crowd erupted with cheers when the centenarian took the stage. The moment had arrived. The Master of Ceremonies asked: "Dear sir, what is your secret to your longevity?" With a strong crisp voice, the man responded: "I never argue."

The crowd went crazy and started shouting, "Impossible! This cannot be true!"

"You are right," he said. And he left the stage.

REACH OUT

Did you know a nonsexual hug can turn negative emotions in a positive direction—and the effects were comparable in men and women? Recent research reported by Carnegie Mellon University studied 400 adults and determined that getting a hug on the day of a conflict resulted in a smaller drop in positive emotions and a smaller rise in negative emotions.

This study confirmed past research demonstrating that hugs and a warm touch help improve close relationships, because they increase one's sense of security and well-being while reducing the perception of threats.

Hugging has been proven to reduce the likelihood of catching a cold; to naturally increase oxytocin, the body's feel-good chemical; and to transcend feelings of anger, anguish and loss.

Give kind, sincere hugs whenever you can. And when you can't? Pick up the phone and tell someone you're thinking about them, miss them and love them. It's the next best thing.

ORGANIC OR NOT

Do we need to buy organic foods to be healthy? The short answer is no. But here's a slightly longer answer.

Organic foods are more expensive. However, if we calculate the incalculable —the cost of our long-term health—they might be a bargain. According to the Environmental Working Group, which bases its findings on thousands of government tests, you can reduce your toxic pesticide exposure by a whopping 80 percent when you buy organic versions of just a few foods. An entire cart might be nice but it's an unnecessary expense.

To enjoy healthier and safer meals by minimizing your exposure to pesticides and other toxins and hormones, start by focusing on organic options of these foods first if your budget allows: Celery. Peaches and nectarines. Strawberries and blueberries. Apples, apple juice and dried apples. Sweet red, yellow and green bell peppers. Kale, spinach, collard greens, lettuce and most other green leafy vegetables. Cherries. Carrots. Pears. And when it comes to eggs, chicken or beef—free range is a healthier choice than organic.

BRUISES

Life has a way of bruising us all, no matter how picture-perfect our upbringings were or were not.

I took five teenage boys to see the movie *Mid90s* directed by Jonah Hill. It's exceptional. While some might think it's a coming-of-age movie or just a flick for skateboarders, it is a movie about getting bruised by life and pushing through anyway. It's about going way off course and finding the way home. The themes are plentiful and addressed with humor and sensitivity. Best of all? The movie served as a catalyst for a deep conversation that lasted well over an hour with all of the boys chiming in—which in adult time is comparable to two weeks of active conversation.

Rough family lives, challenges though our school years, friends who reject us, trying to fit in, figuring out how we're going to support ourselves, intimacy that might or might not have been intimate: The bruising starts early and really never stops.

Our suffering is a direct reflection of whether we see our many life experiences as positive lessons and opportunities to grow—or not. If we continue to view them as open wounds that are unable to heal, we suffer.

Peace and clarity are possible. Both start by not believing and retelling stories of our past. Next, we must accept that whatever happened was not personally directed at us. Then, if we keep our attention focused on what is happening in the moment, life improves exponentially. These concepts are the keys to unlocking our compassionate selves so we can truly love ourselves and embrace others.

Personally

Have you ever noticed how very young kids dance, laugh, wrestle, tell stories, share jokes with no punchline but lots of giggles, and generally seem to have plenty of fun?

Here's the secret to their magic: They aren't self-conscious. They just are. They aren't spending any time worrying about what anybody thinks.

Why? Most children are not yet conditioned to falsely believe that others' reactions are personal affronts to their being. In fact, if we're not enjoying the laughter and silliness right along with them, they're wondering what's wrong with us!

Young kids don't believe in standards of a status quo. They are just in the moment. Even if something isn't going right, they don't perceive it as, "I or someone must be wrong." Instead, it just is. They don't take life personally.

While on a commercial shoot, I got a refresher course in this lesson as I was cast as the grandmother of three kids, ages four, five and nine. It was reinvigorating to get immersed in total silliness and belly laughs.

Figure out a way to spend time with little kids at every phase of life. They're great at keeping all the energy in the moment. If you don't have any of those little guys and gals immediately available, call your local school or house of worship and offer your assistance to the kindergarten or first grade as a reading volunteer. Believe me, it's a win-win for you and the children.

Standards

Have you ever noticed that the standards to which we hold ourselves are sometimes different than what we might accept from others? The opposite happens too, as in cases when we might not tolerate something from another yet give ourselves latitude for the same actions.

For example, why do we encourage other people to take care of themselves when they're sick, yet act like a martyr when we're not feeling well? Or flipping it, what about when we tell a "white lie" yet get angry at another for something comparable?

When we apply different standards to ourselves versus others, we are maintaining an illusion of separateness. When we believe our feelings are wholly separate from those of others, we reduce our abilities to connect and experience greater possibilities and happiness.

RULES

Society creates a lot of rules in an effort to control behavior. Following some rules makes a lot of sense—like looking both ways before crossing the street. Other rules may be up for reexamination.

Rules are forms of beliefs and every rule is followed based on our belief. They hold their power because someone told us or somehow we concluded that the rule was worthwhile.

Let's examine the belief that if we wake up at dawn or stay awake past midnight we'll be too tired to function the next day. While this may be true, we might also be missing some beautiful sunrises or great late-night conversations.

At the root of the issue with this rule is the fact that we might like sleep and want to feel rested.

So what if we created a new rule that stated: When I go to bed, I fall into a deep, restful sleep and awake feeling fantastic.

A while ago, while on set filming some commercials in beautiful Turks and Caicos, I decided it might be time to question my old rule and test a new one. And you know what? For the rest of my life, I'll be seeing more sunrises and enjoying delightful conversations, getting to know all kinds of people more deeply later into the night. And as a result of my new rule, I am also more energized!

Try this yourself—or consider rewriting a few of your own rules.

INSPIRATION

Are you feeling inspired to change or do something different this year?

Inspiration, enthusiasm, imagination, vision, awakening, creativity and motives all start to rumble, spark, arouse, stimulate and trigger thinking about how we can change for the better, leaving behind what we know hasn't been working for us or that which could be improved for our betterment.

We've all likely heard that the journey of 1,000 miles begins with one step. The fact is we can all handle the journey. Any problems along the way are like pebbles in our shoes: distractions that will happen.

As we plot out our goals for making ourselves healthier, stronger or whatever this year, we'll need a plan to counter distractions. It also helps to keep shining the light on Edison's quote: Success is 1% inspiration; 99% perspiration. Ideas are great. But action is the ingredient for turning dreams into realities.

SMOKE AND FIRE

"Where there's smoke, there's fire." Hmm—ever wonder if this is true? Basically, the expression means that if there are rumors or signs that something is true, it must be at least partially true. The expression implies there is some kind of evidence that some event is likely to unfold.

Perhaps when we see smoke, there is a fire—but could it be that we've stepped out of the present moment and are looking to establish some frame of reference to feel more secure or to gain a sense of control over something that's making us feel uncomfortable?

Before assuming the smoke equates to fire, perhaps we need to start asking questions. Being literal, we'd have to ask: Do we smell fire? See it? Feel a lot of heat? Or do we just see what might be smoke—or something else?

The point is that jumping to conclusions might be equally as risky as a fire.

If the situation is potentially dangerous, respond according to those instincts. But otherwise, before we start acting on the belief that "something's burning"—with actions like gossiping, making assumptions, or misinterpreting an innocent situation or remark—perhaps we first need to ask questions and gather information.

A GREAT QUESTION

"How's that working for you?" is a great question to ask whenever we are observing unproductive behavior in ourselves or another. A behavior that obviously isn't working.

By asking the question, we're not being judgmental; we're inquiring, ideally alleviating some tension and acknowledging it might be time to start thinking.

Hopefully the question sets the stage for personal evaluation. It suggests that maybe there are other ways of doing something that might work more in our favor.

At the very least, this question is an acknowledgment that there might be other possible ways to tackle a given situation. This question might be especially handy if we're dealing with anyone who needs to own up to more adult-like behavior.

We can't live another's life and we certainly want to live ours to the best of our capabilities. So with that: How's it working for you?

FAST WHAT?

Did you know one out of three adults in the United States eats fast food every day? And perhaps surprisingly, the demographic breakdown was 32 percent lower income, 36 percent middle income and 42 percent higher income, according to the U.S. Centers for Disease Control and Prevention.

Regardless of financial status, food high in calories, sodium, sugar and fat is not helping our health.

As we age, the downside is that all this extra fat, salt and sugar—along with tons of chemical preservatives—starts to become visible in bigger waists. The extra fat we start to carry exacerbates more serious health problems like Type 2 diabetes, heart disease and metabolic syndrome.

Our health is largely a reflection of our choices. Certainly not always, but often. Maybe it's time to take a good look at our consumption habits of fast foods and ask if we can make some healthier substitutions.

Easy ideas are: Choose water versus soda or juices. Chinese? Order steamed options versus fried if possible. Pizza? Go thin crust and add veggies. Sandwich chains? Order six-inch and a water and fruit versus chips and soda. Mexican? Try grilled lean meats and veggies with soft tacos instead of crispy shells, refried beans, extra cheeses and chips. Burgers? Single patties or grilled chicken. Many offer baked potatoes versus fries. Stay away from fries, milkshakes, nuggets and tenders! Fried chicken chains? Skinless, no breading with a baked potato and garden salad instead of extra crispy, fried, biscuits and gravies.

Choose health!

10 MINUTES

Don't wait until you "feel like doing" whatever needs to be done. Procrastinating won't help. Instead, we need to get in gear and start doing it. My mother used to annoy me by saying: "Ten minutes into the job and it's halfway done."

Literalist that I was at the time, my teenage self thought that her statement was ludicrous! I knew it was going to take me two hours to weed the garden or rake the leaves—so what the heck kind of math was she using to determine that 10 minutes was half of 120?

But now I realize my mom was right then—and she's still right now.

Here's why: Getting started is half the battle.

If we wait for inspiration it might never arrive. But once we start whatever needs to get done, the odds favor that we'll keep going until we finish—or at least make a good dent in the project. Thus, we're already winning the battle.

Whatever it is that you want to do, need to do, think might be good to do—whatever: Get your motor running and do it. You'll be glad you did.

FOCUSING ILLUSION

Focusing illusion is a phenomenon that occurs whenever we fixate obsessively on some person, event or thing and start exaggerating the impact we think it will have on our happiness—either positive or negative. Suddenly it seems we can't imagine *not* thinking about whatever it is.

With focused illusions, most of whatever it is we're obsessed with ultimately loses our interest. Once again, we're on the hunt for something that will captivate our attention, make us want it and excite us to work for it.

Often, when focused illusions kick in, we are processing limited information about objects or ideas yet giving them grand potential to improve or damage our lives.

Believing things like "Everyone who lives in California is happier" or "Owning an exotic car will make me cooler" are examples of focused illusions. While we might move to the Golden State or get those hot wheels, if we didn't feel particularly happy or cool prior to our move or purchase, not much will change.

Focused illusions are not a bad thing. Upon examination, they offer insights into our psyches and can be supremely positive forces used for motivation to better our lives. They may also be telling us that we're giving our thoughts too much attention versus participating in living.

Einstein allegedly said: "Insanity is doing the same thing over and over again expecting different results."

So if we really want to make any changes, a good start is examining the illusions we focus on because wherever we go, there we are.

SLOWING AGING

Want to slow aging? Research published in *Nature Medicine* confirmed that it was actually possible to reduce the burden of damaged cells and extend lifespan and improve health—even if changes are made later in life. How great is this news?! All that is necessary is eating more fruits and vegetables. The research was conducted by the University of Minnesota Medical School.

Today we have all the scientific research we need—and no more excuses like, "But it's too late for me…"

It's a great day to start improving our health by adding more fruits and vegetables to our daily meals.

ROTATING THE SUN

"How old are you?" is a question we each ask and are asked. Why? What it is that we are all trying to compare, reference or determine?

Unless it's the social security office or the discount line at the movie theater, how about from now on, when asked about our age, we simply state, "Ageless." Or, "How old am I? I'm not old at all!" Or maybe, "I'm as young as I feel and today I feel amazingly terrific!"

While I readily admit my age according to the Gregorian calendar, I mostly feel ageless— so the number is irrelevant to me. I don't relate to time other than making sure I meet deadlines and commitments if other people are involved. Otherwise, my days are timeless. In fact, I can't wait to wake up and I often wish sleep weren't a necessity. Even when I get stuck in traffic or otherwise annoyed, it's not like I can really say it was for a long or short time. It just was.

If we met Mother Earth and were able to ask her a question somehow, I don't think the conversation-starter would be: "So how many times have you traveled around the Sun?"

INDIFFERENCE

Indifference might be the most significant cause of failure and pain in our relationships and life.

If we exhibit apathy, callousness, carelessness, disdain, disinterest, inattention or insensitivity toward others, we're sending the message through powerful actions that another is unimportant to us. What our words attempt to say becomes irrelevant.

Aloof, cold and detached are not signs of commitment to another, or anything else for that matter.

It is our attention, esteem, respect, compassion, effort and concern that make another feel loved and gets all jobs done. These are the key ingredients for success in our relationships and our lives in general.

Love and commitment speak through actions. If our actions show admiration, appreciation, care, encouragement, action and honor, nothing else needs to be said.

GRUMBLE-TIME

Nobody is cheery all the time. Happy a lot maybe, but not always full of glee.

Problems often start because we're afraid to admit we're not feeling happy and because whining is not a particularly attractive trait. It was not recommended in Dale Carnegie's classic *How to Win Friends and Influence People*! But if we don't find appropriate ways to release tensions, the risk runs high that we will be hurtful to others or ourselves. It's like a boiling pot with a tight lid—it's going to blow if the steam isn't allowed out to release the pressure.

Scheduling grumble-time can help prevent this! Think of grumble-time as a license to whine. Since everyone experiences rises in emotional pressure, everyone needs a little grumble-time to get back in balance. Here's how to do it: 1) Accept that everyone needs to whine. Ask around and find a whiny partner or friend to sit down with to gripe, moan, wail, grouse and sob. 2) Prepare for the festival: Think about what has been bugging you and building up over the past couple of weeks. Coworkers, spouses, children, weather, driving, the news, whatever—because whining is personal. (Note: We're not talking about trauma; those discussions must be held with a professional.) 3) Find a comfortable living room or public spot where you and your whine partner can let loose with your stories of troubles, angst and annoyances. 4) As each of you shares your stories, add some hand motions: Chop with your hands with exaggerated motions to accentuate your points. Tap with your fingers like an annoying person at a counter trying to get attention. The more physical aspects you can add to your venting with a friendly whine partner, the better. 5) Keep going. Continue until you've air-punched and gesticulated your whiny complaints away. 6) Notice the release of pressure. Observe how you feel better. Nobody harmed, just healthy release. See if you can even start laughing.

There's nothing wrong with having a good grumble. Whining is a normal human activity. It's the body's way of calling for release. The secret is finding a safe place for to let it out. This is what good friends are for! Hey, what are you doing tonight?

GOOD FORTUNE

It's said that if we change ourselves, our fortunes will change. And good things come when we least expect them. Aesop proposed that we could have too much of a good thing.

Considering this, whether you feel fortune is favoring you or not, my favorite expression is: "Save your good fortune." Basically, this means don't boast or squander what you have, whether you believe it to be plentiful or lacking. Value and cherish exactly how things are or we may be regretting if it slips away.

While we all need x amount to pay our bills and celebrate a bit, plenty of research confirms that more does not always equate to happier. Enough is really the goal. The best way to get to enough is not necessarily making more money but watching how we spend. Working more to buy more is a great plan, but it could also be less satisfying than working an average week and enjoying free time, doing more of what we love.

Making and spending money is founded in personal values. On this note, resist assumptions as to what might be in someone else's pocket. When I was 18, managing a health club, there was a charismatic member who had been featured on the cover of a major magazine and he was living life large. My boss, who at 67 was also my first mentor, chided my glorying, saying, "Things might not be what they seem." Naively, I thought, "Hmm. He must be jealous." Long story short: Six months later, that very same member was jailed for a high-profile scam. He had been living off other peoples' money.

The moral of this story? Recognize your own good fortune and don't compare your lot to that of others.

TALK TO ME

Can you imagine a world in which people said, "Talk to me" and really meant it? Envision the changes that could take place within relationships if we could not only listen to others but always do so as if we were trying to understand their thoughts, emotions, perceptions and concerns.

We all want to be heard. But listening is so dang hard because throughout life we've all developed opinions—and darn it, aren't they right?

If we're lucky, with each passing year, black and white seems to fade into shades of gray. Many issues are no longer binary, such as right or wrong. We see nuances—things that make us more open to possibilities.

Maybe our years are necessary to make us ready to sincerely say: "Talk to me."

LITTLE THINGS

Life is made up of big and little things. So are personal relationships and work situations.

Little things in life are often overlooked. We're all busy doing other things so we don't do little things for others or we don't notice the little things done for us by others. While big things might seem grander or more important, are they? Perhaps not if the day-to-day aspects of relating are missed, while we hope a big thing can serve as a substitute.

I'm being vague here, because each of us has personal examples of what constitutes little actions and big actions throughout our lives. I'm really just contemplating the things we do day-to-day, along with what we don't do—because we're so busy coping with life that we hope we can do some big thing to fill-in for what we might have missed in the day-to-day.

Maybe you'll want to think about this as well.

SUGAR SPOTTING

Did you know that sugar is present in countless foods—but without knowing the code words you might not be aware of it, no matter how many labels you read?

If a label says "sugar," it's obvious. But all the ingredients in the list below are also sugar. So if you are consuming too many processed foods with these ingredients, you are unknowingly consuming too many empty carbohydrate calories, which are stored as fat. Additionally, excess processed sugar is the culprit hiding behind risk of obesity, diabetes and heart disease. It can impact our immune systems, create chromium deficiencies, cause tooth decay and accelerate aging!

When perusing a product label, check to see if any of these ingredients are present. Remember that labels start with the main ingredients and work their way down to lower amounts. Here goes. Remember, these are all sugars: Agave, brown rice syrup, cane syrup, cornstarch, corn syrup, dextrose, fructose, golden syrup, high-fructose corn syrup, honey invert sugar, jaggery, lactose, maple syrup, milk, molasses, pulled sugar, rock sugar, sorghum, sucrose and treacle.

This is not about skipping sugar altogether. Rather, it's about being aware of where it might be hidden and staying alert to quantities consumed so that we can keep ourselves as healthy as possible for the long haul.

WATER

Water is essential to our health and well-being. Adequate hydration will: Enhance digestion and metabolism; boost brain function; regulate body temperature; transport nutrients, oxygen, enzymes and glucose to the cells; remove toxins and other metabolic waste from the body; cushion joints and strengthen muscles; and provide natural moisture to the skin and other tissues.

Signs of dehydration include achy joints and muscles, fatigue, headaches, dry skin, dizziness and nausea—and in extreme cases, death.

The amount of water we each need varies greatly based on our physical activity, climate zone, illnesses, medications, hormone changes and poor nutrition.

However, as our bodies are about 70 percent water, a good starting guideline for "how much" is a half-ounce of water per pound of our weight per day.

The most important glass? The first two to four glasses each morning before coffee, tea or anything else. Why? Our bodies used water reserves to function throughout the night and to digest our last meal of the prior evening. As most people lose about two pounds of water between morning and night, awaking and drinking 16 to 32 ounces before consuming anything else will merely be replenishing this essential lost water.

If your day includes plenty of fruits and vegetables, you'll need a bit less water throughout the day (after those mandatory morning glasses!).

However, if you notice yourself feeling too hungry during the day, it could be that you're dehydrated rather than hungry. Reach for a big glass of water first. If you're still hungry after a glass or two, reach for a healthy meal.

Don't wait until you're dehydrated! Easy tip: If your urine is dark yellow (instead of pale) and if you don't urinate every two to three hours during the day, it's quite likely you're dehydrated. Now go drink a big glass of water!

MORAL PANIC

Greasers and slicked hair, pomade, doo-wop, rockabilly, Elvis, motorcycles, moral panic. The Pill, hippies, folk music, fallout shelters, the Twist, surfing, moral panic. Disco music, long hair for everybody, tie-dye, mood rings, leisure suits, safari jackets, moral panic.

Punk rock and heavy metal, spandex, leg warmers, big hair, mullets and hair crimping, aerobics, shags (on carpets and hair), moral panic.

Video games, rap, selfies, celebrities, texting, skateboarding, tattoos, hair straightening and hair dyed silver, moral panic.

The more things change, the more they stay the same. Cultural repositioning is a constant in every society. Each new generation seeks to differentiate itself from the previous one—read that as "differentiate from the rules defined by parents, school and government."

Change pushes, pulls, debates, argues, defies, impresses, glorifies, vilifies. It is crazy and genius. It is thoughtful and unconsidered. It is frustrating and incomprehensible. It is exciting and exhilarating.

"Life is a series of natural and spontaneous changes. Don't resist them; that only creates sorrow. Let reality be reality. Let things flow naturally forward in whatever way they like."—Lao Tzu, 599 BC

GAME CHANGER

Want to know the easiest way to change any relationship, and your health, for the better? Start looking for ways to sincerely offer compliments.

Did you know that researchers at Harvard University have shown that physical and emotional health benefits accrued for both givers and receivers of compliments? Compliments decrease stress, boost our immunity, increase serotonin production (our feel-good hormone), improve productivity and help alleviate pain and insomnia.

Compliments are relationship and health game-changers. Sounds to me like really good reasons to spend more time looking for the positive, wonderful, unique, special, lovable traits in others. And on that note? Thank you for reading my book. I appreciate your time!

HOLIDAY BLUES

When Isaac Newton declared: "What goes up, must come down," he could have been talking about emotions, as they are much like gravity.

Expectations, responsibilities, hopes, conversations, confrontations, emotions, mourning, disappointments and joys accompany holiday times. These are often coupled with indigestion, lack of sleep, too much booze, traffic, crowds and other annoyances.

While some might believe they are headed toward post-holiday blues–whatever the holiday– most likely our emotions are simply coming back into equilibrium after riding high for an extended period of time.

The slowing of holiday bustle leaves some of us tired; maybe coping with frigid temperatures, rain and less sun; colds from getting run down; and more time to reflect on emotionally charged memories that are possibly skewed due to all of the above.

If your emotions are feeling low, this is a good time to try any of the following: Go see a comedy movie. Visit a museum. Take a walk. Have (another) dinner with friends—but ask everyone to bring a dish. Take a bath or allow yourself a shower until the hot water runs out. Go jam on your instruments with friends. Call those you didn't get to see; make plans to see them if possible. Ease back into an exercise routine if you got off track. Add some more fruits and veggies to counter all the sugar you've likely consumed.

Remember emotions are e-motion = energy in motion. When emotions start overwhelming us, it's like they are stuck in our bodies. The best strategy is to give them a physical release that will also make our bodies feel good.

This means a really great housecleaning will leave you not only with a clean house but feeling fabulous as well!

A ROAD MAP

It's disheartening to hear that some believe it's normal to get senile, sick, incompetent or whatever, just because years are passing. I refuse to commiserate and accept any such folly just because we're rackin' up years. Maybe I'm delusional or in for a shock, but this will never be my mindset.

Here's my road map for hitting 120 years at 80 mph at least. I'm going to eat a diet of 90 percent natural foods based on fruits and vegetables, and consume moderately in that other 10 percent of foods and drink. I'll try not to do anything stupid and look both ways when I cross the street. I will not multitask, as everything seems to take me longer when I do, and I might hurt myself. I will not text and drive. I will walk far and often daily. I will start conversations with friends and strangers who might become new friends. I will laugh. I'll memorize jokes to start the laughter, find new vocabulary words and try to learn at least one new thing every day. I will keep working and doing things that stimulate my mind endlessly. I will plant and garden. I will whistle to call the birds and feed them. I will avoid the news, knowing that if I really need to know something, somebody will tell me. I will read biographies about or by anyone I find interesting for any reason. I'll keep trying to speak with everyone who can tolerate me attempting to recall and use mi Española. I'll "vacation" in my own city while making sure I get away to other places when time allows. I'll find ways to help others. I'll keep taking dance classes because they're fun and improve my coordination and mood. I'll try to be better in all my relationships. I'll be so busy, I won't even notice when I hit 120 years old!

Aging for me will be always be defined as the collective of experiences and knowledge that helps us learn about ourselves and our likes more deeply—so we can proudly embrace who we are and encourage others to do the same.

ROUTINES

We all have routine obligations and responsibilities that we must regularly keep to function and move forward in life, like work duties and caring for others. That said, do we have to keep doing everything the same way every day? What if we changed things up and found ways to make the regular, same-old, gotta-get-it-done different?

Let's start with food. We all eat and sometimes it gets boring. Maybe it's time to try cooking recipes from another region of the world, to take a gustatory trip without the travel. Maybe your trip to work in the morning is always via the same route; could the return home be done more scenically and maybe with a stop or two to explore a new neighborhood? What if dinner table discussions started with: "What did you learn today?" instead of "How did your day go?" This could even carry into how we relax. What if, instead of watching TV, we pulled out paper along with watercolor paints or colored pencils and decided to test our artistic abilities? Or maybe we substitute a binge read for a binge watch? Choose a genre and maybe an author who has a character who has evolved over 20 years.

While we each have ongoing responsibilities, there are all kinds of ways we can shake up the routines. By changing things up within the status quo, we're able to add color, adventure, fun, intrigue, learning and more to this thing called life.

Have any ideas?

SPEEDING UP

When I turned 50 several years back, someone gave me a card that said: "Congratulations! You're over the hill. Now life will really start to pick up speed." While it was meant to be humorous, it was actually a real wake-up call. Like so many others, I was at an age and point in time when I was wishing that I could stop the clock and slow the sands of time. In so many ways, life was just dawning.

Speeding through life or not moving quickly enough can cause the same problem: If we are going too fast, we might miss too many things. Yet the same can be said if we're going too slowly: We might miss many things as well.

Since this is our one and only life, we need to find our pace. Ideally it will proceed quickly enough to accomplish all we want to do, yet slowly and easily enough so that we can stop a minute, enjoy, listen and learn. Because it is the minutes where all the details, conversations, insights, understanding and compassion originates. Each day has 1440 minutes. Are you spending yours in a way that provides your best return on investment?

CONCRETE WORDS—AND NOT

Miscommunication occurs in all relationships and usually centers around two categories: The use of words that are either concrete or nominalizations.

Concrete words are specific and definite. Nominalizations are words that are abstract, vague and unspecified, and that cause the listener to search for meaning within their personal frame of reference.

Here are some concrete words: cement; the Atlantic Ocean; "Thursday, January 1, 2020 at midnight EST." Now look at these nominalizations: love, absolutely, trust, loyalty, friendship, tomorrow, later, next year, someday soon.

Here's an example of how nominalizations can cause confusion. Suppose we read: "Keep laughing; it's good for your health." Would this mean to laugh when the biggest, meanest person trips? Probably not, as that might actually be a good way to get knocked out!

Our communication skills improve exponentially once we learn to identify speech nominalizations—and start asking questions versus making assumptions to gain clarity.

So if someone says, "I'll get back to you tomorrow"—but you need an answer by noon so you have time to make other plans—this is the time to get specific and request a concrete deadline. Generally, depending upon the nominalization, start asking questions that clarify and clear up any potential for miscommunication.

Miscommunication is forever a part of communication. As Thoreau said, "The language of friendship is not words but meanings." Not sure of the meaning? Ask for clarification. Unless the words are concrete, rarely will we ever read or hear the same words and draw identical conclusions.

SMILE

Smile, no matter what is happening in life. Practice smiling when feeling sad, angry, depressed, frustrated, lonely or any other negative emotion. This is not denial of the full range of human emotions. Rather, it is a healthy way to remind ourselves that we *do* have an array of emotions—and after hurricanes, tsunamis, tornadoes and every other force of nature, the sun comes out to remind us that it's not all bad.

Smiling is contagious. It's a natural medicine that triggers mood-elevating endorphins and can reduce blood pressure. Smiling attracts others. It's easier to smile than frown and it exercises our facial muscles. Smiling makes us all look more beautiful!

No matter how the winds strike, smile a sunny smile. Give it your 100 percent!

FERRIGNOIT

Back in my early 20s, an idea cemented in my mind that there was only one attitude to have toward living, and that was to "ferrignoit."

Let me explain.

It was the 1986 Ms. Olympia contest at Madison Square Garden's Felt Forum in New York City. Lou Ferrigno, winner of the IFBB Mr. America title and two Mr. Universe titles, and a successful TV actor (he starred in *The Incredible Hulk*), was addressing the crowd.

Yet while Mr. Ferrigno was speaking, a few snide comments and mumbling could be heard about him to the effect that he was "all brawn, no brains."

How quickly the bodybuilding fans had come to disregard his stupendous championships and other successes.

Then somebody finally said, "Shut up! Listen to him more closely. Don't you know he's almost 100 percent deaf since childhood?"

The embarrassment of the chimers around me was palpable as they surely reflected on their own ability to hear, yet their simultaneous inability to listen and marvel at the feats Mr. Ferrigno had achieved—all with a significant hearing disability.

At that moment, a new word formed in my mind that summed up the stamina it takes to be great no matter what disadvantages we might have: ferrignoit.

To "ferrignoit" means to maintain the strength to work harder than everybody else to get what we want, no matter what adversities life might have thrown at us.

I'm not sure if this word is in the dictionary—but it should be.

FIRED UP

Anger and fire have similar traits. Both can destroy, leaving burning emotions and embers of relationships simmering, awaiting the next combustion.

But anger and fire can warm us, too. The very same fire that kills people and is destructive can protect us if it is rechanneled into a stove or coaxed to soar in a fireplace, giving us warmth. And it's the fire in our hearts that we equate with love. Anger and fire are both powerful energies that are important to our lives.

As fire sustains life on a frigid, wintery day, anger is essential as well. Its rising heat can help us realize that misunderstandings and frustrations are hitting a melting point that requires our immediate attention.

If we understand anger as a powerful fire and that something is demanding our attention, we would cool our tempers and be less afraid of it. We'd simply look for a safe way to manage it. Perhaps we would be less explosive and more likely to channel it toward warming our hearts and those whom we love.

Anger scares us when we feel it rising inside us and when we sense it in another. Feeling anger is OK. We can have angry feelings, own them and express them. Anger isn't a moral issue and we don't become more righteous by never feeling it. We are all allowed to feel angry. The goal is to figure out the best ways to feel anger and then express it in ways that don't make us feel guilty. Because when we know we could have managed our tides of emotions better, the aftermath never feels good.

Anger is like the taxman. It gets its due. We need to pay it respect because the anger we bottle up today only becomes like a building fire awaiting just a bit more oxygen to combust.

Reading this book or my blog won't make any of us anger-free. I get angry. You get angry. We all get angry. The goal is to listen to what our anger is telling us.

If we can be grateful that our anger is really a messenger, telling us something needs to be addressed, changed, discussed—anger is less frightening and explosions become less likely. Then we can start to respect the fire of anger and channel it to create warmth within ourselves and our relationships with others instead of destruction.

IRRELEVANT

Does aging make those who are older less relevant to society? The juxtaposition between older versus younger generations is worth contemplation. Does age create a divide at some point? The answer is: no. Years do not create irrelevance.

Rather, irrelevance begins by becoming too inward-focused. We do this by making our worlds smaller, more structured, more scheduled and more defined—because we think this will somehow ensure our survival. Yet it is actually the opposite that happens. We begin to shift into declining relevance. Our life pulse weakens in direct correlation to the strength of our resistance.

We fade because becoming inward-focused is really becoming smaller-minded. We do this because we are afraid of change, of differences, of new ways of thinking. Well, here's a wakeup call: Resisting change because we don't like change will cause us to drown in irrelevance—and we'll like that even less.

Action is the antidote for irrelevance. It's what inspires great music, art, fashion, science, medicine, communication and all advances in every area of life at any age.

Age is irrelevant. The number of years we have lived does not make anyone less relevant. Lack of heart and lack of will does. Resistance to change is the culprit.

By resisting change, we become the proud owners of the best insurance policies for irrelevance. Keep yourself in a constant state of learning, growing and changing and you will always be relevant. If you believe your best days are behind you, you're right. Believe you're just getting started? You're right, too. It's all a relevance state of mind.

THE WRONG COMPROMISE

It's easy to get caught up in life. Work, late nights, family, social obligations: the list is endless. Sometimes it seems there's no time to make that healthy meal or take a walk because there are more pressing tasks and obligations vying for our time.

What we don't realize is that by compromising—by skipping walks, making poor food choices, drinking too much liquor, smoking, stressing ourselves and keeping late hours—we ultimately pay for each and every one of our indiscretions. The price: Our health and energy.

Being born with a healthy body is a blessing. Maintaining it in top form is a major responsibility and task. The challenge is upon us. Take it. Make the commitment. Today you can make choices to build greater health and energy.

STUCK

It's easy to get stuck. We're stuck when we're spending too much time thinking about past hurts, like whether our choices were good or bad, and potential future ones.

We can also easily slip into professional fiction-writer mode as we invent various scenarios to rationalize how things would be different if we had made different choices along the way. Our egos inflate our worries as we ponder the impact we might or might not have had on someone else or ourselves. We wonder where we fit into the equations.

Instead of blaming yourself or anyone else for anything that's happened—instead of trying to rewrite past history—flip your switch to the present.

When our thinking goes backward, we have to practice flipping it.

Ask: How would my partner feel today if I started to do X? Fill in the X with what you think you didn't do or could have done differently.

Ask: Would my children respond differently if I started doing X? (Like practicing listening instead of offering suggestions, or trying to solve another's problems instead of assuring them that they have the skills to find resolutions.)

Ask: Would my boss or client feel differently about my capabilities if I started to do X to change their perspective regarding my work?

Once you have the "X" established in your mind, start incorporating it into situations that arise whenever possible.

The list of scenarios is endless. But by shifting our focus to what we can do versus what we didn't do, we stay real and hold the potential to change things for the better.

Mentally flipping our focus to what we can do differently in any situation, sets the stage for progress, peace, satisfaction and growth.

BRAIN POWER

While technological innovations are awe-inspiring, they pale in comparison to our minds and bodies. The recording and instantaneous recall performed by your nervous system, the ultimate memory chip, is fast and thorough. Since birth, it's been recording everything—which contributes to our reactions, responses and instinctual behaviors. Each sound, feel, sight and word has been stored for future reference, whether it was perceived as pleasurable, threatening or not even noticed as it was being recorded. As water changes shorelines, our experiences and impressions consistently impact our nervous system's responses, guided by our brain, consciously and subconsciously.

Neural pathways are formed as our brains start to recognize familiar patterns of response to our emotions or beliefs. The more these triggers fire, the deeper the neural pathways become. Many of our reactions in the moment are somewhat predetermined because our brains are acting on deeply stored subconscious ideas that have been collected over the years and recorded as our responses to situations.

Science has confirmed that our breathing greatly impacts our nervous system, the functioning of our minds and the health of our bodies.

The reason we want to stop and practice deep, steady breathing on a regular basis is that when we perceive any kind of threat and feel stressed, we tend to hold our breath and it becomes more becomes shallow. Our heart function relies on oxygen, as does our overall health. By practicing "stopping and breathing," we can help our brains create new neural pathways that calm our nervous system's response to stress.

Our minds and bodies are one. With awareness and practice, we can help make our response to stress less stressful no matter where we are, no matter what is happening.

EPITAPH

An epitaph is a phrase or statement written in memory of a person who has died. It's a brief proclamation intended to sum up the highlights of one's existence while on Earth. Have you ever thought about what you might like yours to say?

We're all going to die. Occasionally reflecting on how we think we will be remembered—or want to be remembered—is time well spent. Although we might be perfectly happy with the epitaph that we envision would be written by others as they reflect on our life contributions, doing this exercise ourselves can help motivate us to change our ways and how we spend the remaining days of our lives. Maybe there is something we've wanted to, needed to or thought we should do.

While none of us can physically live forever, there are things we can choose to do to impact the memories of a few or of many for years to come. Time on Earth is finite. The legacy we leave can last forever. Today is a good day to begin acting in ways that will reflect the legacy we want to be remembered for after we pass—which hopefully is a very long way away.

SMASHITUDE

Our expectations in life can greatly affect outcomes. Did you know that believing aging equates to being feeble, absent-minded, weak or forgetful has been scientifically proven to be a self-fulfilling prophecy? Not only that, believing such bunk is more likely to trigger heart attacks and strokes.

The good news? The opposite has also been proven to be self-fulfilling! Believing we're getting better and more fun, while staying healthy and strong, are recurring themes of how lively centenarians see themselves.

So it's time to get real and smash these attitudes!

I've seen positive attitudes materialize as favorable outcomes in all aspects of life, time and time again, for myself and countless others.

Today is a good day to try smashitude thinking! Life has countless phases and each can be uniquely robust and as exciting as any other phase of life—if that's how we choose to see it!

GASOLINE

Offering unsolicited opinions on others is like adding gasoline to fire. Even when we've been asked to share our opinion, it is prudent to ask ourselves before engaging our mouths, "Is my opinion: Thoughtful, Hurtful, Intelligent, Necessary or Kind?" In other words, take the acronym of those words and THINK long and hard before sharing an opinion.

Resisting urges to opine is hard to master. I am not claiming to have mastered it. But I can say this: If we take the time to think before adding gasoline to a raging fire, our more rational self may rule our lips and reconsider whether it's time to just nod instead.

A nod is not necessarily a physical form of agreement. Rather, just like in many cultures, saying yes does not mean, "Yes, I agree"; it means, "Yes, I acknowledge that you have said something."

Proceed with caution!

NO

We all say "yes" to plenty. But sometimes, for various reasons, the answer we should give is "no." This simple two-letter word, which can be so hard to say, is still a complete sentence.

Kids know it. "No" is one of the first words they utter. Not only that, if they think you didn't get the message this simple word conveys, they'll repeat it 10 times. No explanation is offered. Just: No. No. No. No. No.

Say "no" if a request is overwhelming. If it's too much. Doesn't work. Doesn't fit. Feels uncomfortable. Takes you away from more important priorities. Is too time-consuming. Too distracting. Whatever.

Need to say more? "No, thank you" will suffice.

That's enough. Sometimes "no" needs to be said. Try saying "no" as a stand-alone statement. Skip your urge to explain or justify.

No.

Yes. Really. Try it!

That's it! Short and simple.

Moment by Moment

Life gets a lot better when we focus on how far we've come versus how far we have to go. Sometimes just acknowledging where we are at this exact moment is enough.

To illustrate this with an example, let's say we want to eat better, exercise to get in shape, improve communication in our relationships, get a new job or whatever. The victory is in each moment we choose to do something that moves us forward in that direction. Each little choice accumulates and adds up to the end goal. If we can make the right choice in the moment, we will instantly feel happier and we won't be so focused on how far we still have to go. Much of life satisfaction is defined through moment-by-moment decisions.

Boxed In

Now is the time to define who we are. Not who we were, but who we are now in this moment.

Here's a challenge: Try defining "who you are"—which can include "what you do"—in 50 words. If you were speaking it, that would take about a minute, which would be a long commercial, as most are 15 to 30 seconds.

Note that the question is: Who are you? Not who were you!

Stay current in your descriptor. Release the judgments on your words as you spell this out mentally (or even better, on paper). If you want to make your self-descriptor longer, go ahead! Try not to box yourself in. Be broad. Risk using the most important words and adjectives that define who you believe you are today and what you are doing with your life that is fulfilling your spirit.

We place so many judgments on ourselves while telling others who we are—and also on others while listening to explanations of who someone is—that we inadvertently box ourselves in. We do this because faulty thinking makes us believe we can control the reactions of another regarding our statement as to who we are. While this sense of control might work sometimes, it will never work all the time.

While "What do you do?" is a common question asked in the early stages of any relationship, it is one whose answer deserves careful consideration and possibly an update. Get out of the box and become fashionably current in describing who you are!

IMPOSSIBLE TO KNOW

It is impossible to know what it is like to be anyone other than ourselves. Although we might think we know what another's life is like, we are seeing their experience through our eyes and trying to define their feelings through our own.

Our perceptions of others are reflections of ourselves—and our reactions to others are actually a form of self-awareness, whether or not we're aware of (or choose to acknowledge) these self-revelations.

The only way we can really know what another feels is by asking them and listening closely. The flip side for this is true as well. Others will make assumptions about us, but only really know what we share with them.

A few years ago, someone told me that in her country, if someone said to another, "Gee, you look tired," the rejoinder would be, "You must be looking at me through tired eyes." I always found this response fascinating. It was a cultural acknowledgment of how we comment unknowingly about others' experience while actually reflecting our own state of being.

Our tendency to be critical diminishes once we accept that it is impossible to truly know another. Instead, we realize that what we're about to voice might reflect an internal conflict within ourselves—one that perhaps we need to work on or have not really accepted. This, in turn, is why the other person's behavior disturbs us. If you notice anger rising, it's time for listening—something that is difficult to do if we're talking.

A LITTLE BIT WISER NOW

Much of what is happening in our lives today reflects choices we made in the past.

That said, whether you're happy with the current situation or not, the game is not over yet.

Now would be a good time to ask ourselves if there's anything we need to work on changing today so future days reflect our more constructive, proactive, positive, smart, informed, educated, thought-out, wiser choices.

Just sayin'…

Time for Expression

Nothing we do is a waste of time if it expresses something within us we feel is important. Yet what is important to each of us might or might not be relevant to someone else. As a result, others' reactions to what we do with our time must be considered in this light.

Time is an irreplaceable asset. Spending it doing nothing or worrying about what others will think about what we're doing is a big waste of our precious time. No matter how we choose to allocate our time, someone will have comments and opinions. Those comments will often have little to do with what we're doing and will be more likely to reflect the other's thinking and what they feel are important ways to spend *their* time. So when others question what we're doing, although it's always worthwhile to consider the source and weigh the validity of the thought as it relates to our own life, we owe it to ourselves to proceed if our actions achieve some goal we personally feel is important.

Express yourself. Study, exploration and self-expression are at the foundation of life satisfaction. Learning to express what's important to us through actions that fulfill our dreams ultimately benefits not just ourselves but also those around us.

Habit Exchange

Today's a good day to exchange one habit for another. Let's say you really like eating potato chips when you're watching TV. How about exchanging one of those two activities —either the watching TV or the potato chips—for another, healthier habit? Then instead of watching TV or eating chips while watching TV, you don't watch TV or you eat fruit when you are.

Another example could be that maybe you're in the habit of eating on the run. Could you exchange this habit for sitting down at a table to dine? And ideally with others, having a conversation during the meal?

Maybe you make lists for everything—except something important that concerns your health and well-being. Could you add "take a walk" to your "to do" list and actually make sure you cross it off each day?

Nature abhors a vacuum. So, by eliminating one habit and replacing it with another, we fill the hole and get nature to work with us.

Think of it as a game. Try playing to win!

Take some time to consider what behaviors have become your habits. See what you might be able to swap out, modify or tweak with a different behavior. Then go do it!

PASSIVE AWARENESS

Being passive is associated with being aggressive or doing nothing. Although passive can mean "to be indifferent," it can also mean laid back, quiet, unflappable and receptive.

Becoming aware in a passive way, or passive awareness, is to practice watching, observing and paying attention without judging or trying to figure out what's right or wrong with another person or situation.

Instead of thinking: "I'm right, so you must be wrong," the goal of passive observation is to shift our focus from what we think we're seeing—which involves our own thought processes—to observing the thoughts and how they relate to how we feel.

For example, imagine this situation: I'm pretty energetic. I come home and I want everyone else to be on that same wavelength. If they're not, I start wondering "What's wrong with them? What's the problem? Why are they raining on my parade?" In other words, I've made the others wrong.

Now, if I come home to the same situation but try to practice passive awareness, I put the focus on myself and ask: "Why do I feel uncomfortable when others' energy doesn't match mine? Why do I need them to respond how I want them to? They actually seem fine but maybe a bit tired."

With passive awareness, neither party has to be right or wrong. Instead, it's just about observing that different people act differently in different situations.

Throughout life, we've developed coping mechanisms, learning to act in ways we believed would be more pleasing to others. This helped us manage the emotions of those around us while society simultaneously taught us rights and wrongs.

The result? When someone disagrees with how we feel, think or see something, we've been conditioned to believe that one of us must be wrong. We think that if we can just explain our position, the other person will understand their wrongness and our rightness. The argument develops because we think the other person cannot possibly be listening to us if they don't "get" our point or our rightness, or worse, that we haven't been clear—so we start monologuing ad nauseam or yapping until everyone's anger starts to elevate.

Passively observing helps us to see different perspectives, allowing all to coexist and all to be OK—whether we agree or not. Being open to passive awareness opens relationships and new life possibilities. Passive awareness is not being passive but rather observing our thoughts before choosing a path of action.

If we can practice watching, observing and paying attention without judging, we can see others. When we only want to be right, we are choosing our rightness over the importance of the other people in our life. In our hearts, we know this is wrong.

CHANGING OTHERS

We were each born with the ability to change someone's life—in fact, many people's lives. Although this book and my blog are largely focused on changing ourselves so we can have better lives, let's look at how changing another is not that hard to do.

While many will say it's impossible to change another, this is incorrect. If you've ever keenly observed someone during a conversation, you know this to be true. While the change might or might not be permanent, a change does occur. This happens in all our interactions. We change and others do as well.

Think about a time when you were hurt by another. Did it change you? Did it make you become a little more protective of your emotions? How about when your efforts were recognized? Didn't your pride swell a bit, making you feel good? That's a change, too. What about when you felt loved or witnessed the reaction of another to your love? Change occurred. Mutual hearts expanded. The same worked for others during these interactions. We've all hurt others and changed their perspectives, and we've changed their feelings with love and praise, too.

Change occurs over time. The impact of our actions might not be apparent at first. But upon repetition of any behavior, an impact is made. All our interactions have a cause and effect not only for ourselves but others as well.

Today is a good day to figure out ways to ensure the impact of our actions is positive, not just to benefit ourselves but all those around us as well. If we do this, before we know it, more good stuff will circulate, because that's how energy flows.

We each have the ability to help channel anger and sadness into laughter and happiness. Although it's the responsibility of each of us to change ourselves, we also still have opportunities to create a more positive flow of energy that can help change ourselves, others and the world around us for the better.

POSSIBILITARIANS

When we have exhausted all possibilities in an attempt to solve a problem or accomplish a goal, we need to remember this: We haven't.

No matter what we think, until time's up, possibility exists.

Possibility is everywhere. It surrounds us. It's not always out in the open but is sometimes hidden: in a subtle, knowing smile during a conversation; through observations of our surroundings; within the pages of books; in documentaries. Possibility is everywhere! (And yes, I just said that twice because it's worth repeating—and I might even say it again!)

Although our physical being might curtail some of our possibilities, a strong will and determined mind can create endless other opportunities.

If there's something you've been thinking about doing, as you percolate your ideas, continue to hone your skills of observation. All the help and tools we need are often within arm's reach if we carefully think about where we need to look.

Start reading everything and anything related to your goal. Make it a topic of conversation with others, asking what and whom they know who might advance your goals. Make your lists and start checking off your actions so you're prepared when possibility actualizes into opportunity.

Whatever it is that you want to accomplish, while you might not be 100 percent sure on how to make it happen, keep your eyes and ears open.

And in the meantime, I hear the world is in dire need of more possibilitarians. I got one of those jobs—and I bet you can, too!

BEAUTY IS A VERB

A noun is a person, place or thing. Beauty is a verb because it is an action, state or relationship identified by contentment and satisfaction with the person we have become and how we see others and the world around us. Have a beauty-full day.

HABITUATION

Habituation is a psychological phenomenon whereby our response is decreased to any stimulus after having been exposed to it repeatedly. As a practical example, it's how one might learn to ignore the noise of living near a train track, whereas to a visitor the sound might be overwhelming. Basically, think of habituation as a learned behavior that results in our ability to tune out inessential stimuli to focus instead on all that really requires our attention.

The first time we put on pants after a long hot summer of wearing skirts or shorts—or when we put on cologne or perfume—we notice it. Yet over time, we get comfortable and don't notice our scent unless someone else mentions it.

We become habituated because we've been exposed to something frequently and over a long period of time. Likewise, it's usually not something that we found intense—like a deafening, pulsating car alarm, which we'd never really be able to ignore.

Habituation results from exposure to everyday stuff that almost becomes blasé, so we stop noticing it. People who work in a chocolate factory or donut shop become oblivious to the smells, whereas the chocolate or sugar would stimulate another quite differently.

Habituation deserves examination because it's more likely associated with "what we get used to" in life versus what we might really want. Sometimes we habituate—but our low-level satisfaction or acceptance with the situation changes over time. This might be at the root of boredom in relationships or life.

If there's something in your life you are resisting, perhaps it might be worth thinking about how habituation may be having an impact. For example, if you're feeling bored with your significant other, perhaps it's time to notice that they're not the same as background noise. Bored with life? Maybe it's time to shift your attention to what's happening now and what could be happening if you made some different choices.

While we might think life is always the same old stuff, it's not and doesn't have to be. Likewise, if we're habitually lingering over some social blunder we made who-knows-when, maybe it's time to realize that it's only ourselves stuck in that habituation, and most likely others have moved on.

By examining habituation, we might be reassessing what we're taking for granted.

REJECTION

Rejection is a part of life for everyone. Sometimes no matter how we try, our efforts are resisted and met with rejection.

Neuroscience proves rejection is physically and mentally painful because the same areas of the brain where physical and emotional pain are processed, are activated when we feel rejected. Worse is the tendency to torture ourselves by mentally reliving the circumstances over and over, which floods us with the original feelings.

Rejection is often accompanied by a deep sense of disconnect, anger and possibly aggression. These feelings might be projected toward others—while our self-esteem suffers a knockout punch if we emotionally linger on what we did wrong or, worse, what is wrong with us.

Rejection is not a confirmation that we lack worth, talent, value or love. Rather, painful as it might be, what is happening is a lack of real connection. It's better to know connection is lacking sooner rather than later—whether with a mate, boss or client—because maintaining the illusion of a connection is even more hurtful.

When facing rejection, acknowledge it hurts. Admit you're feeling sad, embarrassed, discouraged or disappointed. Pretending it was irrelevant denies your emotions and only temporarily buries the hurt.

Be kind to yourself. Beating ourselves up doesn't help. Reach out to others you trust, who will allow you to vent.

You are not your rejection. You are not suddenly a loser, worthless, unlovable, incapable or any other negative adjective. Maintain your dignity no matter which way the circumstances are heading. Name calling, begging and pleading are not effective forms of communication and at best they compromise dignity, making the situation and sense of rejection worse. A decision has been made; if you can't change it, acceptance is in order.

Rejection is a good teacher. Reflect on what you've learned from the experience, however painful. But keep more of your energy focused outside of yourself, preferably spending time being physically active. Socialize with others. Be kind to yourself—and better yet, get out and be kind to others. Helping another will remind you that you have love to give, are valuable and are valued and appreciated. Remind yourself of your good points. And know this: The pain will pass.

PREVENTABLE

Did you know that out of the top five reasons people purchase medications, almost 100 percent are preventable with healthier habits? During 2018, for example, 41 percent of medication purchases were for blood pressure; 30 percent were for allergies; 29 percent for colds or flu; 29 percent for cholesterol and 19 percent for arthritis. These numbers are striking because the same poll declared that 55 percent of Americans ages 50+ believe they have complete control or are mostly in control of their health.

Could this mean that most believe their control over their health comes from taking a pill instead of making healthy personal choices? Let's hope not. While medicines have a time and place—and science has made phenomenal advances that have benefitted humankind—it is in our own personal best interest to do what we can do, right now, to limit the likelihood that we'll ever have to take medication.

Right now, half of all Americans live with at least one chronic disease like heart disease, cancer, stroke or diabetes. These and other chronic diseases are the leading cause of premature death and disability. But as the U.S. Centers for Disease Control and Prevention states, chronic diseases can be prevented by eating well—which means plenty of fruits and vegetables, being physically active, not smoking and avoiding excessive drinking.

Now here's news: Even if you have been diagnosed with a chronic disease, improving any of your daily health habits will most often improve the condition.

If you needed a reason to change out a bad habit for a good one, there you go! Today is a great day to add more fruits and vegetables to your diet; get up on your feet as often as possible; walk whenever and wherever you can (ideally 30 minutes or more a day); breathe deeply and practice other forms of stress management; get a good night's sleep; avoid smoking; and go easy on alcohol.

The best control you will ever have over health is from diet, exercise and stress management choices—not a pill.

WATCH

Although moments might be filled with a flurry of "e-motions" or energy in motion, we can watch and realize this does not necessarily require our response.

WHAT'S NEXT?

When things go wrong in life, it's important to get into the mindset of "What's next?" as quickly as possible. Challenges will always present themselves. There will be problems no matter how we plan. We can either get thrown like a kite in the wind, swaying back and forth in all directions, or we can immediately elect to get our thought processes into resolution mode so we can make new choices.

When we shift our thinking into "What's next?" we move to solution mode versus problem mode. A challenge has presented itself and with intent, we can earnestly seek resolution. A "What's next?" attitude kicks our gears into action, limits our inclination to linger on doubt and puts us back into bold decision mode.

The reestablishment of a new direction, adjusted with more information when we get it—even if it hit us like a tornado—makes the difference in processing our lessons as failures or routes to success with additional directions or a new map.

Allowing ourselves to linger on a problem means we're resisting normal life, which is ever-filled with challenges. We can change our mindsets to find resolutions, helping ourselves or the situation in the process. Asking "What's next?" is empowering. It's a phrase that becomes a new way of thinking, one that can open us to seeing new possibilities instead of being stuck in stagnant resolution or acceptance of what may not need to be.

The next time something doesn't go quite as planned, adopt a "What's next?" attitude and see what happens! Let go of what's gone and appreciate what still remains while adopting the perspective of looking forward to what's coming next! It's a game-changer!

20 YEARS

A word to the wise is unnecessary and a word to the unwise will likely fall on deaf ears. We all listen and learn when we're ready and not a moment before. This is why it's high time to release the urge to say, "If only I knew this 20 years ago."

We are ready when we're ready.

But with that, now might be the time to ask ourselves, what are we currently trying to get ready for? No doubt there's something we've each been thinking about doing. Waiting another 20 years to do it? Might not be such a good idea.

THE WAY YOU ARE

Remember those cartoons where the character had a devil on one shoulder and an angel on the other?

There's a little of that good guy and bad guy in all of us.

As different as we all are from one another—as unique as we are—we're all actually more the same than different. We are all sets of juxtaposed emotions. This doesn't need to frighten or overwhelm us. Emotions move like the tides, rising and flowing out. Accepting this as early on in life as possible, helps each of us feel more comfortable with allowing our caring, compassionate aspects to shine.

No two people, no two lives will ever be the same. It's life's great mystery. While we all begin life the same way, by birth, and we all leave the same way, by death, the journey in between is vast and varied. The love between parents and children is universal—as are the difficulties and challenges as we grow to become separate individuals.

Laughing and crying. Peaceful and angry. Growing and trying. Living and dying. It's all good. It's all life. All coupled with feelings about our wonderful days and sad ones too. All the while, trying to find healthy ways to deal with our emotions in ways that won't hurt ourselves or others. Figuring out love, which is an active noun like clash, conflict, attempt and struggle. Striving to love ourselves and others.

So let me close with this: Even if you still think you're a tangled mess of emotions, you are lovable just the way you are. Mister Rogers and Billy Joel got that right.

WORK

Throughout life, our work challenges represent a series of character-building lessons that fortify our self-esteem, sense of value and worth. These lessons accrue while learning and managing a variety of jobs throughout our careers, but also while doing the hard jobs of parenting, coping with caregiving and offering time for volunteer work.

Work rewards are not always accompanied by an obvious payday. Sometimes the rewards are subtle or seen over time, like a smile from another as they acknowledge our assistance, or seeing a child turn into a responsible adult.

Hopefully, we've remained positive while working and witnessed how our attitudes helped make what we wanted happen: Work works best when we commit to working at it. We've likely witnessed the importance of appreciation for our efforts and those of others—and how recognition inspired us to work harder. We learned about collaboration, teamwork, weak links and the value of strong ones.

We've also heard time and time again that the only way to do great work is to do what we love. I don't think we have to love everything we do, but no matter what roles we try, we only waste our own time by not committing to doing our best during the time spent on the job. Just to be waiting for the end of the week is a serious waste of time. No matter what the role, each is necessary to society. There is no "I'm just a…" anything. Don't believe it? Watch what your neighborhood starts to smell like if the garbage pickup is missed. Each role contributes to the completeness of life as we know it.

Work provides opportunities to learn about ourselves and others. It forces us to communicate better on countless levels. It challenges us to grow. Learning to think before speaking, being open-minded, discussing versus arguing, watching our tone of voice, the feelings of exceeding expectations and the essential nature of praise. Work has taught us that whether or not our efforts are noticed, we can find a way to persevere and continue regardless.

Today, reflect on all the work you have done in its many forms that has helped make you stronger, smarter, more valuable, bolder and wiser. And likewise, how your efforts benefited many others.

DON'T

Throughout life, we've all been told "Don't do that" by a variety of well-meaning others who shared and continue to share their "Don't do it" opinions. They could have done so in an effort to keep us safe; to control our behaviors; to manage our energy when theirs was lacking due to life demands; and to get us to do what they wanted or were afraid of wanting themselves.

We have been the recipient of plenty of "don'ts." And if we're being totally honest, at this stage of life, we've likely shared well-intended (but not necessarily well-considered) "don'ts" with many others, including our children.

The result of a lifetime of "don'ts" is that deep down, we all question who we are, our abilities, our strengths and even our general likability or worthiness. We may even believe that if we "do" instead of "don't" that others might think we're being selfish.

Trusting ourselves to do what we want to do is not bad. Who we are and what we want is not wrong or greedy or any other negative, judgmental adjective. It is who we are and what we want, period. If you believe otherwise, it's time to get out of this trap, because that's all it is: A trap that keeps our identity stuck in believing that we need to be like others—and that to be liked by others, we need to do what they want.

Today is a good day to begin releasing ourselves from don't-do-it conditioning in any area of our lives where it might still be lingering. Here's why: 1) Holding on to conditioned don'ts, without really considering their impact on our lives today, is a weak attempt to shift the responsibility of living our lives from ourselves to other outside forces. 2) It denies the fact that as a one-of-a-kind being, our self-ish self can know what we need and want to live a fulfilled life, which is our responsibility to humanity.

Next time you hear yourself or another saying "don't," ask "Why not?"

It might be very good, important advice such as: "No, you don't want to jump off a bridge!" But it might also be old conditioning or outdated information about fears—our own or others'— that are worthy of examination.

Only you can decide why you're holding onto "Don't do it." It's your life to decide what you want and need to do—and what you think is right for you.

AWARE

It does not take any more energy to change our ways than we'd spend otherwise. Doubt this? Did you ever wonder how much time and energy we use repeating the same old, same old, no matter how unproductive it is?

Changing doesn't require more energy: It requires greater awareness and different thinking. The energy output is the same. This is why, whenever we recognize something we need to change, this is fabulous first step!

All change begins with awareness. Then, as we choose to start working on something, we need to give ourselves a pat on the back—because committing to changing any unproductive behavior by swapping in a productive one is absolutely fantastic!

We've recognized an unsuccessful pattern and are changing it up.

Don't worry if you stumble and don't do everything perfectly. An imperfect change for the better is preferable to maintaining the status quo that we know is inefficient, ineffective, wrong, counterintuitive, less than it could be or unhealthy.

The old way and the new way both demand energy. Yet when we choose to change a behavior in a way that is beneficial to our being, our energy is empowered to freely flow as it should, which moves us toward new benefits.

Now some of you might be thinking: Wrong! It takes more energy to exercise. Well, this is incorrect. If we don't channel energy to exercise, our bodies feel stress and tension—which are blocked energy that will ultimately demand our energy for repairs.

We each are Energy Directors in our personal United States of Being. Direct these energy forces to your benefit.

RIGHT DECISION

Sometimes we get stuck because we're trying hard to make the "right" decision. What we really need to focus on is making the decisions that we do make, right.

Whether forced or voluntary, decision times are inevitable. Life requires decisions at every phase. For the most part, decisions are made by assessing the desirability of options or their worthiness. Sometimes decision time is forced upon us and we must make our choices in a timely or urgent manner; other times, decision making seems to linger endlessly while we debate pros and cons.

Decisions represent a choice at a moment in time and an attempt to create resolution. While we may be waiting for more information, we won't always have what we think we need to know to make the best decision. Sometimes we must choose based only on what we know in the moment.

In our hearts, we usually know what we want to choose. Still, we might seek the opinions of others in an attempt to reinforce our choice. We're hoping others will agree with what we consciously or subconsciously believe is the right choice—and we're looking for external validation. But who's to say, other than ourselves, what is rational or right for us?

Choices reflect individual beliefs, history, experiences and perceptions. Try as we might to apply the opinions of others, or logic, emotions will most likely impact our decisions.

For this reason, take your time. Decide when you're ready. And when you're ready, that will be good enough to proceed as best as you can. Move forward into the unknown. Remember, regardless of our choices today, life is not written in stone—nor are our choices.

EVERY AGE

Every age of life is equally important. Just as each moment segues into the next, each moment is wholly distinct from the previous one. The aggregate value of these moments turns into years and ultimately is accounted for as our age.

When we think about age, we often talk about wisdom. Yet it would be a mistake to believe that a two- or eight- or 14- or 18- or 24-year-old lacks wisdom. Each stage of life is a window into different understandings, and people at every age are full of unique, wise interpretations. Clinically, these awarenesses reflect the mental state or development of the brain at the time. However, each age also deserves to be recognized for bringing a unique awareness of life and whole immersion in culture as it is evolving in real time.

What age brings is more experience. This is a unique benefit because the more we live, the more experiences can we accrue. Important note: I did not say the longer we are *alive;* I said the more we live. Please note the differentiation. Here's why:

New experiences come our way daily, whether we like them or not. Our reactions and reflections to them aggregate. We can choose merely to live through them, letting them accrue in ways that jade us, closing us off to new ideas and experiences—or we can embrace them (be they good, bad or ugly) so that they assemble to create newfound wisdom and awareness that is different not just from that of our younger days but also from the previous 24 hours!

To maintain a young mind with an experienced brain, we need to keep merging these concepts. Every day gives us a new opportunity to become wiser than yesterday if we choose to reflect and learn from our inevitable daily lessons.

ONE WORD

There's a Zen saying that when we're angry, we should say one word—with our mouths shut.

Research Is In...

Health science consistently proves 11 basic factors can exponentially benefit our health, mental well-being, physical abilities and likelihood of longevity. Here goes. Let's see if you can score 100 percent!

1. Make sure you're eating a variety of fruits and vegetables every day, ideally a variety of five or more.
2. Stop eating when you are full. Work on recognizing that physical feeling of fullness. Not sure what it feels like? Drink four big glasses of water and see what that feels like. For most, this will provide an indication of what a full stomach feels like. Then start noticing that feeling at mealtimes.
3. Keep moving naturally. Walking, stretching and dancing all count!
4. Stop and breathe deeply. Do this regularly. Also do something every day that helps to relieve your stress.
5. Cultivate a sense of purpose. What is important to you? Figure that out. It doesn't have to be earth-shattering. It is all about doing something that is important to you and working on it every day.
6. Love someone—or many. Care deeply about others. Pets count. People are even better, albeit more challenging.
7. Spend time with others. Get out and increase your sense of belonging with a group of others. While this might be difficult at first, the benefits outweigh what might initially be uncomfortable.
8. Believe. God, nature, a higher power—whatever. Believe there is a universal energy always ready to help guide you.
9. If you smoke, quit. Be moderate with alcohol.
10. Look both ways when you cross the street. Don't drink or text and drive. And the most important of all...
11. Don't take anything in life too seriously. Laugh at yourself. Laugh in the moment. Laugh when you cry. Don't wait until illness or death to put life into perspective. Find laughter whenever you can.

INTENTION

Intention is a mental state that represents making a commitment to carrying out an action or actions in the future. To act with intention requires considerable forethought along with planning.

Clarity is essential when setting our objectives, as is a willingness to clearly state to ourselves what we want. Writing it down is even better. Stating the goal, laying out the plan and following through with action are the only ways that intentions can transform from thoughts into realities.

When we're defining our intentions, we need to be as clear and specific as possible. If we want a new job or career, we need to spell out exactly what we want to be doing in a realistic way—and noting if there are requirements whose fulfillment will require educating ourselves. If our intention is to get into a new personal relationship, we need to thoughtfully envision our desired mate. What qualities are we seeking? The more specific we can be, the more likely the relationship will materialize. Simultaneously, we need to ask ourselves what we might need to do to make such an acquaintance cross our paths. If our intention is to become healthier, we will need to set a clear plan as to how we're going to eat more healthy foods and increase activity, while avoiding those foods and activities that defy our intentions.

Boldly declaring our intentions is a first step. Next comes the planning, followed by our actions.

COMPLAINT COUNTER

When we start complaining, we're looking for what's wrong, not what's right. We're contributing to the problem, not the solution. This applies to personal relationships as well as work and everything else.

At this stage of our lives, we've seen the effects of complainers. Their words are poisonous and can adversely impact relationships and environments. No one has ever been positively rewarded for complaining. Accolades result from finding positive alternatives to move situations forward.

I'm not delusional enough to say life is fair or easy. It is not. Still, greater life satisfaction starts the moment we get ourselves off the complaint counter line and instead start appreciating what's going right.

SURFING

Do you surf through life's problems or drown in them? Some people get stuck in glorifying problems, both their own and others. They take excessive pride in perceiving themselves as being tasked with saving others and carrying the weight of all on their shoulders. This is a great way to drown in life. Been there, done that: It sinks spirits.

While wanting to help others is a wonderful trait, wanting to solve all the problems of others isn't.

Greater success for ourselves and others results when we learn to see problems as waves to surf—and by teaching others who rely on us how to swim to the best of their abilities.

Ask a lifeguard or surfer: They will say it is impossible to fight the power of the waves. Instead, one must find the opportunities to go with their energy. Also, it is impossible to save someone who refuses to stop struggling, unless you knock them out. Victims can only be saved when they make the choice to calm down. If they won't, rescuer and victim both risk drowning.

Improving our stance to achieve better balance, enables us to see that calm seas are ahead and the rough waters are only temporary. This is the only way to navigate choppy seas and those times in our lives when we ourselves or others seem to be drowning. There is no glory in drowning.

People who want to live long healthy lives see problems like waves. They know you can't surf every day, but when a good wave comes along, it's an opportunity to master ourselves and our environment.

GOSSIP

Gossip is a thinly veiled attempt to convince others that we would never engage in the same activities as those we're gossiping about. This is ironic in many ways because forgiving someone is really the act of admitting that we are like other people.

As gossip and forgiveness are intimately intertwined, perhaps before we gossip it would be wise to stop and think about how we really are very much like the person we're tempted to gossip about.

Nobody wins in gossip. Nobody feels better once caught in the gossip trap. Rather, guilt via complicity is more likely.

In our hearts, everyone knows gossiping is wrong. Perhaps what we need to practice more is forgiveness and understanding.

ACTIONS

We know we're a member of the Silver Disobedience® squad when we stop listening to what people say and instead pay attention to what they do. We're more guided by the proverbial "Actions speak louder than words."

Our years have toughened us up in the right way by helping us become less judgmental of mere words, so that when someone says something that could be perceived as a slight against us or a wrong, we can breathe. Our sense of self is strong enough so that we resist lambasting another, forgetting and obliterating all the things they've done right.

Valuing our time, many of us are at peace while alone while also preferring to spend it with those who know us dearly and love us for who we are—while they keep us laughing at our insecurities and doubts. Even if we don't see our true friends often enough due to distance or time constraints, just thinking about their existence immediately gives us a sense of joy.

Confidence has grown inside our hearts and helps us to know that what is right for ourselves is good enough. In fact, defining what we like about who we are and accepting it is quite an achievement.

PEBBLES AND GEMS

Have you ever seen raw gems? Rough on the outside. Managing to keep themselves tucked deep in the Earth and rubble, hidden from the untrained eye. Looking mostly like average pebbles, unrelated to their polished siblings. Yet for all their seeming ordinariness, they are sought as they are still highly more valuable than one might initially realize upon their discovery.

Pebbles are like people. As such, throughout our lives, it helps to recognize that however we are feeling about ourselves or others, we are really all unpolished gems.

Life chips away at us. Each lesson removes the unnecessary layers to reveal our value held in disguise, waiting patiently to have us recognize our inherent worth. When we realize that we are gems, it becomes easier to be truer to ourselves and our values. Suddenly we are more able to unveil our shine—glowing bright like a diamond.

It is with the realization of our worth that we begin to radiate light toward the world around us, that in turn allows others to shine. Just as no two gemstones will ever be polished the same, it is our responsibility to shine like the human gems we are. Shine on, crazy diamonds!

MENTAL PROPERTY

Many of you have expressed that you're feeling good about your life—but others keep dumping their garbage on your mental property. Let's break down the issue.

It's important to know that feeling negative is as normal an emotion as feeling positive. I'm not saying it's pleasant to be around negativity—but knowing it's normal is helpful to remember when we're confronted with another's mood that is less elevated than ours.

When living with, working with or interacting with someone who is stuck in negativity, we need to practice selective hearing. Just because someone is complaining, we don't have to listen. Instead, try imagining the person like those cartoons where the annoying character's voice is replaced with a "Wha wha wha…" that says nothing. This is a helpful tactic, particularly if the droning complaints become incessant. In fact, you might even find yourself smiling if you really visualize this.

The big point is to allow the other to vent versus spending your energy trying to stop them. Once you start struggling against their energy, they've sucked you into their abysmal abyss of negativity, which can be hard to escape.

Instead, hold onto your superpower protective shield and do not give the negativity any power. See it bouncing off you.

And if you're really feeling strong, try being your most compassionate, empathetic self. This doesn't mean agreeing or commiserating nor saying, "I know how you feel." Instead, it's saying, "Sounds like you're having a hard day"—or something to that effect, which acknowledges the struggle of the other.

Living with someone negative is not easy. It can feel like an endless dumping of garbage. But here's the thing: We cannot make another change—and negative today does not mean they will be negative forever.

The less we contribute to negativity by giving it our attention, the faster it tends to dissipate. Remember: It's not your job to clean up the emotional states of others. That's their job. Your job is to stay groovy within all the stuff dumped in your own life.

CREATIVITY

Hang on to your creativity. Never let experience replace it or you'll make yourself boring and less relevant.

Knowledge and experience accrue with years of living and working, while being confronted with countless situations that require us to find solutions. When this is happening, we are in high-creative mode. It is this creativity that is identified with youthful ingenuity.

Sometimes as we get older, because we've been through so much, dealt with so many people in so many circumstances—we think we have all the answers. Unintentionally, this is actually a form of laziness or lack of creativity. It is also identified with being old.

No two situations, people, events or days in our lives are the same. New moment, new everything. It might feel familiar. There might be similarities. We might have points of reference to correlate to the situation—but it's not the same as it was and never will be.

The most admirable youthful trait that can be owned by anyone at any age is creativity. It's looking at anything and everything with a fresh eye—the willingness to know that we don't know it all and maybe there is a new and different way of seeing a solution. Be open to change and new ways. Keep transcending traditional ideas, rules, patterns and ways of communicating to create new meaningful ideas, ways, methods, interpretations, approaches and more.

Creativity is the best identifier of life.

UNDER CONSTRUCTION

We are all ongoing emotional and physical construction projects. We benefit from assessing where we've built walls, due to fears or believing in limitations, because by recognizing their presence we can figure out new ways to expand them to make more room for life.

It's our job to own that we are the architects of our lives because as the saying goes, "Happiness is an inside job." So we all need to review our plans regularly, while knowing that nothing great was ever built alone. Plenty of collaborators will be necessary along the way— and we are lucky for that, even though all of them will have their own designs in mind.

Still, by maintaining the right perspectives, we can build our lives in a way that will make the impossible possible. Construction is not always a comfortable living arrangement but it's still the foundation for how dreams are built.

APPEARANCES

A huge benefit of age is that we won't get fooled again. Or maybe we will. But if so, it will be due to a desire to believe in our fellow humans—which is a wonderful trait. It is far less likely that it will be due to being tricked by appearances.

Life teaches us that appearances can be deceiving. While some people are exactly as they appear, sometimes what we see might not reveal the whole story. The jokester may be hurting inside. The one who seems to have it all might be depressed beyond measure. Possessions might be acquired at the expense of debt, sacrifices or an emptiness seeking to be filled. Likewise, the abrasive personality might be a guise for a wounded heart. The argumentative person might simply be uneducated in how to communicate from the heart. The photographs on social media might be highly filtered for maximum response.

To increase the likelihood of survival, all species are somewhat chameleon-like in nature. Yet for most of us, these tendencies seem to be shed with age. Through the passing of time and gaining of experiences, we tend to become more in touch with who we are and what we like. The benefit of this is that we are instinctively drawn to recognize others who also want to reveal what might have been hidden behind a facade for the purpose of self-defense, aiming to avoid exposure to hurtful people or situations.

Walking our individual paths, understanding the ways life has shaped us, we can choose new filters to see ourselves, others and the world. Time has helped us see beyond the surface of appearances. Experience has enhanced our abilities to see beauty as it was meant to be recognized and defined: Comfort with oneself.

CELEBRATION

I'm going to share the biggest, best-kept secret to being really happy. It's so obvious, we all overlook it while searching for happiness and greater meaning in our lives. Are you ready? Are you sure? Here goes: Celebrate your happiness by never questioning it.

That's it. Stop asking, "But am I really happy?" or, "If I did this, would I be happier?" or, "Why do they look happier than me/us?"

Celebrate your happiness. Stop questioning whether you are happy. Happiness happens when we let go of whatever it is that we think happiness is supposed to be like.

HABITS

The more we do anything, the more it becomes a habit. Our brains create neural pathways, which is why repetition of any behavior, positive or negative, becomes thoughtlessly rote. Often, reactions to situations are habits more than conscious responses, because most habits have deep roots in our subconscious mind. As such, they are really reactions to some past trigger. We're often unaware of how we are responding, or even that we have the option of responding differently. We are harnessing a response that has become a habit instead of being "in the moment"—and responding in a way that might be more constructive or positive.

Just because we've always done something in a particular way doesn't mean it's the best way or that it actually "works" for us. Maybe it's based on how our parents acted, which in turn might be rooted in how their parents reacted. But there's good news: If we aren't loving our reactions or habits, we can change them.

Changing a habit becomes possible when we become aware that our rote response is a reaction or a habit. Recognizing this, we can instead move to "choice" mode.

To break a habit, we have to follow a few steps:

1. Specifically identify what it is that we want to change.
2. Identify what might trigger our autopilot reaction.
3. Determine a substitute plan for what we can do when we are triggered.
4. If necessary, look at the bigger picture to see if we need to add other reinforcing behaviors that support our plans to change the habit that isn't working.
5. Set up prompts so that before the habit has a chance to kick in, we're already a step or two ahead—because we've set new, healthy prompts to remind ourselves we're changing up the former status quo.
6. Support the change, either by asking for help from others or by creating new positive rewards.
7. Be patient and kind. Habits build over time. Breaking them and setting new ones will take time, too. Be gentle with yourself if you slip.

Remember, all change starts with awareness followed by willingness to act.

SEEING AGING DIFFERENTLY

Aging is a lifelong process that begins at birth. With each passing minute from the moment we're born, we are aging. Yet aging is not the same as getting old, which, according to the dictionary, equates to irrelevancy.

Based exclusively on biological determinants, the idea that aging implies an inferiority to youth is ludicrous. While certain physical attributes alter with years, many mental, emotional and impulse intangibles arguably only get better. Ageism, a prejudice or discrimination on the basis of a person's age, is as wrong as racism or sexism. To deny the divine nature of any individual for any reason is extremely flawed thinking.

Sadly, for those who believe in ageism, their beliefs might become a self-fulfilling prophecy that reflects in choices and outcomes. Instead of continuing to eat well, stay active, remain social, work, explore, learn, grow, collaborate, party and more, they stop doing—and old creeps in.

Value and worth take on a new significance with age. Virtues, usefulness, caliber and inherent significance become richer by an accumulation of years of experiences.

The fact is that until death the human body and mind are a living system with a remarkable capacity for regeneration and growth, along with enhanced creativity and, frankly, courageousness.

Aging isn't for the weak-hearted. It's a challenge like everything else in life—but we've handled every other challenge to date. Plus, we're in good company! Fifty percent of the United States population is now over age 50. Seventy-four million of us are ages 51 to 69, and Americans 65+ are projected to hit almost 70 million over the next three decades. Thanks to a Silver Disobedient™ attitude, growing health and fitness trends along with medical advances, the 85+ population is the fastest-growing segment—and an unprecedented longevity surge is projected.

There's no reason to be less than confident of living life at this stage. It's time to outgrow the myths of old age.

H.A.L.T.

When we're ready to rip on someone, it helps to recall the acronym H.A.L.T. It's a way of putting a lid on fury we'd likely regret by asking: "Am I H-hungry, A-angry about something that needs to be discussed, L-lonely or T-tired?"

Allowing anger to ignite or linger is comparable to assigning ourselves a personal prison sentence. While feeling angry is as normal an emotion as feeling happy, the problem is when we get stuck in anger or other negative emotions and act on them in destructive ways. Managing anger without damaging all in our path is the goal.

If you find yourself imprisoned in anger, here's a list of "get out of jail" ideas.

Take a walk listening to favorite music and sing along. Take a bubble bath or hot shower. Go to bed or take a nap. Take responsibility for your emotions and refocus. Imagine "flipping off" your anger switch—knowing that keeping the anger on is hurtful. If someone else triggered the anger, try to find compassion for their pain. Get perspective: Remember it could be worse. No matter what is happening, it could be worse. Exercise. Write a letter to yourself expressing all your anger—then rip it to shreds, burn it and flush it down the toilet. Look at yourself in the mirror expressing your anger. Really let it out. You won't like what your face looks like and the horror of seeing your scary expressions might make you recognize the ugliness of holding onto anger. Make a recording of all that you want to say. Listen to it and be empathetic to your pain—but like a good friend, try to share reasons why it's time to let it go. Have a dance party. Call a trustworthy friend and vent in a safe environment. If you can't change the situation, remind yourself you can change your perspective about it and choose to do something positive if possible. If the situation is proximal, take a step back, walk away and recollect your thoughts before responding—or skip responding completely.

Lastly for this list, remind yourself that "He who angers you, conquers you."

GET OUT OF JAIL

When we're stuck in indecision, procrastinating about deciding, we've imprisoned ourselves. What is typically locking up our action is that we're hoping everything will magically align in some perfect way. We're also resisting compromise, accepting partial solutions or progress. The ideal, perfect scenario we're imagining will likely be forever elusive. Life is uncertain and it takes a certain kind of wisdom to keep moving forward, trusting that things will be fine, whatever choices we make.

Wanting everything to be perfect before we act, denies the fact that action, not just planning, is how we get what we want. We all realize how ridiculous procrastination is if we think of it this way: Recall all you've done for work throughout your entire life. Envision the intricacies involved with handling your day-to-day responsibilities and all you learned from trial and error doing your job, day in and out. Now imagine interviewing a 22-year-old who's telling you that they can handle your job. Silly, right? Of course it is. The newbie may be book-smart but they lack deep experience: They are ignorant of the foundation of actions and intricacies of knowing a role, built by a lifetime of showing up, learning and doing the work.

Life passes whether we choose to participate and act—or stay locked up in indecision. There never was and never will be a perfect time to resolve a problem all at once until we make the bold decision to act. Chipping away, we reduce challenges facing us: Finding the things we can act upon, making problems smaller and manageable while setting reachable goals. Waiting for everything to be perfect according to imaginary plans, keeps us locked up in inertia.

At any and every stage of life, we can only create what we want by giving ourselves permission to keep taking little steps forward, moving in the direction we want to go. Action is the key.

Science Behind Living Longer

The evidence is well-established: Want to live longer? Start eating more fruits and vegetables.

Studies of those who have lived 100+ active years of life—not medicated, decrepit ones—eat diets that are 95 percent plant-based.

So how to begin? As I said, put more fruits and veggies in your diet! Eating just five fruits and veggies a day makes a huge difference in longevity and reduces premature mortality. Get to seven a day and the health results become even better. If you can eat 10 fruits and vegetables daily, remarkably dramatic changes in health status can be achieved!

Fruits and vegetables deliver maximum nutrition per calorie, which adds life to our years. Better, the vitamins, minerals, antioxidants and water help reduce heart disease, stroke, cardiovascular disease, cancer and premature death from a variety of other illnesses as well.

Having researched, practiced and counseled others on the benefits of eating well for 30+ years, I've witnessed changes that are remarkable.

Need help to start? Add diced kale or spinach to your meatball batter. You'll never notice. Start eating salads. Make fruit your only food before 11:00 AM and after 9:00 PM. Reach for carrots and cucumbers when craving crunch. Dunk them in ground-up chickpeas with tahini or a bit of olive oil. Thinly slice your favorite veggies in a casserole dish, add a low-sodium tomato sauce, sprinkle the top with your favorite cheese and bake it for one half-hour at 350°F. You'll have an easy, veggie-filled casserole. Make a ratatouille by chopping and lightly sautéing onions, eggplant and squashes with tomatoes. Eat warm or cold. Make a salad and toss it with a creamy dressing made by blending an avocado and a tomato. Season it with pepper. Pick some grapes off the vine and put them in a plastic bag in the freezer. Nibble them when frozen for a sweet treat. Freeze peeled bananas. Once fully frozen, blend them in a blender with a little half-and-half for the best "ice cream" ever!

It's your body. Time to say: The health with it!

COURAGE UP

"Courage," said Hemingway, "is grace under pressure." Maya Angelou declared courage to be "the most important of virtues, because it was required to practice all other virtues," such as "insight, sympathy and solitude," according to Nietzsche.

Summoning our courage in any situation requires putting ourselves at risk. When we risk acting or communicating with another in such a way that requires courage, at the root of our motivation is love. With any act of courage, as we risk our physical or emotional safety, we've acknowledged something to be either right or wrong and we are exposing ourselves, hoping for a meaningful outcome.

Throughout history, the words "courage" and "fortitude" have been used interchangeably. Fortitude, by definition, is our strength and firmness of mind. Boldness, bravery, determination, endurance, grit, moxie, patience, conviction, perseverance, stamina, staying power, tenacity, backbone, dauntlessness and heart are all synonyms.

We are acting courageously when we deal with failures. Admitting we are wrong requires bravery. When we decide to offer help to another even if we're tired or feel as if we're lacking resources, we're summoning fortitude. When we ask for what we need we're strengthening our backbone. When we do unto others first, knowing they might or might not return the favor, we're acting dauntlessly.

Courage is not absence of fear. It's acting even when we're fearful, knowing an unknown outcome awaits. We risk taking those chances if we believe the outcome might be more important.

Today is a good day to ask what situation or relationship might change for the better if we summon up our courage to act and take a personal risk.

RONG

When we risk being (w)rong, new possibilities open up for us.

If we're willing to gooph-up, make miztakes, do something that might be in earor, be less than pressice, take a chanze—life improvs because we've stopped trying to be perfek and possibilities become possible because we might fail and be rong, but we might be rite.

It takes a lot of time and energy to always feel like we need to be right. Shoot, even riskin ritin' this paragraf was very hared since I'm someone who rites and ed-uts for a livin and thinks spellun is importunt.

Try it. U can do it. Let's do it 2gether. Lettuce let go of being perfek and see what happens. Tell me all abow't it.

PROBLEM SOLVED

Problems often resolve themselves in ways we least expect. On the flip side, we can't expect problems to be solved only in the ways we propose. There are usually many ways to solve the same problem.

I look at problems as a form of communication. For more than 25 years, I've owned a public relations firm. We've been hired to help companies and individuals communicate their developments—whether they were positive or less than. My entire amazing team has been working with me for more than 10 years. I think one of the reasons we get along so well and have been able to work together is because, as a leader, I've learned that how one person might write a press release or relay a story or say something to offer an answer or do something in an attempt to solve an issue—might be entirely different than the way I would have written, said or done it. Yet their approach works. It might not be the way I'd have done it, but I cannot deny its end effectiveness. So I've learned not to edit, interrupt or stop the flow and process.

The more we can let go of our need to control and step out of the way to allow others to exercise their creative problem-solving skills, the better we become as a group and as individuals. This principle works with spouses, children and other family members as well.

We don't have to "do it all." We don't have to be "experts in everything." We do have to do what we do to the best of our abilities and let others do the same. When we manage to do this, we all enjoy the benefits of more successful relationships on all fronts. If we ask or simply allow others to help solve the big or small problems that inevitably arise because this is life, everything tends to unfold better.

THE BEST DAY

The best day in your life is today. Not yesterday. Not tomorrow, no matter what you're planning. Not the future day of some major life event you're anticipating celebrating, either.

You might be questioning this truth for any number of reasons. No doubt there are many issues pending in your life, just like mine and everyone else's. Here's a mental readjustment tip: While we think happiness is a kind of joy we attain, this is illusory—and actually a mind game that keeps happiness elusive. Greater joy and life satisfaction are really about doing our best to reduce our stress levels in the life we're living now.

The more quickly we can flip our mental mindset to seeing ways we can reduce our stresses, the greater happiness we will feel.

Having studied the power of the mind and hypnosis for 20+ years (I am a card-carrying member of the Hypnotherapists Union and the American Counselors Association), I can firmly say: Although we cannot completely rid ourselves of stress, we can change our mindset about who and what is stressing us—and bring our body into the reduction-equation through breathing.

To get our mindset under our management, we need to accept that everyone is on their own journey. We're the tour director of our journey and everyone else is responsible for theirs. Yes, our paths cross and intertwine. But major levels of stress are reduced if we keep the focus on ourselves and what we can do. When we do, our sense of empowerment grows.

None of us knows what's coming next, other than what we choose to do. Make the choice to focus on choosing, following through with action, instead of worrying about what everyone else is doing around you. Doing this offers the best guarantee for greater happiness and joy.

FNA

Anger from another is not an affront to our being. The fact is that anger is intimately entwined with fear. When we start getting angry or notice someone else is, it is a worthwhile goal to try to remember that what we're really feeling or witnessing in another at some level is fear.

If we could recognize that fear is at the root of most expressions of anger, we would be far more compassionate and understanding in the moment. Sympathetic tenderness would also allow each of us not to take another's anger personally. Rather, we would see the anger as a problem that can be resolved with kindhearted discussion—or understand the action that triggered the sense of fear to arise.

DAM(N)IT

We often unconsciously put a lid on our hearts, which are our own unlimited sources of power. We seal up our potential for greater enjoyment and rewards in any relationship or circumstance by blindly allowing our minds to roam. This is why stopping to do nothing except breathe and clear our thoughts is vital to increasing our sense of happiness and satisfaction.

Our heart is our source of power. As long as it is beating, we are alive with potential to fulfill our greatness. Envision your heart as a spring of water or a fountain: Energy ready to flow forth into the world, refreshing all in its path. Our thoughts are like streams. As such, they can get blocked. Maybe it's not a coincidence that obstructions in a river are called a "Dam(n)?!"

Our thoughts are immensely powerful. When we allow our energy to flow forth, springing up from our hearts, our thoughts stream positively. When we plug our energy with negative thinking, the connection between our hearts and minds becomes obstructed (dammit!), and life, people and situations feel like they are drowning our spirit.

The only way to keep the heart and mind connection flowing with positive energy is to stop and breathe. To take a moment to clear out all thoughts. To allow our hearts to fulfill their role of helping to move fresh oxygen into our lungs, through our veins and into our brains.

If there is only one extra thing you can squeeze into today to make your life a bit better, do this: Stop and breathe. Take the minute. Even better, take three to four one-minute breaks throughout your day. When you can, do this for two minutes or longer: Nothing but breathing with eyes closed or while looking at a pleasant image. Stop, breathe, clear your head. This is how we reconnect our hearts and minds.

TEACHERS

While we might not like the lesson, everyone we meet and interact with is a teacher.

Teachers come in all kinds of packages. Although we might like our life lessons to be associated with beautiful locations filled with pleasant people who are equally delightful to look at and hang with, this isn't reality. A fact of real life is that the teachers who really put us to the test are those whom we find annoying throughout our day. These are the folks who say and do things we'd never say or do. Those with traits we so very much dislike. Those who act in ways we find annoying, distasteful, outlandish or basically unacceptable. These are our gurus. They are teaching us lessons about ourselves and life in countless ways.

When our beliefs clash with others, this is when we really have to stop. And then breathe our way to greater acceptance of the other—and dare I suggest, ourselves as well.

Acceptance doesn't mean we have to like whatever has irked us. Rather, it means we try to recognize it as a sign of suffering and maybe we can see another human working through their own journey, as are we.

In life, we don't get to connect only with those we think are groovy and cool. Everyday life requires interactions with every kind of person. And each interaction deserves our respect and peaceful response, which might be best displayed by our silence while quietly (and without drama) taking several deep breaths. Not easy. But that's why Zen—which means "a mind not fixed and open to everything"—is called a "practice." We practice so that when the moments arrive, maybe we'll get just a little better each time at being kinder and more understanding of another in this game called life.

SPEED OF LIGHT

Although one way to look at age is to hope we don't die before we get old, far better is to actually grow up without growing old. To be 80 years young is way better than to be 40 years old.

Since "now" passes at the speed of light, or 186,000 miles per second, today is a good time to do the things that keep you young at heart. If you're not sure what those things might be, ask yourself what is it you do that when you do it, time passes like the speed of light.

Whatever "that" is will give you the answer as to what will keep you young at heart—and you want to be spending more of your time doing more of that!

VIBRATION

Vibrations are waves of energy, emotional states, the atmosphere of a place and associations to something as communicated and/or felt by others. Vibrations can be well-received—like the feeling we have when listening to music—or, conversely, unpleasant as vibrations from loud machinery squealing through the air.

As energy vibrations come in many forms, we each must consciously attune ourselves to the positive vibes that flow through the universe via the godliness in each of us and in nature. Waves of love, hope, joy, wisdom, courage, equality, justice, fairness, strength, healing, abundance and progress will flow continually if you choose to tune into their wavelengths and become a receiver.

Send out positive vibrations and the same returns. Vibrate at your highest possible frequency by consciously striving to reduce your negative thoughts. Do this by recognizing them, then visualize changing your emotional channel in the direction of a positive thought about the same person or situation (or anything else if this is too difficult) so you can vibrate higher.

If you think I'm getting flaky, listen to Einstein, who said: "Everything in life is vibration. Match the frequency of the reality you want and you cannot help but get that reality. It can be no other way. This is not philosophy. This is physics."

Appreciation is the ultimate way to raise your positive vibrational energy. How you vibrate will determine what waves the universe sends back to you. When heartfelt prayer for the good of us all becomes the vibration of the mind and self, we can create miracles.

ENERGY INVENTORY

Is your energy dipping? It might be time for an energy inventory.

Life force equals energy. When energy falters, this is a sign we are focusing on, consumed by or doing too many things that drain energy. Signs of this include: increased agitation; short tempers; throat tickles and coughs; skin blemishes; poor sleep; headaches; heart palpitations; circles under the eyes; weight gain or unexpected weight loss; flu-like symptoms and general malaise.

Everything we do demands energy. But poor diet, lack of physical activity, saying yes when we need to say no, late nights, too much alcohol, drugs (prescribed or otherwise) and smoking all drain our energy. These, plus too many negative emotional thoughts, steal energy.

When we do an energy inventory, we ask ourselves what situations, activities, habits and obligations are causing our life force to bleed away. Once identified, we need to decide if these draining aspects can be modified or eliminated, and how.

This is not assuming that a quick fix is necessarily imminent. Nor is there a solution to propose that fits for everyone. However, while you are working on finding your personal solutions, there are a few things we can all do: Take a nap. See a friend. Read a book. Prioritize your "to do" list and remove inessentials while adding something specifically for you at the top. Spend as little time as possible with those who steal your wind. If these involve work or caregiving situations, try to schedule set times when you will fulfill the obligation. Keep a list of the good things in your life and refer to it immediately before and after dealing with those who thrive in negativity. Take a class that is for you alone—you don't have to tell anyone you're doing it. Explore artistic or musical endeavors. Get out in nature. Take a drive and play music. Cook a meal with five or fewer natural ingredients. Enjoy eating it by candlelight.

While we can't control time, we do have the power to control our energy levels. One measure of life is how long we live—but the more significant measure is how much energy we have when we're living it.

CARS AND HORSES

Just because we can get behind the wheel of a car built to go 200+ mph, doesn't mean we should drive that fast. Same for riding horses: Although we might wear a cowboy hat, this doesn't mean we should jump hurdles unless we have been adequately trained.

What we can do and what is prudent to do may be two different things. Knowing the difference is maturity, which can come at any age—and which is also a synonym for adulthood or the state of being fully developed in mind and body as a person.

Now, this is not to say we shouldn't race in the Indy 500 or the Kentucky Derby! However, to do either, or anything else we desire, we need to study and prepare, understand the risks and be willing to fail in our endeavor.

But on that note, remember that any initial endeavor may be coupled with failure. Still, this is not the same as defeat. I've failed many times and so have you. We all have! Failed in relationships, controlling tempers, business, healthy diet choices, exercise—the list is long and personal.

Yet as long as we haven't allowed these failures to defeat us, we've grown. We've dusted ourselves off and tried again. Frankly, in many ways, we've won the race and earned our place in the Winner's Circle of life. It's time to notice your achievements—of which you have many—and enjoy a bit of a victory celebration!

Don't wait. Rejoice in your life's triumphs to date. Count them. Don't linger on the failures, except to find the lesson and confirm your strength. Acknowledge your achievements. Honor who you are and who you've become as a result of rising up after getting bucked time and time again.

EASY AND HARD

Life is hard if we only want to do what's easy. But if we're willing to face all the challenges and do what's hard even when we don't feel like it, surprisingly life gets easier. I have a lot of theories and examples as to why and how this is so, but not enough space to expand upon them. Nonetheless, I know this to be true and it's worth thinking about carefully.

MEAN

Want to know the number one way we are mean to ourselves and others? It's this: Recalling over and over in our heads—or spitting out to another—something that happened in the past that nobody can change and can't be taken back. Doing this is how we beat up those we love—and this includes putting ourselves in that category of those we love. All of us have said and done things that we wish we hadn't. Yet mentally repeating or bringing up old news halts every form of progress in any relationship, including our relationships with ourselves. Everyone just feels bad. Today is a good day to think long and hard about what benefit we could possibly be getting from holding onto past hurt and anger. Personally? I can't think of any benefit at all. This means it's time to forgive ourselves and others so we can get on with living life in the present, which is the only place we can make different choices for better outcomes. As Forrest Gump reminds us: "You've got to put the past behind you before you can move on."

TOMORROW

While the only guarantee in life is the moment, be optimistic about tomorrow. No matter what is happening today, go to sleep with your last thought of the day being: Tomorrow will be a better day.

This puts your faith to the test. Believe that today was better than yesterday and tomorrow is going to be your best day ever. Instead of worrying about tomorrow, we can each train ourselves to believe an even better day is coming.

Just imagine if we could each start practicing this and—even better—putting our faith to the test and becoming believers. Smiles would be on every face. Enthusiasm would be bursting forth. Eyes would be sparkling and hearts would be open to giving and receiving more love.

Practice saying: Tomorrow is going to be even better than today. Remind yourself of this whenever possible. Remember, your mind will strive to move in the direction of what you repeat with conviction. Say it to others too! When you meet people who are struggling, look them in their eyes, hold their hands and assure them: Tomorrow is going to be a better day.

Happiness is found in the moment while believing the future will be bright. Youbettabelieveit!

FLOW

Energy fills each of us individually and collectively. This energy is the power source that flows through the veins of the universe, connecting each and every one of us, heart-to-heart. We can either keep the flow going or shut it off, much like a tourniquet stops the flowing of our blood and will ultimately deaden a limb if not released.

Like any form of energy, we can either welcome this life force flowing through humanity or resist it. Our happiness lies in welcoming it and sharing love—even when we don't necessarily feel like it.

We harness this energy for our own benefit and that of others by showering happiness onto others in any ways we can and, by example, teaching these others how to share their happiness energy.

When we notice our flow being adversely affected, we have turned off something in our minds via our thoughts. Anger toward another is the surest way to stop the flow that creates our happiness. Likewise, focusing on what we don't have will halt the flow as well.

Seeing the godliness in each other, while thinking about all that we have, are the surest ways to reap universal positive energy for greater life force.

Together, Silver Disobedients, we are a life-force, super-empowering, collective consciousness of higher intelligence and love!

DANCING

Whenever we feel stuck in a rut in a relationship, it's because—figuratively speaking—all parties are waltzing through. Somehow the status quo has been deemed acceptable, even if it's not, and nobody is attempting to change things up. If this is the case, why would we experience anything different? If we want to interact differently with another, we have to risk changing the dance moves. It might be time to get radical and do the hustle.

In all relationships, the minute one dance partner risks changing up their moves, the other notices—and possibly resists (or at least starts asking a lot of questions!). Regardless, the dynamics shift. Suddenly, new conversations can start because they are no longer silenced. Changes become possible. Life can advance in new ways.

If we want changes, we don't have to wait for our dance partners to change it up for us. Instead, try taking the risk of leading the dance of life by testing out some new moves.

PERSPECTIVE

In art, perspective is showing the right (or wrong) relationship between visible objects. In communication, perspective reflects our attitudes toward things and an understanding of their relative importance.

Either way, perspective provides us with a sense of proportion. And at all times, it helps to keep the relative proportion of any discussion, situation or event—or the comparative relationship of it to the entirety of our lives—in perspective.

Whatever is happening at any moment is merely a part, portion, bit, piece, percentage, fraction, segment or share of the entirety of our life—even when the moment seems like it is everything.

The perceptions we have regarding our lives and the world-at-large can change at any moment based on our perspective and whether we choose to see things positively, negatively or neutrally.

It's helpful to remember that the primary cause of our unhappiness is rarely another person or a situation, but rather our thoughts about it.

As such, when moments requiring perspective arise, our goal needs to be to keep the event, comment or situation in proportional perspective: Not making it bigger or smaller.

Our reality about our lives reflects our personal perspective.

THE COAT

A man was hosting a banquet. He invited all the wealthy friends he had. One arrived dressed in a torn and dirty hooded coat that he had worn all day while he worked side-by-side with his men, tilling the land of his vast fields. The host, not recognizing his friend, chased him away without extending a kind gesture. The man went home, changed into his formal coat and returned. With great respect, he was then welcomed by all. As he entered the banquet room, he put his fine coat on a chair and said: "I expect you invited the robe since you showed me away a little while ago," and he left.

When I think of this little Zen parable, it reminds me of so many perceptions today, many of which are magnified by social media.

Life is about people, not possessions. Although possessions are nice, they do not define our value.

REASONABLE

"The reasonable man adapts himself to the world; the unreasonable one persists in trying to adapt the world to himself. Therefore, all progress depends on the unreasonable man," wrote George Bernard Shaw.

That's a lot to consider!

Most of us were raised being asked to be reasonable and cooperative. Not drawing too much attention to ourselves. Fitting in. Being seen, not heard.

A survey of the news suggests some people are either rebelling against these expectations or they've been raised differently. I'd like to propose that—somewhere between these extremes— communication, peace and happiness can improve on personal levels for all.

The idea is this: For our most important relationships, it's up to us to set certain ground rules for ourselves and others, defining what we want and asking for it directly. We are old enough to know what we want and strong enough to handle the rejection if the answer is no, but smart enough to know the answer might be yes!

Further, owning our "unreasonable" natures means it's prudent to stop assuming we think we know what others want. If someone is important to us, it's time to risk asking about their preferences. Sharing our thoughts and asking others to share theirs constitute investments in the health of our important relationships. Nobody benefits when a missed opportunity to ask a preference becomes a matter of, "I didn't ask because I thought you wouldn't want to." (This can actually be perceived as passive-aggressive, which is not a great trait.)

When we accept that it is our responsibility to ask for what we want and need, others might or might not be receptive. But it will put an end to guessing games that can lie at the root of disappointment. Speaking up moves conversations out of our heads and into the realm of new possibilities.

SLEEP

Happiness, strength, memory, fitness, weight, anxiety, moods, skin, health and our emotions all benefit from rest.

As we age, health risks from lack of adequate sleep can become serious.

While there are no guarantees for avoiding heart disease, heart attacks or diabetes, seven to nine hours of sleep every night might keep them in abeyance.

There aren't many people who don't actually like to sleep. However, there are many who have trouble falling and staying asleep.

Here are a few tips for helping us when we hit the pillow and decide to call it a night:

- Avoid caffeine six hours before bed and alcohol at least two hours prior.
- Exercise—walking more counts. Avoid napping after dinner. Try a warm evening bath or shower.
- Read a book, which will tire your eyes, instead of surfing the web, which will stimulate them.
- When you notice you're sleepy, get in bed if you can.
- Break the habits of working in bed or watching TV.
- If possible, get yourself up every day at the same time regardless of when you went to sleep.
- Before getting into bed, write down anything worrying you or that you don't want to forget, so you don't wake up worrying you're going to forget something.
- When you can't sleep, get up and read until your eyes get sleepy again.
- Eliminate as much light as possible in your bedroom during sleep time.
- Turn off electronic dingers on phones and other devices.
- Keep the temperature of your bedroom between 65°F and 68°F and use light, cozy covers.
- Ask your doctor if a melatonin supplement is suitable for you. Past age 50, melatonin, the brain hormone that acts as a sleep agent, declines.

Lastly, if you find yourself waking and feeling distressed, keep a pen and paper by your bedside. Write down whatever you're thinking about. Then tell yourself that this is sleep time and you can work on the issue in the morning.

THE DEVIL'S ADVOCATE

The term "devil's advocate" describes someone willing to take an opposing position in a debate that they might or might not necessarily agree with, just to explore the position further. For some people (like my children), this is a really annoying practice—and I've been ailing from it my entire life. Maybe it's because I was born under the zodiac sign of Pisces—those fish swimming in two different directions that can't make up their minds.

Although I've often wondered why I want to argue the contrarian perspective as if it were my own, I know it's helped me learn and be far more open-minded to ideas to which I might have otherwise never considered or given credence.

If someone states something that I agree or disagree with, by immersing myself in the opposite perspective for a debate, my thinking is forced to become clearer, aligned or totally flipped around.

Genuinely trying to find points to validate an opposing position enables us to see things from a different light. (It also sometimes upsets the counterparty, who might not really be up for a debate, so it pays to ask to share another perspective before charging forward.) By doing so, we acquire new information and an education, while biases are forced to be confronted.

By looking at something differently, we can see why the issue might be mired in misunderstandings. Those who risk seeing all sides of an argument have quite different perspectives than one who only sees one side. By challenging ourselves to see both sides, the likelihood of understanding any person or situation increases.

Experiences and debates throughout life combine to make us who we are. Yet we are not concrete. If we allow our conversations (and life) to flow, our thoughts are more like water: Able to form new shapes based on the "containers" or situations to which we open ourselves through willingness to hear different perspectives. Suddenly we may find ourselves exploring new ideas— freed from habitual thinking, breaking out and trying new things—because it expands our perspectives on what is possible, right or the proverbial "only way." We gain new ways to see ourselves, others and situations. Exposure is growth. Growth is invigorating.

REVIEW MIRRORS

Inside everyone older than 50, there's a 20-year-old wondering, "What the heck happened?"

We got older—and that's better than not having this opportunity. The really great secret that aging allows us to understand—which is at the root of our disbelief about our age—is that we really haven't changed that much in our 50, 60, 70 or 80+ years and we still retain much of our 20-year-old selves. Of course our bodies change, but the essence of who we are—our spirit—doesn't change that much.

Yes, we get knocked around and build back up by living. We cry a little and hopefully laugh a lot more. We sometimes stay and other times move on. It's the continuum of life. The time flies by every day when we're not even noticing (unless we're sitting in traffic or late for a meeting).

We got older.

Now, lots of old people don't get wiser with age—but aging is a catalyst in the process of accruing greater wisdom along with appreciation for others, life in general and a more spontaneous, childlike sense of fun.

So, for those wondering, "How can I accept aging?" Or more importantly, "How do we ignore any negative thoughts we might have about age?" We start by reminding ourselves we are still the very same person we always were.

Think of it this way: We're not getting older—we're becoming classics!

Don't stop looking forward and living your life—and while you're at it? Forget your age.

OLD IS IN

"Savage" is an old word with a new meaning these days. According to teenagers, if you call someone "savage" it is a form of compliment. It means that although the delivery of the message might be a little rough, they admire that the person says and does what they want to say and do without worrying about what everyone else thinks they should be saying and doing.

Do you think it's a coincidence that the "cool" associated with being savage has to do with the fact that getting comfortable with being who we are—and doing what we want—is directly related to the root of the word "age?"

Looks to me that what's old is in. Go have a savage day!

WHATCHAGONNADOABOUTIT

To increase the odds that exciting new outcomes will present themselves to us, we have to stay in the present. If we're feeling sad, pessimistic, mournful, sorrowful, bitter or melancholy, we're likely spending too much time thinking about the past. When we start to feel anxious, nervous, afraid, apprehensive or scared, it's likely we're focusing too much on the future. Yet neither the past nor future will give us accurate guidance about what is going on right now.

While the importance of appreciating our limited time on Earth tends to become clearer with each year of living, it's a characteristic we can hone at any time because it's a matter of choice.

It's only right now that we have the opportunity to decide what we're going to do to make a difference in our relationships, health, work lives, personal lives or anything else. We can spend hours contemplating, but it's our actions in any given moment that will make the difference of a better life or not.

While the winds of change might not always cooperate with our plans, we can still use their force to propel us to where we want to go. So whatchagonnadoaboutit now?

TAKEN

If you need a good reason to be yourself, here you go: Everyone else is taken.

Yup, you. And me. And all of us. We've never existed before and will never exist again. No two people have ever been the same, nor will they ever be. Not today. Not ever.

More amazing? Because of this, there's nothing holding back all that is defining who we are or what we can be. This is our play. We get to tell our story, play the game, whichever way we want. No rules except our own—along with a few laws that probably make sense to follow. Think about it.

SITUATION

"We've got a situation" is a stock phrase for saying we've got a problem that needs a solution. Often when a situation arises, our tendency is to look for who is at fault as we seek to assign blame.

When this happens, we're experiencing a form of spiritual interference. Instead of recognizing our connectedness and the fact that—like it or not—we're all in this thing called "life" together, we begin to separate. This separation is at the root of loneliness, depression, hurt and a whole slew of emotional states that none of us particularly enjoys.

When we have a situation, perhaps it might help to stop and carefully consider whether the fault-finding we immediately resort to is really our own foundation of beliefs—or maybe, just maybe, something we picked up along our life journey that is worth examining.

Fault-finding thinking is usually rooted in learned behavior. But that doesn't make this an opportunity to blame our parents or other teachers. After all, that would be fault-finding thinking too. Rather, the idea here is to stop and think about the judgments we make, because this is the way we can begin to understand how our past conditioning impacts our present relationships for better or for worse—and maybe it's time for a thought-audit.

Before assigning blame in any situation, it's a worthwhile exercise not to react but rather to ask ourselves: Do I have an old issue that's still lurking around in the recesses of my mind that's making me immediately defensive, angry, frustrated and ready to blow a gasket?

Old pipes and steaming can create all kinds of destruction that will impact our relationships. So before we blow our tops over a situation, stop and silently ask: Do we really need blame or is this a good time to work together to find a compromise or solution?

REINVENTION

The best way to define our future is to reinvent it. There is absolutely nothing concrete and predictable happening in the next minute. Not in the next hour. Not tomorrow either. So there is nothing stopping you from reinventing yourself right now. We each get to decide if we want to change in any way for the better and move forward or not. Just like well-known brands hire agencies to update their images to stay vital in the eyes of consumers, we ourselves benefit from updates, refreshing new looks and even extremes of total self-reinvention—like new careers, moves and more.

The more we put our inventing abilities to the test in the present, the more likely we will increase our feelings of being invigorated as we up the daily ante for the possibilities of greater life satisfaction.

It's never too late to say, "Today's the day I'm reinventing myself." Try it! It's very addicting and invigorating to allow yourself to be different every day.

Although your reinvention could be something large—and we'll leave the definition of "large" to you—it all counts! A new haircut, wild nail polish color, driving down a different road or being more observant on the one we're on, risking a conversation with someone, scribbling and doodling to explore our artistic side, writing a poem, penning a love letter and maybe even giving it to someone, sharing a new idea with the boss or a client, sporting a new pair of eyeglasses, wearing a shirt in a color we've never considered before—whatever.

Nothing can stop us from reinventing our future right now. Self-reinvention is actually an excellent example of hope in action.

A NEW LOOK

Whenever we start acting a bit snappy toward another, it's typically triggered because of how we're perceiving their behavior.

Upon noticing that we're feeling irked by someone, it really helps to try recalling how hard it is to change ourselves and our own behaviors.

By channeling our frustrations into a personal self-assessment about our abilities, challenges, successes and the time invested into changing our own habits (successfully and unsuccessfully), we begin to understand the low likelihood of changing another's.

Suddenly, like putting on glasses, our focus can shift back to looking at our perspectives and judgments—and what about them might need to be adjusted or released.

WRONG

At some stage of our lives, we picked up a slew of worries about being wrong.

Babies don't worry about being wrong—they just are. They're not worrying about wailing their opinion about a soggy diaper, hunger, loneliness, distress or anything else. It's natural to newborns to wake up a household without any worry about being wrong. But as we progress through life, for any number of reasons, we begin to fear doing those things we want to do that might not meet the full approval of others.

Nobody likes being in a position whereby we're exposed as incorrect, mistaken, inaccurate, imprecise, faulty or just plain off the mark. But here's the thing: We need to risk being wrong. Here's why: By allowing ourselves to be wrong, we're actually removing a lot of pressure that we put on ourselves. It's a heavy burden to think we must always be right. People often won't take the risk of being wrong because they think by stifling an idea, opinion, thought, creation or otherwise—all so they can't be wrong—that they will preserve the status quo. But it doesn't work that way because there are no guarantees in life that anything will be preserved, period. Likewise, there are no guarantees that if you risk being wrong that you *will* be wrong. Maybe you will be off-the-charts, supercalifragilisticexpialidocious right! In fact, better than right! Because no matter how you calculate being right, trying to please the world of others with your every move—your "maybe right" gets dull, loses its punch and gets boring.

Risk speaking up about what you want. Share your crazy idea. By allowing ourselves to be wrong, suddenly everything becomes possible. Trust me on this. It works in every kind of relationship—business or personal—more often than not.

PRODUCTIVE PANIC

We can all learn to panic productively. To do this means being patient—because patience can wait, ask questions and make decisions based on the whole picture.

Not everything we'll need to consider can be made sense of. Still, we're old enough now to trust our instincts and make moments of panic productive by stepping back and looking at the situations with patience—knowing that life is somehow unfolding as it should. Now we just have to take all the new information and calmly figure out what to do with it!

Remember: Panic and stress are never good outfit accessories!

TIME

Time is the indefinite continued progress of existence and events that occurs in apparently irreversible succession from the past through the present to the future, according to a collaborative definition found on Wikipedia.

Philosophers have long debated whether it is a fundamental facet of the universe—a dimension independent of events—or a purely intellectual construct existing only to allow humans to sequence and compare events.

Whatever we believe, how we use each of our 24 hours will determine who we become. More valuable than money, time cannot be borrowed from others. We only have our own time and how we use it will largely impact our peace, happiness and success.

Many people speak about "killing time," which is a rather disturbing thought at any time of life, considering its finite nature in respect to a lifetime.

Many don't know where their time goes. If this is you, try recording it. Keep a log of hours and activities. Analyze it so you can see how you actually spend this precious commodity.

Often, we think we lack time to do things we want to do. Yet once we actually start recording what we are doing on a daily basis with our time, quite often we realize ways we're squandering it.

Upon reviewing our "time spent" list, we can prioritize the time we're spending. Did it provide a return on our investment? Did we become happier, smarter, stronger, wiser, relaxed or something otherwise constructive? Or did we merely fill gaps?

How we choose to spend our time is a highly personal choice. But the best way we can spend it is doing something that makes us intangibly wiser: building our joy, strength, focus, attention, care, consideration and capabilities.

Doing what we must. Eliminating the unnecessary. Delegating if possible. Prioritizing whatever is important to us. Time has a wonderful way of showing us what really matters.

CURIOUS

Curiosity and inquisitiveness—the urge to investigate and learn something new, different and not wholly known—is one of the characteristics of youth. Note: Curiosity is not a characteristic exclusive to the young; it is a characteristic of youthfulness, which is anyone's for the taking.

Einstein said, "Do not grow old no matter how long you live. Never cease to stand like curious children before the Great Mystery into which we were born." That's great advice from a smart guy.

In life, we can be curious about anything and everything. Maybe we're curious about the workings of our minds or those of others, and opt to make it a lifelong study in our free time. Aspects of nature. Alien life. Art and its origins and creators. Parallel universes. How to make cheese, why it gets moldy but we still eat it. Whether Jung was right about collective consciousness. What language will help us communicate best and how can we learn it. Technology and coding. Electricity. Peace and how it begins with "me." What dreams really reflect about life, ourselves and others—or not. Building, architecture and the engineering that keeps bridges suspended and buildings erect. The ingredients that make a meal most memorable. Why some people make yarn into sweaters versus knots. The flow of water and modern plumbing. How a boat stays afloat. How seeds actually produce foods and flowers. And my favorite: What we learned from our mistakes—and if they really were mistakes or actually essential lessons.

When we're curious and learning, we're expanding our minds. Keeping our minds curious is one of the best ways to maintain function for the long haul. Curiosity is also a great indicator of our passions. What we're curious about often shows us the pathway to greater life satisfaction. When we're exploring something that interests us, we feel more engaged and alive.

We're all curious about something. Maybe many things. What are you curious about? Are you exploring all you can learn about it?

OXYGEN

Anyone who's ever flown in a plane has heard the flight attendant say: "Before trying to help anyone else, put on your own oxygen mask." This advice is important not just for surviving midair disasters; it is also common sense for living a long, healthy life.

For many, the reason we don't prioritize ourselves is that we're afraid others will view us as being selfish. The idea of putting our self-care first on our list of priorities is perceived as running counter to the positive traits we try to uphold.

Let's break down this false thinking: First, we can't control what anyone thinks about us. And second, don't you think everyone benefits if we're less stressed, happier and healthier?

Putting ourselves last is kind of an extension of sometime long ago when we didn't finish dinner and someone shamed us by saying: "Don't you know there are starving people in the world?" While this is true and we don't want to waste food, this thinking originates from fear of scarcity versus joyful abundance.

Taking care of ourselves doesn't take time away from anyone or anything else. It actually enhances our stamina, giving us more oomph to spend better quality time with those we love, and hopefully adds energy to do more things that increase our life satisfaction, which also would make us each more pleasant to be around!

When life stresses are building from all that we manage daily, if we haven't allowed time for exercise and preparing proper, nutritious meals, we're gambling and playing health roulette.

Taking care of our health needs to be everyone's number one priority. We each need to figure out how to rewrite our schedules.

Don't forget: We can't get to work and care for our families if we get sick. So first things first: Remember that what we eat, how we move our bodies, getting adequate rest, laughing and having fun are as essential as breathing.

NEGOTIATIONS

Life is a series of negotiations, starting with our parents, then teachers, friends, work environments, the mating game and ultimately with new families we might create or inherit. I once read that the first thing to decide before walking into any negotiation is what to do if the other party says "no." While it's always good to have a plan, it's equally important to have a plan if the answer is "yes."

Not getting what we want often makes us work harder, develop new plans, reach out to new connections or makes us decide: It's just not for us.

Getting what we want? That's a whole new conundrum. Thus the expression, "Be careful what you wish for because you might get it."

When we get what we think we want, the stakes are raised as are the insecurities. Are we ready to do the work? Do they really know who we are? Can we handle it? What if we're not ready?

We've all had these situations of doubt. While success might be defined as getting what we want, we need to really think about: What do we want?

When we feel like we're not getting what we want, often it's because we're actually not willing to do what is necessary to get it. Possibly the price is too high personally, emotionally, physically or otherwise. When observing people successful in careers, activities, relationships, and more, it might seem like they really want whatever it is they are succeeding at. It's very important to them and they understand that if they want it, there's nothing to lose by going for it and giving it their all. They're not sitting back, waiting for anything. Rather, whether it's courting a customer, mate, job or anything else, they're getting out there and making it happen. The dreams are now grounded in the reality of doing, which might result in dreams coming true.

Now, the person who's been "doing" to achieve a goal might not feel like "their dreams are coming true," while observers might trivialize it as such. Rather, the doer is likely to believe they have found something that's making them happy and that they're getting rewarded for working toward a goal. It's not luck. It's commitment to try and try again—even when we're tired of negotiating and wondering why someone doesn't just do what we want and notice how great we are. People are noticing. Unfortunately, too many of us quit because we stopped believing that what we want is ours for the taking, if we work for it, and possibly with a lot of compromises along the way.

Keep negotiating and finding new ways to get your vision recognized. And when it's not being noticed, recognize that not getting what we want is actually a priceless experience that tends to make us stronger, better and more creative—assuming we choose to keep finding new ways to negotiate our daily challenges.

REVEALS

Do you overprotect your heart? Many of us miss out on a lot of wonderful relationships—with lovers, friends and colleagues—because we've become jaded from past hurts and/or we are afraid that we can no longer trust our own judgments.

If we ever get stuck in this reaction mode, three primary things are happening: 1) We are stuck on a replay of past experiences and reenacting our role in those past experiences while casting others in our played-out plays; 2) We are focusing on imperfect words instead of actions; and 3) We are rushing the relationships and forgetting to allow time to unfold on its own accord. We most often do this when we're trying to get to some form of intimacy or deeper trust that we're craving, yet the nature of trust takes time to develop so we can genuinely feel secure.

Trust that time and your real eyes will realize real lies.

Real reveals itself with time and our observation of actions. All good things take time to grow. Right now, the ground and trees might appear gray, dull and dormant. Yet with time, nature reveals where beauty might lie.

DISAPPOINTMENTS

Have you ever considered that disappointment might actually be a doorway to opportunity?

We tend to feel disappointment if our hopes or expectations have somehow not been fulfilled.

Expecting is not a crime and disappointment need not be a punishment. Instead, expectations and disappointments can both be opportunities to assess our personal realities.

I don't mind disappointments. They really get me thinking. What did I expect? Why did I think it would be so? How could I have possibly altered or improved the outcome? Was I adequately prepared or committed? When might I be ready to try again? Who did I expect to help—did I put more weight on another than myself? Where did I expect to get to/go—and is that still possible if I alter my expectations, choices or actions? How can I improve so my expectations are rewarded in the future?

We're all old enough to know that we won't always get our own way. Yet we're also wise enough when we put on our rose-colored glasses to figure out new ways to improve our outcomes in the future.

REFRAME

Can you imagine life if we each chose to stop using past negative experiences and emotions that are associated with our recollections of others, as present-day references? Certainly, it would take a lot of practice, but if we're not individually in control of our thoughts, words and actions, who is?

There is rarely a benefit in holding onto hurtful or painful memories related to others in our lives, past or present. It's faulty thinking to believe these memories will somehow protect us now or necessarily apply in the future.

The only reason we might want to recall an adverse past experience with another is if we can reframe it as an experience that contributed beneficially to our growth and helped to make us the wonderful beings we are today. If professional help is necessary to accomplish this, it's a good investment.

The practice of waking up and reframing (or visualizing) each day, ourselves and others as "clean slates" helps us see the opportunities, uniqueness, spontaneity, joy, happiness, potential and more in the moment.

Reframing is not easy but it's the root of love.

GOBEYOU

An original mind is rarely understood, so get used to being misunderstood. We are all originals, which means to some degree we'll all be misconceived by others in one way or another.

Originality is the entrance of personal style and expression in every sense of the word. It is creativity at its finest and creativity is a like a spigot—the more you turn it on and use it, the more new, original ideas will flow.

Don't fret about having your originality misinterpreted: Only those stuck in unoriginal thinking will oppose you. Perhaps you'll kickstart their thinking and they will thank you.

Originality is essential to inspiration and change. Be the change. As Nietzsche reminds us: "No price is too high to pay for the privilege of owning yourself."

The more we own up to our originality, the more confidence we gain in our abilities. We learn to trust ourselves instead of looking to others for our answers. Remember the root of the word of originality is "origin"—the fountainhead from which we spring.

Now, Silver Disobedients®, here's the word of the day: Gobeyou!

APPROVAL

Approval is a powerful stimulant. It's a fertilizer of personal growth. Approval is giving ourselves and others the blessing, confirmation, consent, endorsement, go-ahead, green light, support and permission to be who we are and do what we want to do.

Although we don't need others' permission to be or to act, and they don't need ours either, everyone enjoys the feeling that their choices are supported.

If we've been withholding approval of ourselves, others or various decisions, it's time to ask why. If we don't have a really great answer to that question, it's time to grant our seal of approval and get on with it—whatever it is.

A lifespan is brief. I don't know if we get to do it more than once but if we do, it won't be as who we are this go-round. So I'll once again declare: It is our responsibility to approve of who we are or change as necessary so we can share our "be-ing" in its full glory.

STEPPING UP TO CHANGE

As we reflect on making changes in our lives at any time of the year, we benefit by understanding the steps that make change possible.

Change begins with our awareness of what might not be working. Next, we need to clearly identify all the reasons we would benefit from making the change. Then we must assess, analyze and confront any fears we're associating with the change, remembering that fears, underlying anxiety or worries about changes are rarely more than False Evidence Appearing Real. Lastly, we'll need to act and overcome our inertia to make the change possible.

While all this might seem like a tall order, the number one reason we often won't initiate a change—even one we believe would be beneficial—is because we're afraid of what others will say and how they'll react.

This is faulty thinking for a few reasons. 1) We'll never be able to predict exactly how others will feel and react to anything, including ourselves, now or at any time in the future. 2) The only way relationship dynamics can improve is by taking the initiative to change things that aren't working. And 3) When we commit to change, those surrounding us notice, have no choice but to accept our decision and often begin to change for the better as well.

Although time changes some things, many of the changes that might actually be most important to us must be changed by our choices and actions.

I'm a Believer

I'm often asked if I really believe all that I write about when it comes to fulfilling our dreams.

Here's my fivefold answer:

1. Yes.
2. Plan to work harder and longer than you imagine, because "doing it" takes stamina.
3. Anticipate the strong likelihood that you might fail many times before you succeed, but you'll be figuring out ways to get closer.
4. Expect doubters and haters.
   But...
5. Giving your dreams your all—from reshaping your body with diet and exercise to becoming a rocket scientist and everything in between—is always better than wishing you did.

Going for what we want is like a racing a horse: It requires putting on blinders and staying single-mindedly focused on crossing the finish line. Plenty of people will scoff at the plans of others, share their own experiences with failure and offer all the reasons to quit. Listen if you feel like it; extract any golden nuggets from their advice that might apply and charge forth. Commit to spending as much time as possible "doing" every day. Whatever it is you want to do.

Your personal challenge or calling is yours. Do it if you believe that accomplishing it will create a more personally fulfilling life. Every minute you spend pushing your idea or plan forward is one more step toward proving yourself right.

Failure will always be a possibility. I might even say it's a likelihood unless there is a real iron-will commitment to just keep finding new ways to create results. Self or formal education will be required. Every choice needs to move you in the direction you want to be going in. Risk speaking about your plan and asking for help—knowing others hold the right to decline. Visualize what you want clearly and often. Believe whatever you want can happen by your actions. That's how I see it.

What I mostly regret are those times I quit (or when I lost my temper). I don't like regrets. So to anybody else reading this: Yes, I'm a believer. Now go give whatever you want your best shot. Just do it.

DEEDS

Kindness, love and generosity are no-obligation, one-way transactions. It's our choice to give them to others.

Yet if we are keeping a mental list of what we are doing for others and believing our actions are somehow obliging, we're missing the big picture. When we doubt this concept, it's helpful to recall times in our past when we were on the receiving end of generosity from others. Those times may have been quite obvious—or not. For example, we're receiving not-so-obvious gifts if a stranger lets us have the parking spot when we're in a rush or when someone allows us to cut the line when we have three grocery items and everyone else has cartloads. Or it could even be that random smile we receive when we ourselves, might be feeling less than smiley. Remember those moments.

There is balance in the world—if we choose to see it. The people we give to might or might not be the ones who return generosity to us—but others will. The more we notice random acts of kindness, love and generosity, the better life gets. This is how good will works.

Good actions are like currency for a Universal Bank of Deeds. We all make deposits and we all make withdrawals. If we're worried about whether we're getting our fair share of good will, it's time to make more deposits.

HUBS

A hub is someone who generously creates introductions for others within their collection of friends and associates. It's important to be one. Some people do hubbing very well and they regularly reap the rewards that go around and come around from being a good hub. Others don't and they have no idea what they're missing. Then there are those who are offered introductions by hubs and are reluctant to recognize the opportunity.

Life is all about people. The more you meet, the more interesting life gets. Opportunities for love, friendships, work and new experiences all increase when we choose to graciously find ways to introduce and connect all the people we know with other people.

When we choose to act as a hub, we have to remember that it's not a one-for-one transaction. We might create introductions for someone and they might be unable to respond with their own hubness. However, other hubs will open doors instead. It's a generosity thing that grows. The more we seek to create connections in any way, the more connections come back in ways we can never imagine. Trust me on this. Be a hub and watch how your world opens.

VIBRATIONS

Everything in the universe is made up of energy vibrating at different frequencies. For as long as I can remember, I've been fascinated by physics, medicine and psychology, as well as the frontiers of other scientific disciplines. Add in my enthusiasm for world religions and music, and you've pretty much got most of my personal interests covered.

A personal research project I am currently conducting in a very un-clinical way is: Raising vibrations. Since some people find the holiday season and its wide variety of gatherings stressful, maybe you want to try this test with me. Perhaps we can even prove statistical clinical significance if enough of us join this experiment.

I want to raise my vibration and that of all those around me, upward toward feelings of greater love for ourselves and each other—particularly when a state of frustration or anger is vibrating high. My experiment involves mentally envisioning and hearing, "I love you." I want to see how others are affected when I keep repeating "I love you," quietly and without telling the person, when I know they are not loving themselves. More so, I want to see how it affects my emotions.

My thesis is that by becoming conscious of our emotions and understanding that they are really just fleeting thoughts, we can learn to harness our energy and shift it to something more beautiful.

Maybe we can collectively raise the love vibration. How cool would that be?! As Joe Strummer of The Clash signed all his autographs, let's "Love it live!"

OPTION 3

Want to really open up your thought processes? Start considering Option 3.

Most often when we are faced with a decision, we focus on dualities such as 1) staying or 2) going. When we choose, we are likely thinking we have to select one and give up the other. These situations tend to make one or all parties dissatisfied with the conclusion.

When confronting these situations, instead of thinking we have to choose between Option 1 or 2, what if we told ourselves the following instead: Either there is a compromise between 1 and 2, or we can find a unique Option 3 that reduces the worry we might have about choosing one of the other two.

We can't avoid problems or decisions but we can use our creativity to continue thinking up new solutions. By trying to find alternate solutions, new paths usually appear.

The more we practice this way of thinking, the less often we feel threatened by the dilemma of making a choice. Practice it regularly enough and we might find ourselves noticing opportunities everywhere instead of situations where the possibilities feel limited.

FOUR STEPS

There are things we all do that we might complain about but really don't intend to change. If we did want to change, we'd start changing.

Instead, we make excuses, rationalize and pretend we'll get to it—but the fact is: On some level we've decided whatever "it" is, it's just not a priority.

At our ages, if we're not already doing so, it's time to accept all of our choices.

Here are the four steps to practicing acceptance of those things we really have no intention of changing:

1. Stop the denial about whatever "it" is that we say we're going to change but haven't and aren't.
2. Stop judging ourselves for our choice. Just accept this is our choice and it doesn't require justification to anyone.
3. Get real. Life is not slowing down for any of us. We're all getting older. As such, we might as well accept the who, what, why, where and how we are.
4. Be attentive to what we are choosing and doing. Remember, actions speak louder than words.

Everyday life is filled with things we don't necessary like but that require acceptance. This goes both for ourselves and for the world. I'll give you two examples, general and personal: First, we know death is a part of life. We don't like this but we have to accept it. Second, for years, I beat myself up over five pounds: That I couldn't lose it, how I needed to eat or exercise to lose it, that I was weak for not taking it off and keeping it off. Then I practiced the steps above:

1. I really wasn't willing to do what was necessary to lose the five pounds and keep it off.
2. I cut myself five pounds of slack and stopped judging myself for it.
3. I accepted that my face actually looks better with the five pounds because it plumps up my wrinkles!
4. I chose to become a moderate healthy eater versus someone who "diets." So far, it's working out just fine!

MASTERPIECES

Each life is like a gigantic canvas that's just waiting to be transformed into priceless art by our individual expression. Let us all create masterpieces by adding our unique "personality paint" into the mix and seeing what happens!

CONCLUSION-JUMPING

Do you jump to conclusions? Of all the high-risk moves we might make in life, conclusion-jumping is one of the riskiest. It lies at the root of all miscommunication, whether in our personal lives or work lives.

While we might think we know exactly what another meant by what they said—do we?

The easiest way to get more peace in day-to-day life, while simultaneously improving communication, is this: If someone says something that makes us feel defensive, startled, hurt, confused, extra-excited or unsure regarding any comment directed toward us, it is far safer to ask for clarification versus jumping to conclusions.

When we jump to conclusions or make assumptions in our interpretations of another's words, we risk the proverbial problem with "assume": it makes an "ass" out of "you" and "me."

Rarely is communication or expression by any of us concrete. Most is subject to interpretations—and our assessment of the words is most likely reflective of our wants, desires or fears.

I always think of my mother telling me I wore out the seat by the phone because some boy in high school said he'd call me and I would sit waiting. She'd ask, "When was he calling?" I'd reply, "I don't know, but he said he'd call!" Needless to say, plenty of those calls never came.

If you're not sure what someone said, if you question the intent of their words, if you doubt the meaning—ask if you really want to know!

It's simple: "Can you please explain what you mean by that?" Asking the question that begs to be asked can solve a world of problems.

STIMULATION

Did you know the white matter in our brains, myelin, actually becomes denser whenever we challenge ourselves to learn a new skill? Committing to being a lifelong student is one of the best ways to stay sharp throughout life and ward off memory loss as well as dementia.

Learning stimulates neurons in our brains and forms more neural pathways, which means our electrical impulses can travel faster. In turn, this makes it easier to process new information and learn more readily. Interestingly, science shows that knowledge builds on itself. In other words, everything we learn helps us to add layers of new knowledge with greater ease.

Research has also concluded that building up all these neural pathways makes us less likely to develop dementia. This is because active brains seem to have less of an opportunity to demyelinate (or lose myelin)—since the neural pathways remain in better shape for the electrical impulses traveling along them.

Clearly, these are all great reasons to keep learning. Then add the fact that we become more well-rounded and interesting, which makes life more interesting and each of us more attractive to boot—and who wouldn't want to be more attractive?

The challenge is issued: What are you going to do to learn more and brain train?

MISTAKES

Did you know that our mistakes and stumbles might actually be perceived as making us more lovable?

Back in 1966, Elliot Aronson, a social psychologist, conducted some research that determined that those who are perceived as smarter or very competent become more likable when they perform an everyday blunder, pratfall or stumble of some kind.

Long story short, in the study, 48 men were recorded while answering game show-style questions. The listeners were told the men were divided equally by intelligence. Of the contestants who were in the highest-scoring group, some could be heard saying, "Oops! I spilled my coffee all over my suit." When the listeners were asked which contestants they enjoyed listening to the most, it was those clumsy coffee spillers who were ranked as more likable.

Mistakes seem to make us all more human, relatable and nonthreatening. Since we're inevitably going to make mistakes no matter how perfectly we plan, why not stop worrying about the mistakes we might make and just start messing up right now? Whether our plans work out exactly as planned or not, maybe just by showing the effort and trying, we'll become even more endearing through the process. That sounds like a win to me!

EXPECTATIONS

Expectations about any situation or person—including yourself—can be a way of avoiding the reality of what is.

Expectations are all about assumptions and leaving things to chance. They are promises of possibilities that are not necessarily based on substance. Often, if we are in expectation mode, our thoughts have shifted to some future event that is out of our control. At their worst, expectations can become premeditated resentments that steal our happiness from today.

In the present, lots of choices can be made—but not if time is spent dreaming about future expectations. We must act without expectation.

At every stage of life, dreams and visions for the future can be guides for setting a course, but realities materialize with action. Although we cannot predict the future, peace begins and disappointments end when we lose our expectations.

Today to expect more from yourself than others.

PERCEPTION

Perception is the ability to see, hear or become aware of something through the senses. When we are perceiving, we are regarding, understanding and interpreting through our senses with intuition and insight.

The word "perceive" comes from percipere in Latin, which means to seize or understand. Perceptions are formed using all the signals that course through our nervous system and result in physical or chemical stimulation of our senses. All of this comes together to shape our learning, memory, expectation and attention.

Although perceptions gather physically, sensorily, computationally and philosophically, all together the information from these perceptual systems form realities in the mind of the perceiver.

I use the word "realities" loosely, because perceptions can change—often and like the breeze—which means our realities are quite malleable and flexible, too.

Although we all seek to form opinions because they make us feel secure, it is our experience and motivational and emotional states that contribute greatly to those opinions—which are not necessarily real as they might not be universal opinions for all. Further, they may be assessed based on a series of prior events that no longer constitute relevant or current information with the situation or relationship at hand.

Questioning our perceptions and realities is always a worthy endeavor. After all, reality is philosophically defined as existence that is absolute, self-sufficient, objective and not subject to human decisions or conventions. That means not much is real—except for the moment.

CALM DOWN

While we can't avoid all stressful events, we can greatly impact the ways we respond to stress—and how it impacts our health.

Stopping at regular intervals throughout the day to practice steady breathing helps reduce stress. Practicing steady, even breaths before bedtime—or the minute we notice our stress levels rising—can help us fall asleep more peacefully and help us manage our reactions in the moment.

Here's how I like to do it. I close my eyes and take a deep breath. Then I let it out. But now the next time I breathe in, I mentally say the word, "calm." Then, I exhale while mentally saying the word, "down." I repeat, breathing in on "calm," steadily releasing on "down."

I find that a minute of these deep, even breaths with the words "calm" and "down" added to the process helps me calm down more effectively.

Learning to breathe and calm down can significantly lower cardiovascular risk and a whole cadre of other stress-related illnesses, particularly as we age.

Please give it a try and see how you feel!

DIGNITY

Divorce and separations are highly charged personal topics. As such, the best advice I can share if faced with the ending of a relationship—voluntary or not—is to maintain dignity.

Our dignity is a great asset. Dignity is how we hold ourselves, conduct our actions and speak in a way that indicates our self-respect while honoring and considering the gravity of the situation. It is acting with elevated character that acknowledges our own worthiness, that of the other person as well as anyone else affected by the situation, particularly children.

To act in a way that does not uphold our dignity, regardless of how a relationship is collapsing, belittles oneself and implies a lack of self-worth. Maintaining dignity respects what the relationship once was.

Being dignified is not being rude or distant. Dignity involves maintaining character and acting in a way that warrants respect.

Dignity is not false. It is not disloyal to what was. Dignity is not petty or small.

If a relationship is ending, it is paramount to be dignified.

WISDOM

We're all born with wisdom, although socialization tends to put it to sleep. We can reawaken our innate wisdom at any time because while it might be in a dormant state, wisdom is not something external we need to gain, earn or realize.

Think about the phrase, "Out of the mouths of babes." Perennial bestselling books (like the Old and New Testaments of the Bible!) recognize that young children share profound insights with us. We marvel in response, as children prove daily that wisdom comes with birth.

While we might lose touch with our wisdom throughout our lives, we don't have to wait to be old to find it again. We awaken our wisdom by trusting our intuition. It is our intuition that helps us adapt more quickly and comfortably to new situations and people. Past experiences and intuition combine to strengthen wisdom—if we choose to see the past as a series of lessons that make us less likely to make the same mistake twice.

Wise people see life as a continual education process. Additional traits include discipline, the ability to admit mistakes and learn during the process (whether we're liking the process or not), patience, the ability to roll with rejection, understanding that failure offers many lessons, and mastery of emotions.

Being honest about who we are is the first step to accessing our wisdom. The second, paraphrasing Socrates, is that true wisdom is found in knowing we know nothing. Gee, Socrates sure enough provided generations to come with some whopper thoughts for contemplation!

PROOF

Some people need proof before they believe anything or anyone.

Suppose someone believes they have a new idea or invention that will change the world. Or that animals talk to them. Or anything else that might be beyond another's personal reality.

Is casting doubt necessary? Do all beliefs need to be based in hard realities—our own or another's? And if proof were necessary, what would that look like? For example, how could someone prove that animals talk? Maybe they do, but they don't like the attitude of the person demanding proof, so they refuse to comply.

The point is: You don't have to prove your belief in yourself or your capabilities to anyone. If you believe something—that's good enough. Just keep doing you. Trying to prove a point wastes a lot of valuable breath. People only listen when they're ready, no matter how the evidence stacks up.

We are each unique. While we might find commonalities with others, we're completely different from our friends, parents, siblings, other relatives and acquaintances. With our differences, we are each entitled to maintain our private beliefs that are not hurtful to others, without worrying about conforming, unless of course that's what we decide to do.

We don't have to prove ourselves to anyone. Others' opinions, altering ourselves to comply, trying to fit in boxes that are constricting—no. Those are all attempts to prove our worth. Be you. You are worthy as is. Be honest with who you are. No proving is necessary. Just believe that you are working every day to be the best you can be.

THE PRICE OF TIME

I once read that time is free but it's priceless. We don't own it but we can use it. We can't keep it but we spend it.

Time is nonrefundable, so it's best spent by concentrating on our better intentions for maximum returns. As we get older, time really seems to show us what matters. Both the years we've lived and the life in those years have been excellent teachers, if we paid attention.

Hopefully, sooner rather than later, we learn to value our time and recognize that we'd better be enjoying the finite amount we have. Because the trouble is, we think we have time. But we've only got the moment.

One day or day one. It's a daily choice.

YOUNGER LONGER

We become older before we realize it, yet we can feel younger longer than we are young.

Our sense of enthusiastic happiness with our years largely depends upon our perceptions. If we recall our pasts with fond memories or at least acceptance, and hold onto excitement about our futures—all the while keeping our focus on whatever is happening today—this will all add up to a greater sense of contentment.

Staying present while seeking to witness and admire the good in ourselves and others: These are the things that keep hopes alive. Doing so is immensely important, because what we never want to do is allow parts of us to die while we're still alive. Instead, we must choose to remain rooted in our purpose with faith that life is unfolding as it should. This is the essence of eternally youthful energy.

Waking up is good. Better is embracing the day with the enthusiasm it deserves. This is the secret of feeling youthful enthusiasm longer. And "youthful" does not necessarily mean "young." Grammatically, "youthful" equals "enthusiasm," which to me equals "any age" plus "excitedly happy about a new day!" If we're lucky, we add years to our time collection. Young is wonderful. Older is amazing, too. A spirited attitude that welcomes every day? Priceless. Make it a great day!

TRUST

Trust or lack of it largely comes from our sense of self. Our trust of others is usually strong if we feel confident regarding our own capabilities. Contrarily, lack of trust develops when, for whatever reasons, doubts arise as to who we are and what our worth is within the relationship.

We trust when actions align with words. When we are trusting in any situation, we are showing love and respect for another.

Most of us don't trust easily. We want to be in love yet we're afraid to trust. The two walk hand and hand.

Without trust, there is no love. Love is really deep trust.

Ernest Hemingway summed up trust this way: "The best way to find out if you can trust somebody is to trust them." Scary prospect. But still, it's really the only way we'll ever know who's trustable—and how deeply we can experience love.

People (and we all fit in that category) disappoint. But today, we can only love by choosing to resolve regrets and release fears. If we can't find it within ourselves to trust someone with whom we are in an important relationship, it's time to try again or be honest. We must own up to our limitations and speak up about our inability to trust. We cannot betray ourselves.

Although hurts can run deep, choose to live with the full belief that everything is possible. Go forth with trust. As Anton Chekhov said, "You must trust and believe in people or life becomes impossible." Live for possibility.

No Gym Pass

Exercise is very important but nobody gets a gym pass for poor diet.

Diets filled with solid fats and lots of sugar are hard calories to burn off. While exercise beneficially impacts stress levels and cardiovascular health, it's pretty impossible to use exercise as a means to eradicate the impact of too many poor food choices.

Using 150 pounds as an average weight, here is a list of the walking time required to burn off the calories of each of these common fast foods. If you weigh in above 150, a little less time would be required; below 150, you'd have to exercise a bit more—but whatever you weigh, this average will help tell the big picture story.

Quarter-pound burger with cheese: 1 hour 19 minutes of walking

Large fries: Another 1 hour and 17 minutes

Large soda: 43 more minutes

Large sweetened iced tea (16 oz): 27 minutes

2 pieces of fried chicken: 1 hour 14 minutes

Half a frozen pizza: 1 hour 40 minutes

Small bag of potato chips: 49 minutes of walking

20 oz "sports" drink: 20 minutes of walking

Cinnamon rolls (just one): 2 hours 14 minutes of walking

Large cookie: 34 minutes

Candy bar (not supersized): 38 minutes

Ice cream (without chips, cookies, syrups): 46 minutes of walking per cup

Now, let's juxtapose:

A mixed salad with olive oil and balsamic vinegar dressing: About a 6-minute walk

An apple, banana, peach, plum, cherries or pretty much any fruits or vegetables: 12 to 15 minutes.

Calories are required for all our activities throughout the day and nobody eats a perfect diet. I love good homemade cookies, pies and cakes. The point here is about balance and understanding that if the scale isn't reading what we prefer, it could be because there's no way we are burning off the number of calories we're unconsciously consuming. Making conscious food choices is our best health defense.

FENCES

All of us have the ability to recall painful situations in our pasts that might still feel like they're blasting at 11 on the volume dial—and not playing a particularly pleasant tune.

Although we might believe we can't escape our pasts—that somehow we're fenced in on all sides—this belief triggers a question: Why is there a tendency to blame other people in our lives for our dysfunctional behavior while we take all the credit for the aspects of our lives that are going well?

Everyone does this to some degree or another. Yet the fact is that everyone's past has involved dysfunction and poop that nobody wants to step in. We're only kidding ourselves if we believe otherwise. The underlying issue is accepting responsibility for our choices at any and every age.

For example, having just reread J.D. Salinger's *The Catcher in the Rye* for about the fifth time—for my own education and that of my kids—it's clear that growing up and taking responsibility for our choices is something that has been a challenge since at least 1951! Heck, Shakespeare and Plato wrote about this theme as well. That makes it an old and recurring issue!

If you really want to hold onto your past, ask yourself why? What's the benefit? If you can't find a clear-cut one, get present. Your past is untouchable. Your future? That's yours to own and mold with no excuses.

BOREDOM

Boredom is a very interesting thing. I once read that it is fear of ourselves. Don't do boredom. Ever. There's no time for it. Instead, get to know yourself.

Not sure how to get to know yourself? Imagine two of you: You today and you at 120 years old. What would you ask your older self? Would you be proud of your 120-year-old self? Would your 120-year-old self be proud of how you've been using your time or encourage you to try a few more things with your time remaining? If so, what might that be? Would the conversation be about all the exciting things you did and how you really seized every opportunity? Or would you both be discussing all that you wished you had done?

No matter what age you are, no matter what your physical condition, no matter where you live, no matter what your financial situation—both the world and our minds offer vast unexplored territories that can keep life exciting both in the moment and upon reflection.

ASK

What is it that makes asking so difficult? Do we feel disadvantaged, incapable, less than or weak? If so, there's some faulty thinking that requires realignment.

A truism of life is: If we don't ask, we don't get. Life is designed in such a way that asking is an integral part of all of our lives. Sometimes we're the asker and other times the answerer. Life is never always one way or the other.

Too often we desire, long for, crave and maybe suffer, when all we needed to do was speak up and ask whatever we felt needed asking. Although there might be nothing more difficult than asking, we progress much faster in life when we accept the reality that asking is OK.

Asking becomes easier when we learn that every request must be made without a concrete end or expectation set in our minds. The universe, God and the godliness in others gets to decide what is within their capabilities to give when called upon.

Here's a story: When I first moved to New York City, I worked in the automobile business. I did a fantastic job selling the cars—because I really like cars and believed in the line. But my customers often left carless because I was afraid to ask. Honest truth: How I finally got used to asking was when we'd sit down at my desk to go over details, I'd drop my pen and while my eyes were focused on looking for it on the floor, I'd ask: "So are you ready to buy this car?" My closing ratio went up exponentially and so did my confidence! Plenty said no, but enough said yes that I was able to bank enough money to start a lifelong career of self-employment. Eventually I learned to be more direct.

It's OK to ask. We might get a no, but then again we might get a yes—or more information to move our lives forward. What can you ask for today?

RAINING

The worst storms occur when we are raining self-doubts, insecurities, fears and worries about the future. When we are raining inside, quite possibly the storm of emotions has made us forget how strong and powerful we really are, while instead we feel stuck in a situation that feels insurmountable as it is soaking up our joy.

Perhaps we're really just getting wet from another's bad mood. Maybe we've drifted into some future moment instead of staying present with whatever is happening this very moment. Possibly while dealing with something that is sad, the flood of emotions feels as if it might never pass. Such tempests could temporarily drown and drain the best of spirits if we chose to allow it.

Yet nowhere on Earth does it rain forever. The sun comes out. Bob Marley said, "Some people feel the rain. Others just get wet." So yes, some of us experience the force of emotions more strongly than others. Yet Eeyore reminds us that, "The nicest thing about rain is that it always stops. Eventually." And all the way back in 550 BC, in assessing the emotional swings of the human condition, Aesop wrote, "After the rain comes the fair weather."

Whenever it rains, remember: We need that rain, just like the plants require rain to grow. All growth comes after the rain. On that note, Eric Clapton reminded us: "Let it rain... Now I know the secret; there is nothing that I lack... Let it rain."

TWO LISTS

Make two lists: The things you have to do and the things you want to do.

Which one is longer? Do they intersect? Does the "have to do" list have any fun things on it? Do you have a plan as to how you'll get to do the things on your "want to do" list?

Ideally, our days include a combination of doing what we have to do and time spent checking off and enjoying things we want to do.

Make the lists: Have to/Want to. Next, create your own personal business plan for merging the two for greater daily satisfaction.

PERFECTLY KISSABLE

One of the best parts of age is that personal insecurity and angst are largely behind us. Of course, we all still have moments when we slip into anxiety about ourselves and how we relate to situations within our worlds, but hopefully we've released ourselves from the majority of the angst that teenagers are associated with. That "Oh-I'm-so-misunderstood" has been largely replaced with a "Who gives a hoot?" attitude. And you know what? This may actually be one of the biggest benefits of age.

The quest for perfection is stressful and can backfire! While aiming for personal excellence or desiring to do the best we can is a motivating goal, perfection tends to be an elusive ideal—if not downright imaginary— that prevents us from feeling satisfied with what we have accomplished along the way.

According to research that was published a few years back in the *Journal of Health Psychology*, "perfectionistic seniors"—those moving into their 50s and beyond—have a 51 percent higher mortality rate than those who approach life with a more laid-back attitude.

In light of this, it would be both kind and wise to do a self-inventory to assess those areas where we're driving ourselves too aggressively, and maybe figure out some ways we can ease off the pedal. Ultimately, we all arrive at the same destination—and let's hope it's a long way away—but how we get there will vary greatly. Life will be remembered in the end as a wonderful or stress-filled journey based on how we chose to treat ourselves during the ride.

CONTEXT SWITCHING

Where we focus our attention will determine whether we believe life is going well or not. In a fast-paced world, it's easy to get focused on what we don't have, and feel deprived. If the news bombards us with stories of violence, we might feel fearful.

Is the answer to move to a cave or develop a positive attitude?

I don't think either.

Instead, it is far more helpful to look at what is it that rises within us and flips the trigger when we are confronted with situations where emotions of deprivation, fear, loneliness, worry, anxiety or anything else of the sort begin to rise.

By trying to think about the who, what, when, where and why of triggered emotions, we can notice how our attention works and start seeing the differences between how our lives have conditioned each of us to process things versus what might actually be happening in the moment, in our home or backyard.

Observing our mishmash of thoughts, emotions and physical sensations can actually help us relax and separate our physical being from those emotions that are really just thoughts. While we might think our brains are great multitasking machines that are perfectly processing everything accurately, we're actually "context switching" and splitting our brain's resources, which triggers erroneous thinking and stress.

In computing, a context switch is the process of storing the state of a process so it can be restored or executed upon at another time. In a multitasking context, this is really pausing one thing so we can start or resume another thought or action. Context switching often is triggered via an interruption (which is also what usually triggers stress and emotional reactions in daily life). Whether in computing or in processing our daily lives, context switching has a cost in our performance. Instead of staying focused on what is actually happening, we get into a state of recalling a series of data that we are trying to layer into the moment, while there is a strong possibility it doesn't compute.

The key to managing stress, emotions and our lives in general is staying focused on the task or moment no matter what is circling around us. This is our biggest challenge and within it lies our greatest successes for whatever it is that we want. The journey of life is ideally a long one. Sometimes our hardest challenges come by deciding what we are not going to focus on.

BRAINPOWER

Our brains control motion, thoughts, sleep, dreams and nightmares, breathing, heartbeat, muscle contractions and blinking. As the ultimate high-speed computer, the brain also decides in a split second to swerve to avoid danger coming in our direction.

Brains require a steady supply of oxygen-rich blood to maintain optimal reaction time and avoid memory loss. This said, eating the right foods can help prevent a mind-altering stroke, which is most often triggered by atherosclerosis (clogged arteries) and high blood pressure.

Research shows that the top 10 daily foods for increasing the calcium, magnesium and potassium we need for blood pressure control, while also boosting brainpower nutrients, are the following: 1 cup milk or yogurt; 1/2 cup spinach; 1/2 cup black-eyed peas; 1/2 cup acorn squash; 3 oz. pink salmon (canned is fine); 1/2 cup kidney beans; 3/4 cup orange juice; 1 medium papaya; 1/2 cup bok choy; 1/2 of a baked potato. Runners up? 1/2 cup broccoli; 2 tbsp. wheat germ; a banana; 3 oz. firm tofu; 1-2 oz. of raw, unsalted nuts (like walnuts and almonds); any mix of fruits and vegetables that you like, ideally 5-7 per day.

Researchers estimate this type of diet would reduce stroke by 27 percent in the United States. Imagine the impact if we all added some oxygen-pumping exercise—even something as simple as 30 minutes of brisk walking. Sounds to me like it's time to get smarter!

GROWTH

Although we might think we know ourselves or someone else, we are each always changing. It's virtually impossible to claim to "know" anyone. While this can be a disturbing concept, it is also immensely exciting!

By recalling life between birth and 18 years of age, we easily understand the constant changes of growth. Although our changes might become less obvious in later years, it does not mean we've stopped changing. And here's the kicker: Changing is what every other person alive is doing too, whether we realize it and accept it or not.

Because of this, when we or someone we love expresses a desire to change things up, it does not need to be feared or perceived as a threat. Instead of striking resistance mode, perhaps we can try to honor the urge to experience something different. To test capabilities. To reach new heights. To learn something new. To explore.

Although the status quo might feel safe and secure, we are all changing. The goal is to keep learning about ourselves and those whom we love as the changes are happening. To use these times as opportunities to gain deeper understanding. Not to corner or box ourselves or another in, trying to define how "we know them"—but instead to allow room for expansion of ideas and growth for all.

Few things can be contained in life. If we give respect and room for growth, we increase the likelihood that our relationships will flourish.

FREE WILL

We often avoid making decisions in important areas of our lives. We do this because we believe that by not deciding, we might alter the outcome. In reality, we are really attempting to evade, flee, shirk, duck or ignore our responsibility in the situation. It's faulty thinking to believe that we can push things off when we know we would be better off with making a decision. Choosing to not act is not without consequences.

One of my all-time favorite wisdom-loaded song lyrics is one by Rush. The song is "Free Will" and the line says, "If you choose not to decide/You still have made a choice." It's funny, I can't even type that line without wanting to sing along with Geddy Lee because the essence within the words is so powerful. (But about my singing—I've cracked car windows trying to hit those notes!)

It's worth asking yourself: Am I hurting myself in any way by not making a decision that needs to be made? If so, it might be helpful to give yourself a deadline. A new day is coming tomorrow. Maybe it's a good time to set some plans in motion today with active decision making. It's rarely good to put ourselves in a position whereby others are making our decisions for us.

KUDOS

Although social media has all kinds of icons to say "Bravo," "Nice job" and "Kudos," it's sincere words, delivered at the right time, that can inspire maximum-voltage smiles and the warmest of warm feelings.

Next time it's time to offer a sincere compliment to someone for whatever they've done that you admire, try any of these lines: Stop—what you said/did was genius! • I might not tell you all the time but your efforts haven't gone unnoticed. • No matter what's happening, you continue to amaze me. • I like the way you put that! Can I quote you on that? • You always share a positive (healthy) perspective. • I appreciate all you do. • Could you repeat that so I can write it down? I want to remember it forever! • Whatever you do, you do with style. It's really impressive. • Thanks for being flexible. I appreciate it. You helped make my day easier. • You brightened my day with your smile. • You are absolutely right! • Do you have any idea how awesome you are? • I love your laugh. You make me smile all over. • I'm grateful to know you. • You're strong. Probably even stronger than you realize. • And my favorite, with a nod to Spinal Tap: Silver Disobedients: On a scale of 1 to 10, you're all 11s.

Thanks for joining me on this journey! Kisses and hugs!

EXTEMPORANEOUS

The word "extemporaneous" comes from "ex tempore" in Latin, which means "to do something out of time," improvised without advanced preparation. Extemporaneous actions are unplanned and spontaneous.

While our years have taught us the importance of planning, our ability to be impromptu is a youthful trait that can still be ours at any age.

To act instinctively, breaking loose, being free-spirited, letting our urges and impulses lead to snap, spur-of-the-moment, wing-it, harmless and fun decisions.

This is not the same as being irresponsible. But it is: Calling old and new friends at the last minute to see who's available for a dinner party; jumping into a pool with a bathing suit (or not); being the one to get the party started by dancing up a storm; singing however you sing at the karaoke mike; buying that bus ticket to head to the nearest city for a day of exploration; having a sit down, candlelit dinner at 10:00 PM instead of a rushed one at 6:00 PM in front of a TV; making a gourmet meal from whatever ingredients are in the fridge and closets; adding an accessory to your outfit that just seems like fun; banging a drum to the best of your abilities when other accomplished musicians say, "just try it."

Find your moments. Extemporaneous improvisations come without instructions. No rules. Just your gut inspiring your next action. Try it. The more you trust that it's OK to be extemporaneous, the more invigorated you will feel. This is the best prescription for adding life to our years at every age.

YOU AND I

Have you ever noticed that when someone says, "I (fill in the blank)..." the tendency is to come back with an "I"-statement as well? For example, if someone says, "I'm hungry," we might respond, "I'm hungry, too." Or if someone said, "I'm feeling sad," we might respond, "I know what you mean," or "I know how you feel."

Here's a challenge: What if we could remove our "I" from these conversations? Our goal could be just to hear what the other is trying to express without internalizing or trying to extrapolate another's experience into our personal collective frames of reference.

What a challenge worth accomplishing if we could really learn just to listen and let another express what they want without the need to bring "I" or ourselves into their experience—unless, of course, we are specifically asked to do so.

This would take lots of conscious effort. But perhaps every relationship would benefit from it. Although you and I are similar, we are each experiencing life uniquely.

IMPATIENCE

Patience running low is an expensive situation. Its costs include annoyance, anxiety, agitation, haste, stress, decisions we regret, snappy words we wish we'd never said and accidents. When impatience runs high, its tolls on our relationships, in the present and in the future, can be costly.

Harsh responses. Passing that slow car in front of us, risking an accident and possibly impacting lives forever. Going into debt when perhaps we could have saved a little longer or reconsidered the purchase.

There are reasons patience is considered a virtue. Sometimes we underestimate the value of slowing down, taking our time, considering carefully, thinking and maybe even waiting or stopping altogether—whenever it is necessary to get our perspectives back in balance.

Twice in a single year, my impatience resulted in concussions: I tripped on the street, face-planted and needed surgery, and less than a year later I got wacked in the head by a ceiling fan while stringing lights. Both times, I was having a deep discussion in my head and not paying attention to my surroundings.

When patience is running low, when we're rushing and on edge, it's time to stop, breathe, have a tea, maybe even ask for help—and consider the cost of rushing, overthinking, worrying, searching, demanding, insisting and pushing.

Don't wait for life to smack you in the head. Practice patience, which is a trait of the wise.

FEELING VERSUS BEING

There's a big difference between how we might be feeling and our state of being. Because a lot of you have asked me to address anxiety, let's use anxiety as an example to explain.

"I am feeling anxiety" and "I'm anxious" are not the same statement.

One allows for the possibility that we are feeling something that will pass. The other is kind of like a judgment or label as to who we are, i.e., I'm an anxious person or I'm someone filled with anxiety.

But it goes deeper. When we switch to thinking about the "feeling" of anxiety, or any other emotion that we might feel, we start looking for reasons for it.

Neither labeling ourselves as anxious beings nor looking for reasons triggering anxiety are very beneficial to the situation.

How about trying to observe what's happening when we feel anxious because if we're prone to feeling anxiety, pretty much anything can trigger it.

Observing is: I'm feeling sensations of anxiousness. My stomach feels uncomfortable. I feel a tightness in my chest. My thoughts and emotions are swirling. Fill in the blank…

Stopping and identifying these observations helps us separate ourselves from the emotional state. We are not our emotions. Our emotions—the entire range of them, from the ones we love to the ones we fear—are not us. They are fleeting thoughts and sensations that can be identified and acknowledged.

By learning to see our emotional states without believing we *are* our emotional states, we can move through, relax, chill and get on with the good stuff that is happening in the moment as we get ourselves into gear with beneficial choices and actions.

GIFTS

What are your gifts? Each of us comes with special distinctions that are uniquely our own. They are not what we buy, but innate aspects of who we are.

Our gifts deserve nurturing. Our gifts need to be exercised; enticed out over and over again; shared with others; and showcased when possible. Our gifts also need to be protected against annihilation by others who may feel threatened or insecure, perhaps because they haven't yet recognized the powers of their own personal gifts. Maybe certain others haven't realized that gifts are plentiful for all to share.

Although some of our gifts might be obvious, others perhaps are not so. Possibly we were uncommunicative yet with an instrument in hand we've spoken volumes with music. Perhaps we've been called bookworms while in fact we're scholarly. Maybe we've been told we're pushovers when really our gifts are fair-mindedness and compassion. A tinkerer who was fascinated by circuitry who can light up a city. A mechanic who keeps us revving and arriving in our vehicles without incident. A nurturer who has keenly observed and encouraged the gifts in children and others.

The range of gifts is as unique as all of us. If you are not sure what your gifts are, or the gifts of those around us whom we'd like to encourage, ask a friend to tell you what they've observed about you when you're not on-guard. Observing others during times of relaxation and play showcases our gifts because we're in action instead of thinking about how we should be.

We are never too old to nurture our gifts and those of others we love. We owe this to the world.

Silver Hair Secret

Because I am often asked: Yes, silvery white is my natural hair color. And here's my secret #DIY recipe that I use to keep my hair silvery white. I do this every two to three weeks. It rinses away the copper, sulfur and other chemicals that are naturally in water and cause that yellowish buildup:

1. In a small jar, mix equal parts of 3% hydrogen peroxide, water and your favorite white-colored conditioner (or 1/3 hydrogen peroxide (3%), 1/3 water and 1/3 conditioner).
2. Stir or shake up the mixture to blend thoroughly.
3. Apply the mixture to your clean, damp, unconditioned hair.
4. Comb through the hair with a wide-toothed comb or pick. Leave on hair for 10 minutes before rinsing thoroughly.
5. Repeat once every two weeks to prevent mineral buildup.
6. Enjoy your whiter, shiny and very conditioned hair.

Disclaimer: I take zero responsibility for your personal outcome—particularly if you don't follow directions or mistakenly decide "more is better" and you leave this mixture on your hair for too long. Remember, it does use peroxide.

Also and very important: It is not appropriate to do this until your hair is at least 85% silver, white or gray. Remember, the peroxide will lighten your other base color hair!

What Silver Disobedients™ Say About Dian Griesel aka @Silver Disobedience®
Continued

"Always inspiringly on point, Silver Disobedience advice and opinions transcend age." @parkwestrose

"Because Dian always sees the positive side of things, I find Silver Disobedience posts very uplifting!" @cristinalula

"Because of Silver Disobedience, I feel fabulous! Never, ever, did I think being 70 would be a door to a new adventure, a new thought pattern and breaking away from a grumpy old lady to become a fun, positive, silver-haired woman who is now looking forward with a best-of-everything attitude." @cathy_jeanne

"Silver Disobedience is a daily reminder for those of a 'certain age' that our voices and contributions are vital." @maryjoczar

"I thought I'd heard it all before but I was wrong. Silver Disobedience is thought-provoking and unique, full of fresh ideas to take in and questions to consider. I love you whether or not you post my review!" @d_rolon_cope

"When I found the Silver Disobedience blog, the daunting 50th was around the corner. Dian's words were so on point that I didn't believe they were written by one person. I asked in a comment if she was a real person—and she answered! Now, that's dedication and sincerity in a world full of virtual reality. I don't think Dian can imagine how many she helps." @randitravisdisney

"Wise and valued perspectives." @bakerdezine

"Silver Disobedience showed up in my life at just the right time. Not only that, but Dian always says what I need to hear when I need to hear it!" @eggersm

"I commented once that I think Dian is so cool. She responded: 'You are cool and kind, a great combination.' I love Silver Disobedience. Not only is Dian cool...she makes total sense." @DebraPretti

"An uplifting nudge for being the best we can be." @gardner133326

"I am a health-related professional in my 21st year of successful practice. While Dian's silver hair caught my attention...intelligence, wisdom, general cultural knowledge, beauty, sensuality, pity, humility, common sense, happiness and a sense of total fulfillment that is contagious are reflected in each blog! All of this makes @SilverDisobedience my favorite Instagram account. What Dian shares makes my day, every day, happier and easier!" @eojguel78

271

"Authentic and beautifully bold." @libbiekayt

"Silver Disobedience rocks!" @feliceisbebe

"Silver Disobedience helps me be the best version of myself as the wise words get into my head and stay there."
@julieisinthegarden

"Thanks to Dian sharing her life, I am comfortable where I am in my life at 66, which now includes no more hair coloring and going part-time in my 'big girl job' as a nurse to pursue my passion of antiquing and photography!" @muddycreekantiques

"Silver Disobedience's daily inspirations helped me realize that age is just a number and that women 40 and beyond can still make a difference in this world." @michele_mf2002

"I've often said to myself that Dian will run out of material to write about—but daily, she comes up with something that everyone can relate to in a clear and concise manner that should make us all THINK...and if that's not enough, she reads all responses, responds when needed and is open to listening to alternative ideas."
@photomaker54

"Dian's insight and inspiration are required reading each day. I appreciate her thoughtful connection to my soul and gentle push to embrace these years...to be as beautiful as I can be." @tamerinco

"Silver Disobedients know that Dian is a 'savage' woman with lots of love and compassion for other people's feelings. And she knows we're 'totally savage' too! How she shares her life gives everyone else the opportunity to share theirs. Dian reminds us all how we can be living our lives without the walls and barriers that we've likely built around ourselves. Silver Disobedience keeps the love flowing!" @danastoltz

"Silver Disobedience is my must-read each morning. Dian's balanced presentation of ideas that seem to be synchronized with current consciousness is wise, compassionate and authentic." @professor_qi

"Dian's insight into the thoughts of our generation is spot-on. I've thought exactly what she's written. Silver Disobedience posts have made me 'feel alive' again and helped me pick up my aging pieces and move forward." @ssheavin

"I am 61 years old and new to Silver Disobedience. I love how inspirational the posts are. For me, Dian is helping to take the worry out of aging and replacing it with inspiration. With deep appreciation for the experiences and wisdom I have accrued from my years, I am now more motivated and excited to continue to love and to live my life with intent." @jonbyr

"Being an older person doesn't mean you succumb to older ideas or mindsets or that you stop growing, thinking and learning. Silver Disobedience reminds me of this quietly—and sometimes not so quietly—which feels fantastic." @daphdog77

"Food for thought on those later years." @marty123ohio

"My daily dose of comfort food for the soul." @j.collins_7

"Connecting with @SilverDisobedience has allowed me to share the joy of living, doing, being." @daisygrlisme

"We are silver and yes, perhaps disobedient is how we roll. Thanks for photos and ideas that rev up our souls. I'm old but I'm loving it!" @newjoyze

"Thank you for being honest and encouraging to me in those times when I didn't have any idea of what to say, do or think. Often a little simple word in your writings changed my whole day! I am glad I found @SilverDisobedience on Instagram. I was looking for intelligent and exciting bloggers 50+ just like you. Dian, you are a blessing to many women and every day I look forward reading your blog." @mariadenbow65

"Dian constantly reminds us to be kind and proud of who we are and where we are in life. Bless you, gorgeous lady." @pammcelrath

"You make me feel, you make me feel, you make me feel like a natural happy older person. Much love, Silver Disobedience!" @lamp.artz

"Short and sweet.... Where were you in my 20s! I've often told my daughters, had I been wiser and known more about life, I could have had less to fear and suffering in my early life. That is what we get from Silver Disobedience blogs…what we wish we'd known then! Thank you!" @aascorpio

"Silver Disobedience has been a beacon of light through my twin sister's journey with breast cancer. Thank you." @cristinamigpapa

"Thank you for sharing your wisdom and loving thoughts. I started reading Silver Disobedience when you started this journey. I can only say I wish you were around when I was in my 50s but I'm glad to be here with you in my 70s, Dian. I'm looking forward to another year! Silver Love." @avis.hardy.733

"Silver Disobedience is spot-on the pulse of our age." @tomassetti.michael

"Day by day your words capture the beautiful truth." @dee_eubanks

"Silver Disobedience is thought-provoking at a human level and a daily wakeup call for your brain. Coffee and Dian's words are the best way to start each morning." @mary_adamski1

"While my eyes and hearing are not what they used to be, along with an occasional ache or two, aging has never been better. My daily medicine from Silver Disobedience's inspiration is a breath of fresh air every morning. So glad I discovered Dian's blog. Love it!" @officialpoppatl

"Feeding my soul, encouraging me to stretch my boundaries, to live with love and joy! Forever young!"
@susan.ketterer

"Silver Disobedience is like mile markers on a journey, keeping us focused on living in the moment! You rock!"
@hurt_covington

"Reading Dian's Silver Disobedience post every day is my coffee break happy time! She never disappoints to hit the mark on a topic that provokes and enlivens me. Dian is the smart best friend I can always count on."
@carolebethshaw

"Dian brings to light so many of the thought processes that we ponder, that have never been put into black and white on a page. Thank you, Silver Disobedience, for your positive inspiration to be a better you! Let's all be thankful and celebrate life!" @mamajules62

"Dian's words bring clarity to my thoughts and actions. They resonate on a daily basis. Profound! Love your daily Silver Disobedience posts. Thank you—and you have a great sense of fashion! Lol"
@kookla718

"For me, in Dian's words I find daily reinforcement, sometimes a challenge, and then humor or a light at the end of the tunnel. While sometimes I'm not open to new ways of thinking and exploring myself, others and experiences, I always find kindness, graciousness and wisdom with Silver Disobedience."
@amvofpimi

"It's always fun to see Dian's interesting locations and fashion choices showcased in her daily pictures. Silver Disobedience posts are inspirational, always uplifting and thought-provoking. I look forward each day to checking in and seeing what she's shared with us." @jank1146

"Always giving me something to ponder and meditate on." @shaneei92

"I am a hairstylist who started following Silver Disobedience because of Dian's beautiful natural hair…. I showed the blog to my bold and beautiful clients to encourage them to quit coloring their hair. Yet to my surprise, I found each post is much more than just beautiful hair: It is full of wisdom to instill self-reflection and empathy."
@not_bald
"Awesome job, my friend." @roberson9702

"Dian has started a revolution of personal thought and joy in accepting ourselves for where we are—for it is where we are supposed to be at this moment and we must celebrate every stage of life."
@birdm1

"Silver Disobedience: One of my favorite things about the morning!" @pollyanna.59

"Dian's profound insights and wisely chosen words give me inspiration, renewal and motivation to embrace ALL the moments of life. With gratitude." @mafaray

"To be a forever badass woman despite all. Love your messages!" @mommamunkee

"Silver Disobedience is a very good way of life: Inspiring, creative and makes the golden years look like silver! A good habit to read it daily." @jeffsanson

"I catch up with Dian over morning coffee. I'm at a stage where I don't have to read and run. I can digest, be introspective and give thought to how each Silver Disobedience blog applies to my every day with their many takeaways, which are much appreciated." @marycontrary10

"I look forward to Dian's posts daily! Sensible, imaginative, wise words and the Silver Disobedience followers are sensible, imaginative and wise, too!" @kerrymoment

"Common sense and down-to-Earth is the thread of each post, which are always good reminders." @uschris.art

"Dian puts into words that which we probably know on a deep level but don't always practice." @debicollins11

"I look at Silver Disobedience every morning and it starts my day off right. Love it!" @rellisherrera

"Silver Disobedience serves up a healthy dose of moxie! Dian is reprogramming the old school of thought on aging. I've learned to embrace my gray!" @karenwettstein

"Inspirational and aspirational." @neldaisyfreeman

"First and foremost, thank you for your giving spirit. You are a comfort to me and for me." @wrxdion

"Every morning while having my coffee, I peruse Instagram and look forward to Silver Disobedience posts, which are almost like a daily devotional to me. Since I am 61—and for the most part on Instagram that makes me a dinosaur—it is so refreshing to be reminded daily how much we 'silvers' have to offer. I have never and will never think of myself as old—my spirit is forever young! I love how encouraging Dian is and even when talking about the less pleasant aspects of aging she points out the positives! I am always enthralled by her honesty, integrity and authenticity. @SilverDisobedience is a beautiful woman—inside and out!" @bethcarlpicard

"My Silver Disobedience takeaways are: Always be prepared to learn and don't be afraid to make mistakes; rather, make them and learn from them. Always push yourself to grow. Forgiveness is key to moving on to our next level. Thank you, Dian aka @SilverDisobedience for keeping me on-point and reminding me that each day really does count. Find the joy in ALL things and laugh out loud!" @hippiegirltoo

"Silver Disobedience has done a lot for me. I've just turned 52 and was feeling a bit depressed about aging and maintenance (and honestly, mourning my period, my fertility and what I perceived as my youth). Dian has helped me see that I was still the same, still valuable, still zany and that life isn't over. That there is still so much time and that I'm in a better place than ever to take advantage of that!"
Toni Sand

"I like to read Silver Disobedience daily because each post reflects the thoughts of women like me in a clear, direct and wise way. Do not stop writing to us." @lilyboohart

"When I saw Silver Disobedience posts, it hit me: Hip Cool Real. SilverDisobedience: the New Sexy Smart! Anyhow, it seems to sum it all up for me!" @jsb_getting_healthy

"I enjoy all of Dian's views and information on different subjects or topics. Silver Disobedience is very inspiring and a breath of fresh air whenever I read it. Thanks for keeping me young in mind and spirit. Continued blessings." @gloria.claiborne

"Silver Disobedience is a voice that resonates to any age. Dian's mindful perceptions inspire us to recognize our own light within; she is a mirror of beauty that ignites hope as we all walk our own paths, which are so different yet one and the same, prompting a feel-good gratitude attitude!" @hartldy1

"I love @SilverDisobedience blogs and look for them every day!" @suss0047

"Dian's posts get me thinking out of my paradigm, and I love that. Daily, Silver Disobedience is a breath of fresh air." @trthorseranch

"I don't even have to agree with the Silver Disobedience post to be inspired to be my best self. Dian has a gift and I thank her for sharing it. Let's rock!" @diane_mazurek

"Most often the Silver Disobedience posts are about something I am feeling. I think: 'Do I really have this much work to do on myself?' But I also think, maybe we all are struggling to find our way— and some have more, some have less. Either way, it's nice to come to @SilverDisobedience and find encouragement in a moment when others may not be around or just to get what I feel is a healthy perspective. Thank you for creating this space and continuing to post your perspectives." @eclecticlife

"Dian is a darling whether she's dressed up as a model or standing naturally in front of colorful graffiti. Her words reflect those poses and teach humility, self-control, personal strength, empathy and a whole slew of attributes that gets one to thinking about life and our position in it. I read @ SilverDisobedience every day and it's made me more respectful of others and of myself. Thank you!" @jimy4261

"When we begin to feel invisible, Dian's inspiring words define our soul and fill our spirit with color." @diannafacci

"I work with 'at-risk' teens. I've been doing this for over 10 years. It's an emotionally draining job and I was thinking of quitting when I stumbled upon Silver Disobedience during the summer. It's renewed my inner positive strength. I'm back at work full force! What I gain from Dian daily, I pass on to my students through my actions and guidance. Thank you!" @megdecker60

"When I read Silver Disobedience each and every day, I am able to refresh my mind and remind myself how to think and respond to everyday life, family, friends and even the strangers I meet. Dian's quotes and stories are like a personal freedom seminar and they have become part of my daily life." @keith_miller_shred360mb

"Dian is always 'reading my mind, thoughts and feelings.' Silver Disobedience has helped me to acknowledge myself, instead of 'waiting on others.' I've come to realize that age is just a number, that life is a journey to be savored, moment-by-moment, instead of endured—as I have often felt since being in my 50s with aches and pains that can't be helped—but beat the alternative. My new can-do attitude makes the day so much better." @teresa.j.napier

"Thank you for putting into words how I often feel but have trouble articulating. Reading Silver Disobedience daily not only inspires me but motivates me to totally be myself and find joy in all I do. I just turned 57 and thanks to you, I am also growing out my gray after coloring my hair for 30 years." @kimsblair

"Dian's outer beauty and sophistication evinces the soul of a woman who loves life—making her essence irresistible." @heavenandbeauty

"Silver Disobedience makes me happy." @iamdeaszy

"Dian is helping to turn thought into action with Silver Disobedience. Thank you." @whalen555

"Silver Disobedience is a voice of reason." @purplecow56

"I have always felt as though aging is the best thing that has happened to me. I am 47, letting my hair go grey and embracing my age.... Reading Dian's perspective on aging via @SilverDisobedience has reinforced everything I believe in.... It is all about perspective and a positive attitude that makes life beautiful." @jasminekracken

"Dian unlocks the ways we can all be Silver Disobedients in a society that needs to catch up with aging. She reminds us we can enjoy growing up and remain forever young." @gramma_suz_

"Never be afraid of who are. Embrace, 'breathe' and know how blessed you truly are. Be yourself and love who you are. Let others see you glow. This is what I read in the words of Silver Disobedience. Thank you! @robincp54

"Thank you for 'choosing' to share your insights. After all, as Silver Disobedience reminds us, most everything in life is a choice." @amy_lang_1

"There is no time but now…. Silver Disobedience wisdom goes perfectly with my daily morning coffee!" @peaceoflisa

"Clarity: Silver Disobedience is not the traditional motivation post; it's real and inspiring." @suedborst

"Silver Disobedience posts are giving me the permission I needed to let my voice be heard…to express myself finally…to change the way I live the next 50 years, which will be much differently and more boldly than I lived the first 50." @amylynn2223567

"Dian is speaking to our generation, being honest and telling it like it is. It's so refreshing to hear the truth and have higher expectations of ourselves presented to us in such a beautiful way by such a classy lady!" @themer3

"Dian provides highly prolific and inspiring insights and advice that continually broaden my perspectives on life. Silver Disobedience is a must-read blog for everyone who's becoming wiser and better by the day!"
@debrapickrel

"Silver Disobedience is encouragement for positive living. I look forward to each day's message." @linda.w.moran.3

"Daily inspiration for better embracing life and living each day to fullest. @SilverDisobedience is truly a blessing!" @mbuedel

"Silver Disobedience is a daily reminder that we women can continue to reach our personal best for as long as we are here. That happiness is not synonymous to youth only. That the relationship we continue to have with ourselves deepens daily and enriches our lives. That the art of living continues and is not attached to a number. That those who know this look forward to time lived and its incredible rewards." @atlorishome

"With each post, I feel Dian has reached inside my soul, challenging me to release the better parts of myself! What a great way to begin each day! Nothing but gratitude for the Silver Disobedience gift of this wisdom and insight!" @4_momma_di

"Silver Disobedience is a daily reminder that we have much more living to do and wisdom to share." @katiepoo62

"Reading Silver Disobedience is an act of self-love. It is my daily dose of clarity." @luckygirl814

"I like to follow smart women because they send wise words to other women and make us strong and positive. I love all of Dian's messages!" @silvia_what

"Coffee and Silver Disobedience is the breakfast of champions!" @heymair

"Dian presents a wise perspective every day while mindful of humor and compassion." @angelinawilson54

"Silver Disobedience reminds us all that if you've ever felt invisible, even for a moment, you are not alone and you're not invisible!" @anne_welham

"I look forward to Silver Disobedience and love Dian's daily gold nuggets.... My pockets are now overflowing and I'll need a bucket!" @debbierichardson913

"The name 'Silver Disobedience' drew me in. As a real baby boomer hippie and a grown-up woman in my 60s, my first thought was 'You go, girl!' Now, after reading Dian daily, I say '...and I want to go with you!' I share many of Dian's posts so I can tell my peers that they can come, too!" @notedbynancy

"Before following Silver Disobedience I just existed; now I know I can live!" @ernie.gonzalez.1969

"Dian's Silver Disobedience represents the epitome of beauty in us all, inside and out!" @dmarienichols

"Silver Disobedience touches deeply into one's soul through each conscious and mindful essay...reaching right into the core of what we call existence and brings forth such clarity and understanding." @cvnp44

"I love @SilverDisobedience blogs. They bring positivity to my life." @chey14810

"Dian is cool." @steve.keeler

"As I believe I can still be described by all the adjectives I value—fit, active, vivacious, fun, adventurous, spiritual, kind and more—no matter what my hair color, I'm grateful for Dian's daily loving posts." @jcoxie26

"I was attracted by the first pic, then amazed at Dian's words, ultimately reeled in by her perspective and self-help instructions. Silver Disobedience is a great daily read. Please keep it coming." @choppagang
"Silver Disobedience is redefining aging as a woman in America." @annjam

"The Silver Disobedience blog is full of authenticity and words of wisdom...thought-provoking for an inner journey toward peace and happiness. The inspiration Dian provides for others is plentiful. I find myself checking the blog daily for deep perception and aha moments." @mdcphotographystudios

"I love the positive essays. Reading Silver Disobedience daily makes me feel good—and I know I'm feeling better about being ageless!" @jaynestime

"Every morning I look forward to Dian's motivating and inspiring posts. They are beautiful and always touch my heart!" @pattianz1054

"I've been feeling discouraged about getting older: like not feeling sure about how to handle and accept the changes in my body. I pray and read the Bible, which helps. Yet @SilverDisobedience also reassures me that I'm not alone: It is and is going to keep helping me tremendously during this journey of my life." @michellegsphotos

"Since discovering Silver Disobedience, I haven't been able to stop reading each of the uplifting and positive posts." @nserafini57

"True and very informative!" @kimannhulon

"Fell in love with Silver Disobedience the minute I saw the name, read your words and found a soul sister who loves aging like I do!" @graceandme7356

"I'm almost 58 and Silver Disobedience definitely speaks my language. I so look forward to Dian's positive, informative, and inspire-y messages! P.S. Love her hair...my stylist and I are working on a plan to work toward platinum!" @cocosab27

"Aging is a privilege and should be embraced. We are beautiful in each decade of life. We don't need someone telling us we must use their product to be beautiful and that to me is disobedience to the status quo."
@lelensmalley

"Thank you Dian! After numerous requests from me and others, you have written your book 'by popular demand.' Now we can carry your tender encouragements and insights about living life agelessly with us wherever we go. Excited!" @judykatz

THE AUTHOR: DIAN GRIESEL

Dian Griesel is a perceptive human behavior analyst, businesswoman, social influencer, model, wife and mother who has developed a keen understanding of the way written, verbal, visual and body language communication triggers opinions, actions and responses. For 25-years and counting, via her company Dian Griesel International, she has been sought after and engaged by more than 1,000 people, including 350+ CEOs of publicly traded companies, for her strategic, game-changing advice and counsel.

As blogger @SilverDisobedience, Dian's daily posts engage on an extraordinarily deep level with hundreds of thousands of followers across all social media platforms. AARP Magazine described Dian as a "Model-Philosopher," and named her one of the nation's leading "Over 50 Social Media Influencers." Via her company Silver Disobedience Inc., Dian helps marketers better understand and connect with the 48+ demographic. In addition to her blog and this book, Dian has written seven other health, business and communications books. She is a columnist for Forbes.com and a contributor to a variety of publications. She is a member of the Authors Guild, the Hypnotherapists Union and the American Counseling Association.